Comhairle Contae Fhine Gall
Fingal County Council

Items should be returned on or before the last date shown below. Items
may be renewed by personal application, writing, telephone or by
accessing the online Catalogue Service on Fingal Libraries' website.
To renew give date due, borrower ticket number and PIN number if using
online catalogue. Fines are charged on overdue items and will include
postage incurred in recovery. Damage to, or loss of items will be charged
to the borrower.

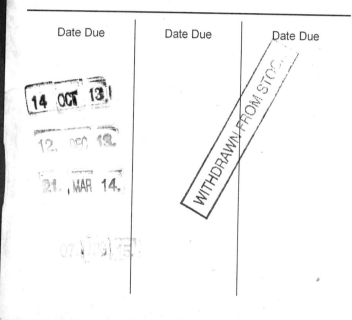

Tom Kerridge's
PROPER
PUB
FooD

To my lovely wife Beth: the most amazing person I have ever met and also my best mate. Big thanks to man's other best friends, Marley, Sponge and Inky, for always making me laugh!

Tom Kerridge's
PROPER PUB
FOOD

First published in Great Britain in 2013 by
Absolute Press, an imprint of Bloomsbury Publishing Plc

Absolute Press
Scarborough House
29 James Street West
Bath BA1 2BT
Phone 44 (0) 1225 316013
Fax 44 (0) 1225 445836
E-mail office@absolutepress.co.uk
Website www.absolutepress.co.uk

Publisher
Jon Croft
Commissioning Editor
Meg Avent
Art Director
Matt Inwood
Project Editor
Alice Gibbs
Editor
Beverly LeBlanc
Photographer
Cristian Barnett
Photography Assistant
Roy Barron
Food Styling
Tom Kerridge, Nicole Herft and Anna Horsburgh
Props Stylist
Cynthia Inions
Indexer
Zoe Ross

A catalogue record of this book is available from the
British Library

ISBN: 9781472903532

Printed in Italy by Printer Trento

A note about the text
This book was set using Helvetica Neue and Clarendon.
Helvetica was designed in 1957 by Max Miedinger of
the Swiss-based Haas foundry. In the early 1980s,
Linotype redrew the entire Helvetica family. Helvetica
Neue was the result. Clarendon was designed in 1845
by Robert Besley for the Fann Street Foundry. It was
refreshed by Edouard Hoffmann and Hermann
Eidenbenz at the Haas Foundry one hundred years later.

CONTENTS

2013 so far has been a big, beautiful, busy year for me. Developing and writing recipes for my first cookbook and TV series has been a lot of hard graft – but you know, in the same breath it has sort of been effortless as well. Of course, it's centred around doing what I love most of all – thinking, planning, creating, cooking and eating food. It just doesn't get any better than that.

The process of creating **Proper Pub Food** has taken me on a similar journey to when my wife Beth and I opened our own pub The Hand & Flowers in Marlow back in 2005. Until then I'd worked in Michelin star restaurants for the whole of my career, but when I had the opportunity to open a business myself, I wanted to open something that felt more like me. I love pubs, and it just felt like a natural place for me to be. The one thing that I didn't want to do was compromise on the quality of the food. One thing lead to another and the pub became a reality through our striving for constant reinvestment and the drive to get better every day.

In just under a year we were awarded one Michelin Star and 3 AA Rosettes. And then, in 2011, The Hand & Flowers became the first pub in the UK to be awarded 2 Michelin Stars. I've been very fortunate to be able to surround myself with some incredible, inspiring and highly motivated staff, where we all push in the same direction.

For me, really great pub food should be accessible to everyone without having to compromise on standards. It should offer value for money – notice I haven't said that necessarily always means cheap, but it certainly means value for what you're eating.

As you leaf through the pages of **Proper Pub Food** you'll realise that I like to take ordinary, even everyday dishes and make them extraordinary. I'm not interested in pretentious food or bells and whistles – for me it's all about the food being approachable and available to everybody. Not to mention good, honest dishes with the flavour and taste that's the result of taking a little more time, care and attention to prepare them. The quality and intensity of ingredients plus precision every time is the key – keep it simple and let those ingredients speak for themselves. The result? Robust, delicious, interesting, good-looking dishes that people can't wait to eat.

I've included a whole range of my absolute favourite pub food recipes suitable for any occasion, time of year, or event. They're intended to showcase great, simple cooking that brings a smile to the face of everyone at your table.

OK, here's a preview of just some of the dishes I've put together...

If you're feeling like a particularly English menu, look no further than Asparagus with Duck Egg Yolk Dressing (page 56). English asparagus in season is one of the joys of being a chef!

Or what about a firm family favourite like Proper Baked Beans & Soda Bread Toast (page 16) – everyone loves baked beans and these are really worth the effort.

My Slow-Cooked Shoulder of Lamb with Pommes Boulangère (page 176) is the perfect family Sunday lunch! I've embraced the French origins of this recipe where long, slow cooking produces deliciously moist, flavoursome lamb that in turn brings a rich layer of potatoes that form the base of the dish.

My Warm Tomato, Onion & Bread Salad with Beef Dripping Dressing (page 50) makes great use of leftover beef dripping. This is a tomato salad with all the sunny flavours that everybody knows – I've simply given it a new-look salad dressing to lift it to a new level.

Hay-Baked Chicken with Whole Roast Celeriac & Cider (see picture, opposite, and recipe on page 190) is, if I'm honest, probably my favourite of the recipes I've gathered for **Proper Pub Food**. It's so clean and simple and stands for all that food should be about.

And no cookbook would be complete without something sweet! Date & Toffee Pudding with Caramelised Bananas (page 211) is one of my classics – very easy to make and really good when served warm. Or indulge in Plum Fool with Pink Peppercorn Shortbreads (page 213). You can change the plum purée in this recipe for any other fruit flavour if you like and move the dish with the seasons.

The majority of recipes I've selected for this cookbook are deliberately not overly complicated. We've made sure that they've been simplified for the home cook so they're all very do-able, as well as including a few other recipes that may require a little more experience.

You'll notice that often I like to use some kitchen gadgets like a blowtorch, a mandoline, a cream whipper gun and a cook's instant-read thermometer (see page 11). They don't cost much and are good fun – trust me, they will make all the difference.

My main goal for **Proper Pub Food** is to show how achievable fantastic pub food can be to prepare – right in your own kitchen (not to mention your barbecue for that matter). And to take it further, I'd like to see more pub chefs around Britain putting their particular stamp of care and understanding on the recipes they include on their menus, continually striving to improve the brilliant British pub food scene just a little bit more.

The important thing is chillaxo relaxo, be inspired and feel good about whatever you prepare. Remember, proper food is the result of treating quality ingredients lovingly and with respect. They won't let you down!

x Tom

EQUIPMENT

Pop to a good local cook shop or look online for these fantastic bits of kitchen kit. They will make a difference to the quality of the food you produce – I guarantee it!

Blowtorch
Using a blowtorch gives an extra dimension to dishes. It's great for adding colour, but most importantly it gives an incredible charred taste.

Crab pick
This useful little instrument is perfect for getting fiddly crabmeat out from the small parts of the shell.

Cream whipper gun
A home-use cream whipper gun is inexpensive, lots of fun and makes a real difference to the final texture. Give it a go!

Chinese steamer basket
The only way to make authentic steamed buns is to use this simple, but effective piece of traditional bamboo kit.

Fine sieve
I use a fine sieve a lot to get the smoothest texture possible for proper sauces, soups and purées.

Japanese mandoline
This is a great gadget for slicing fruit and vegetables very finely. It's a tool that will take your food to another level.

Cook's instant-read thermometer
It might sound a bit cheffy, but this really is an essential piece of equipment. It's easy to use and cheap to buy – you'll never look back.

Microplane grater
This looks like a grater, however it shaves much more accurately and delicately. Use a microplane grater for a finer effect with things like garlic, fruit pith or nutmeg.

Meat mincer
A meat mincer is a great addition to your kitchen for making a range of dishes, from terrines and sausages to burgers and Bolognese.

Mouli-legume
This French kitchen kit is a cross between a sieve and a food mill. It will quickly grind food into a coarse or fine texture.

Muslin cloths
I reach for these finely meshed cloths time and time again when I cook. They are essential for straining and filtering, and have unlimited other uses including keeping roast chicken really moist.

Salad spinner
A basic salad spinner will get your salads off to a proper start. No one likes watery leaves diluting a dressing!

Spice grinder
My homemade curry powder is unbeatable and well worth the investment of a simple spice grinder.

PROPER
BREAKFASTS

Homemade granola

I love granola, and handmade really is proper lush! This will keep for ages in an airtight container, and just with ice-cold milk it is amazing. You can even add it to desserts. Once you've made this, you won't buy supermarket packets again!

Makes a whole bunch of servings

75g flaked almonds
350g jumbo oats
100g sunflower seeds
100g wheatgerm
75g demerara sugar
100g runny honey
75ml rapeseed oil
100g raisins
75g bran flakes
40g ready-to-eat dried apples, roughly chopped
40g ready-to-eat dried apricots, roughly chopped
ice-cold milk or Greek yogurt, to serve

Preheat the oven to 180°C/Gas Mark 4 and spread the almonds in a single layer on a baking sheet. Place the baking sheet in the oven and toast the almonds, stirring and turning them over once, for 3–5 minutes until they are golden brown. Remove the almonds from the baking sheet and leave to cool. Do not turn the oven off.

Mix the oats, sunflower seeds, wheatgerm, demerara sugar, honey and rapeseed oil together on a large baking tray. Put the tray in the oven and bake the granola, stirring every 10 minutes, for 30–40 minutes until it is crunchy and golden brown. Remove the tray from the oven and leave the granola to cool.

When the granola is cool, stir in the raisins, bran flakes, dried apples, dried apricots and toasted almonds. The granola is ready to serve with milk or Greek yogurt, or to store in an airtight container.

"Once you've made this, you won't buy supermarket packets again!"

Warm buckwheat blinis with summer fruit

I love these tiny buckwheat pancakes! This is a straightforward, basic recipe you'll keep coming back to because they also make a great, easy accompaniment to fresh or cured fish for a quick starter, and they go very well with soured cream, crème fraîche or clotted cream.

Serves 4

50g strawberries, halved and hulled
50g blueberries
50g raspberries
50g redcurrants
50g demerara sugar
2 tablespoons chopped mint
icing sugar for dusting
thick Greek yogurt, to serve
runny honey, to serve

For the buckwheat blinis
150g plain white flour
75g buckwheat flour
2 teaspoons caster sugar
10g fresh yeast, crumbled
300ml milk
1 egg, separated
2 extra egg whites
vegetable oil

To make the blinis, mix the white flour, buckwheat flour, sugar and yeast together in a large mixing bowl and make a well in the centre. Warm the milk in a saucepan on the hob until it is blood heat. Make sure it is not too hot or it will kill the yeast. Pour the milk and egg yolk into the flour mix and whisk together to form a thick paste.

In a separate bowl, whisk the egg whites until stiff peaks form, then fold them into the batter mix. Cover the bowl with clingfilm and leave in a warm place for about 30 minutes until frothy.

Meanwhile, place all the fruit in a bowl. Add the demerara sugar and mix together. The sugar will start to break down the fruit.

When the blini batter is frothy, heat a thin layer of vegetable oil in a large non-stick frying pan over a medium heat. Drop small spoonfuls of the blini mix into the pan and fry for 3–4 minutes on each side until bubbly and golden brown. Continue making blinis until all the batter is used. You should get about 20. Keep the cooked blinis warm in a low oven while you cook the rest of the batter.

Mix the mint into the fruit. Place the fruit on top of the warm blinis, dust with a little icing sugar and serve with the Greek yogurt and runny honey on the side for people to help themselves.

Proper baked beans on soda bread toast

This is one of the first dishes that I ever cooked, albeit from a can! Everyone loves baked beans and my homemade version is really worth the effort. These will keep for three or four days in the refrigerator in a sealed container. They are also very good as part of a Full English Breakfast, or you could add curry powder when frying the onion to make curried beans.

This soda bread has been served at The Hand & Flowers throughout both Michelin star awards, so I call it the Michelin starred bread. The joy of this soda bread recipe is that it is so easy to make. It's not proven bread, so it won't sound hollow on the bottom if you tap, but you'll know when to take it out of the oven because it will be golden brown and smell fantastic.

Serves 4–6

400g dried white beans, such as haricot
5 tablespoons rapeseed oil
200g smoked streaky bacon in one piece, diced
200g chopped onions
2 garlic cloves, grated
2 x 400g cans chopped tomatoes
2 tablespoons tomato purée
150g soft dark brown sugar
200ml red wine vinegar
500ml water
salt and pepper, to taste

For the soda bread
340g plain wholemeal flour
340g strong white flour, plus extra for dusting
45g butter, softened, plus extra for spreading
2 teaspoons bicarbonate of soda
$1\frac{1}{2}$ teaspoons salt
1 teaspoon cracked black pepper
625ml buttermilk

To begin the baked beans, cover the white beans in cold water and soak overnight.

Meanwhile, make the soda bread. Preheat the oven to 200°C/Gas Mark 6. Put both flours, the butter, bicarbonate of soda, salt and pepper in a large bowl. Stir in the buttermilk and use your hands to mix all the ingredients together until a soft dough forms. Transfer the dough to a greased baking sheet, pat into a loaf and dust with a little extra flour. Put the baking sheet in the oven and bake the bread for 45–50 minutes until it is wonderfully golden. Transfer the loaf to a wire rack and leave to cool completely.

After the beans have soaked overnight, drain them and put them in a large saucepan. Cover them with water and bring to the boil. Drain the beans again and return to the pan. Cover with fresh water and return to the boil, then reduce the heat to low and simmer, uncovered, for about 1 hour until the beans are just tender. Top up with extra boiling water, if needed. Drain the beans and set aside.

Heat the rapeseed oil in a large saucepan over a medium heat. Add the bacon and fry, stirring, for about 5 minutes until it is crispy and the lovely bacon fat and flavour is in the pan. Add the onion and garlic to the pan and continue stirring for 3–5 minutes until the onion is softened.

Add the canned tomatoes, tomato purée, sugar, vinegar and water and bring to the boil, stirring to dissolve the sugar. Add the beans, reduce the heat to very low and leave to simmer, uncovered, for $1\frac{1}{2}$–2 hours until the sauce is thick and the beans are soft. Season.

When ready to serve, preheat the grill to high. Slice the soda bread and toast until crisp and golden brown. Spread the toast with butter and serve with the baked beans.

Proper Pub Food

Sweetcorn pancakes, dry-cured bacon and maple syrup

The sweetness of the sweetcorn goes so well with the strong, salted kick from the bacon in this recipe. It really is worth buying the best bacon for this dish, as it does make the difference between a good and a great breakfast.

Serves 4

200g canned sweetcorn kernels, drained
50g plain white flour
2 teaspoons baking powder
125ml milk
2 large eggs, separated
salt and pepper, to taste
3 tablespoons rapeseed oil
12 rashers of the best dry-cured streaky bacon
top-quality maple syrup, to serve

Preheat the grill to high.

Put half the sweetcorn kernels in a food processor and process until broken down. Add the flour and baking powder and process again. Add the milk and egg yolks to the blended sweetcorn mix and blend until incorporated. Transfer this batter to a bowl and stir in the remaining sweetcorn. In a separate bowl, whisk the egg whites until soft peaks form, then fold them into the sweetcorn mix. Season.

Heat the rapeseed oil in a large non-stick frying pan over a low heat. Add spoonfuls of the batter and fry for about 3 minutes on each side until golden brown and small bubbles appear on the surface. You can make the pancakes whatever size you want, but you want at least 4. Beware, however, the mix will spread a little as it cooks. Cook the batter in batches if you need to and keep the cooked pancakes warm in a low oven until ready to serve.

Meanwhile, grill the bacon under a hot grill until crispy. Reserve any bacon fat that comes from the grill and brush the pancakes with it. Serve the pancakes and bacon immediately with maple syrup drizzled over.

Tom's Tip

These pancakes also work well with white poultry, such as chicken and poussin, or partridge. Serve them with Rye Bread Sauce (see page 242) and a lovely iron-rich green vegetable, such as spinach.

Toasted oat porridge and hot-smoked salmon

Try this dish for a proper, hearty start to the day. It's packed with flavours that go very well together. If you fancy – and live life on the edge a little – a wee dram of whisky tastes delicious with this! The porridge is also good served with fresh fruit, rather than the salmon.

Serves 4

250g porridge oats
750ml milk
25g soft dark brown sugar
4 hot-smoked salmon fillets, about 100g each, skinned
75g butter, cubed
2 tablespoons chopped dill
finely grated zest of 1 lemon
salt and pepper, to taste

Preheat the oven 180°C/Gas Mark 4. Put the oats on a roasting tray and toast, stirring occasionally, for 8–10 minutes until dark brown, but not burnt. This can be done several days in advance.

Place 200g of the oats, the milk, brown sugar and a pinch of salt in a saucepan over a high heat and bring to the boil. Reduce the heat and simmer, stirring constantly, for 5–6 minutes until the porridge is creamy.

Heat a dry non-stick frying pan over a medium heat. Add the salmon fillets and fry for 5–8 minutes until they are crispy on the edges. It is OK if the fillets break up a little.

Stir the butter, dill and lemon zest into the porridge. Taste and season if you think it needs some. Spoon the porridge into bowls, place the fried salmon on top, sprinkle with the remaining untoasted oats and serve.

Warm ham, parsley and sheep's milk cheese

Sometimes the simple things are the best. If you have a couple of great ingredients and treat them with love and respect they will love you back! Try it....

Serves 4

200g stale bread
rapeseed oil
200ml water
100g butter, cubed
4 slices of British cured ham
1 bunch of flat-leaf parsley, leaves only, roughly chopped
2 tablespoons small capers in brine, drained
150g hard sheep's milk cheese, such as Parmesan or Pecorino
salt and pepper, to taste (optional)

Preheat the oven to 180°C/Gas Mark 4.

Tear the stale bread into small croûton-like chunks, place in a roasting tray and drizzle with oil. Place the tray in the oven and toast the bread for 8–10 minutes until golden brown. Season the croûtons with salt as soon as you take the tray out of the oven so it is absorbed, then leave them to one side.

Bring the water and butter to the boil in a large frying pan over a high heat. Reduce the heat to low, add the ham and simmer for a couple of minutes until it is warmed through.

Remove the ham and put it on warm plates. Add the parsley to the liquid in the pan and season, if needed, but the liquid might be quite salty from the ham, depending on the cure, so taste before you add any. Spoon the parsley over the ham and sprinkle with the capers. Add the crusty croûtons and then grate the cheese over the top and serve.

" Sometimes the simple things are the best. If you have a couple of great ingredients and treat them with love and respect they will love you back!"

Black pudding and sautéed Cornish new potatoes with homemade brown sauce

Brown sauce was the staple of my childhood and is by far the best thing ever with a Full English Breakfast. It is the flavour of the day in cafés up and down the country, added to the bacon rolls, sausage baps and hash browns. It is the taste of the Great British working public, the builders, plumbers, van drivers and, of course, chefs!

This is my version, served with sautéed potatoes and a spicy black pudding, but you could serve it with anything. This dish also works well with a poached egg and a little cracked black pepper. You could make your own black pudding, but the best black pudding for me is either from Laverstoke Park Farm, in Hampshire, or Stornoway, on the Isle of Lewis. Both are delicious.

Serves 4

bacon fat or rapeseed oil
500g Cornish new potatoes, cooked and sliced
1 onion, finely chopped
2 tablespoons finely chopped chives
8 thick slices of black pudding
salt and pepper, to taste

For the homemade brown sauce
250g pitted dates, finely chopped
2 Granny Smith apples
$1/4$ teaspoon ground allspice
$1/4$ teaspoon ground ginger
$1/4$ nutmeg, freshly grated
200g soft dark brown sugar
150ml Cabernet Sauvignon vinegar
150ml red wine vinegar

To make the brown sauce, put the dates into a heatproof bowl. Peel the apples and grate them on a coarse cheese grater directly into the bowl, then mix in the ground spices and leave the bowl to one side.

Put the sugar and both vinegars into a saucepan over a high heat and bring to the boil, stirring to dissolve the sugar. Remove the pan from the heat and pour the mix on to the dates and apples, then cover the bowl with clingfilm and leave to cool at room temperature. The dates will absorb some liquid and become soft.

Pour this mix into a heavy-based saucepan over a very low heat and simmer, stirring occasionally so it doesn't catch on the base, for $1^1/_2$ hours, or until soft and pulpy. Transfer the date and apple mix to a blender and blend until it is smooth. Pass it through a fine sieve into a bowl, then leave to cool completely. Store in a covered jar in the refrigerator until needed, or for up to 2 months.

Heat about 4 tablespoons bacon fat or rapeseed oil in a large frying pan over a medium heat. Add the potatoes to the pan in a layer about 1cm thick and fry for 8 minutes, or until you get crispy edges. Add the onion and continue to fry until it becomes a little caramelised. Add the chives and season. Keep warm in a low oven.

Heat about 2 tablespoons rapeseed oil in another large frying pan over a medium heat. Add the black pudding and fry, turning once, until crispy on both sides.

Serve the black pudding with the potatoes, and add the brown sauce at the table.

Proper Pub Food

Eggy bread with chocolate and orange sauce

Perhaps this is a little too much work and maybe a bit posh for a wet Monday in February when you are already late for work, but on a Sunday morning when you have more time and fancy a posh French breakfast, crack on and make this. I know this is French, but they are very good at this cooking stuff!

Serves 4

4 eggs
200ml milk
2 tablespoons Cointreau
2 teaspoons ground cinnamon, plus a little extra for sprinkling
4 big, thick slices of bread
100g butter, cubed
icing sugar for dusting

For the chocolate and orange sauce
120ml double cream
80ml milk
50g caster sugar
225g 70% dark chocolate, broken into small pieces
1 orange

To make the chocolate and orange sauce, put the double cream and milk in a saucepan over a high heat and bring to the boil. Add the sugar and stir until it has dissolved. Remove the pan from the heat and stir in the chocolate, stirring until it has melted. Grate the zest from the orange into the sauce, then pour the sauce into a pot and leave to cool a little. Segment the orange and leave the segments, peel and membrane to one side.

Meanwhile, whisk the eggs, milk, Cointreau and cinnamon together and pour into a deep baking tray. Place the bread into the mix and leave for 2 minutes. Turn the bread over and leave for a further minute.

Melt the butter in a large non-stick frying pan over a medium heat until it is just foaming. Add the soaked bread and fry for 1–2 minutes on each side until golden brown. Remove the eggy bread from the pan and dust with icing sugar.

Add the orange segments to the pan and quickly fry them in the butter remaining in the pan. Squeeze a little juice from the orange peel and membrane over them and stir for 1–2 minutes to warm through.

Serve the buttery orange segments on the eggy bread with the chocolate sauce, and lightly sprinkle with cinnamon.

PROPER
SOUPS &
SALADS

Celeriac and Bramley apple soup

Celeriac and apple are great bedfellows and work so well together as a soup. This really is one of the dishes where you will recognise all of the flavours – celeriac, blue cheese, apple and walnuts. In the kitchen here at the pub we gain maximum flavour by infusing the celeriac skin in the stock.

Serves 4–6

500g celeriac
1 litre chicken stock
3 tablespoons rapeseed oil
1 onion, finely chopped
2 Bramley apples
freshly squeezed juice of 1 lemon
200ml double cream
salt and white pepper, to taste
150g salty blue cheese, such as Roquefort
walnut oil, to drizzle
4 tablespoons walnuts, toasted, to garnish
celery leaves, to garnish

First, peel and finely chop the celeriac, but keep the peel. Pour the chicken stock into a large saucepan over a high heat and bring to the boil. Add the celeriac peel, then remove the pan from the heat, cover the top with clingfilm and leave to infuse for 20–30 minutes.

Heat the rapeseed oil in a large frying pan over a low heat. Add the onion and a pinch of salt, cover the pan and leave the onion to sweat for 10–12 minutes until softened, but not coloured.

Meanwhile, peel and dice the apples and mix them with the lemon juice so they don't oxidize and turn brown.

When the onion has softened, add the apples and any juice and the celeriac. Strain the infused chicken stock into the pan and bring to the boil. Reduce the heat to low and simmer, uncovered, for 10–15 minutes until the celeriac is tender. Add the double cream and return the liquid to the boil. Pour the soup into a blender and blend until smooth. Season, then pass the soup through a fine sieve.

When ready to serve, reheat the soup, if necessary. Crumble the blue cheese into soup bowls, then pour the hot soup on top and finish with a drizzle of walnut oil, toasted walnuts and celery leaves.

Tom's Tip
You can make this thicker by using less stock, and instead serve it as a lovely purée to accompany meats, such as pork, venison or pheasant.

Curried parsnip soup and pickled apples

Although there are a few complex flavours in this soup, they all marry well and this is a very easy soup to make. Curried parsnip soup has become a classic, and this is the version you will come back to again and again. We often have this on our set lunch menu at The Hand & Flowers.

Serves 4–6

100g butter, cubed
1 onion, finely chopped
3 tablespoons Curry Powder (see page 241)
700g parsnips, peeled and diced
1.2 litres chicken stock, vegetable stock or water
freshly squeezed juice of 1 lemon
2 Granny Smith apples
200ml Pickle Vinegar Mix (see page 241)
4 tablespoons plain yogurt, to garnish
1 tablespoon chopped mint, to garnish
celery leaves, to garnish

For the curry oil
500ml vegetable oil or groundnut oil
1 onion, finely chopped
2 garlic cloves, finely chopped
1 green chilli, finely chopped – with seeds and all
1 fresh red chilli, finely chopped – with seeds and all
4 tablespoons Curry Powder (see page 241)

First, make the curry oil. Heat a large heavy-based saucepan over a high heat until it is very hot, then pour in 75ml of the oil. Add the onion, garlic and green and red chillies and fry, stirring, just until the vegetables are starting to brown. Add the curry powder and stir for a further 4–5 minutes, stirring all the time so the spices cook but don't burn. Add the rest of the oil and heat until it reaches 80°C on an instant-read thermometer. Turn the heat down to very low and leave the oil to simmer for 30 minutes. Pass it through a fine sieve to remove the vegetables, then pass through a sieve lined with muslin or a tea towel to remove any remaining curry powder. Leave to cool completely, then cover and keep in the fridge

until needed. This should keep indefinitely.

To make the soup, melt the butter in a large saucepan until it reaches a beurre noisette, or a hazelnut-brown stage. This will give a lovely, roasted depth of flavour to the soup. Add the onion and fry, stirring, for 2–3 minutes until it is softened. Stir in the curry powder and cook over a medium heat for a further 4–5 minutes. Throw in the parsnips and stir so they get a good coating of the butter and spice mix. Pour in the chicken stock and bring to the boil. Reduce the heat to medium and leave the soup to simmer, uncovered, for 15–20 minutes until the parsnips are very tender.

Pour the soup into a blender and blend until very smooth, then pass it through a fine sieve. Adjust the consistency with a little water if it is too thick. Season with salt, pepper and the lemon juice. The soup is now ready to serve, or it can be left to cool completely and then kept in a covered container in the fridge until needed.

Meanwhile, peel and dice the Granny Smith apples. Place them into the pickling mix in a non-metallic bowl and leave for at least 20 minutes, but no longer than 30 minutes, to infuse them with the vinegar.

To serve, reheat the soup, if necessary. Ladle the soup into bowls and drizzle a little curry oil over the top of each portion. Spoon the diced apple from the pickle mix into the bowls. Mix the yogurt and mint together and add a spoonful to each bowl, then sprinkle a few celery leaves over each bowl. Serve immediately.

Cockle and potato chowder with sweet vinegar

Here is a play on cockles and vinegar, the English seaside classic. This is the sort of dish that I would love to be able to eat... sometimes having a shellfish allergy is rubbish! This is packed full of flavour, with so many simple layers of taste – sweet, sour, salt, richness and a little spice. It's an example of how I love using shellfish, be it cockles, mussels or clams, and its cooking liquid to help bring an underlying saltly and savoury flavour to dishes. The chives are added at the end for freshness and colour.

Serves 3–4

1kg cockles
500ml water
100g butter, cubed
6 celery sticks, chopped
2 bay leaves
2 leeks, split lengthways, rinsed and thinly sliced
2 onions, finely chopped
750g floury potatoes, peeled and diced
300ml double cream
175g canned sweetcorn kernels, drained
2 tablespoons chopped chives
cayenne pepper, to taste
salt and white pepper, to taste

For the sweet vinegar
100ml malt vinegar
75g demerara sugar

To make the sweet vinegar, put the vinegar and sugar in a saucepan over a high heat and bring to the boil, stirring to dissolve the sugar. Remove the pan from the heat and leave on one side to cool.

Meanwhile, discard any cockles with broken shells or any open ones that don't snap shut when tapped. Wash the cockles thoroughly under running cold water to remove any grit or dirt.

Heat a large saucepan over a high heat and pour in the cockles. Add the water, cover and cook, shaking the pan occasionally, for 5–6 minutes until the shells have opened. Discard any cockles that remain closed. Strain the cockles through a colander and keep the cooking liquid. When the cockles are cool enough to handle, remove them from the shells and keep to one side. Strain the cooking liquid through a fine sieve lined with muslin.

Melt the butter in the washed pan over a medium heat. Add the celery, bay leaves, leeks and onions and fry, stirring occasionally, for at least 5 minutes until the vegetables begin to soften but not colour. Throw in the potatoes and cook, stirring occasionally, for a further 5 minutes. Pour in the cockle cooking liquid and bring to the boil. Turn down the heat to low and simmer for 10–12 minutes until the potatoes are soft.

Using the back of a large spoon, break up the potatoes a little to thicken the chowder. Stir in the double cream and bring back to the boil. Turn the heat down and add the sweetcorn kernels, chives and the cooked cockles, then simmer for 1 minute to warm though. Season with cayenne, salt and white pepper.

Ladle the soup into bowls, drizzle with the sweet vinegar and serve.

Proper Pub Food

Chicken and sweetcorn soup

This very easy and quick recipe is for a super-tasty version of the classic Chinese soup. We get that little bit of extra flavour by roasting the sweetcorn and then caramelising it with honey and soy sauce. You could make the soup more substantial by adding egg noodles to the broth.

Serves 4

3 corn cobs
4 tablespoons maple syrup
4 tablespoons soy sauce
1.2 litres chicken stock
4 tablespoons rapeseed oil
2cm piece of fresh ginger, peeled and finely chopped
2 garlic cloves, crushed
200g boneless, skinless chicken breast, diced
2 tablespoons water
2 tablespoons cornflour
freshly squeezed juice of 1 lime
1 egg
salt and pepper, to taste
spring onions, finely shredded, to garnish

Bring a large saucepan of salted water to the boil over a high heat. Drop in the corn cobs and boil for 5–8 minutes until the kernels are tender. Remove the cobs from the water and set aside to cool.

Meanwhile, preheat the oven to 180°C/Gas Mark 4.

Cut the corn kernels away from the cobs and set aside. Chop the cobs into small pieces, then put them into a roasting tray and roast for 10–15 minutes until they are toasted and a little singed.

Place the maple syrup and the soy sauce in a pan over a high heat and bring to the boil, stirring to dissolve the maple syrup. Continue boiling until the mix begins to caramelise, then pour in the chicken stock and return to the boil. Add the toasted corn cobs, reduce the heat and leave the stock to simmer, uncovered, for 15 minutes.

Heat the rapeseed oil in another pan over a low heat. Stir in the ginger and garlic, then add the chicken breast and continue stirring for a further 4–5 minutes until the meat is cooked through and the juices run clear. Strain the infused chicken stock through a fine sieve into the pan and bring to the boil.

Stir the water into the cornflour to make a paste, then whisk this into the stock. Return to just below the boil, then reduce the heat and simmer for 2–3 minutes until the soup thickens slightly. Add the sweetcorn kernels and the lime juice and season.

Whisk the egg, then pour it into the simmering soup, whisking all the time so they egg cooks into thin strands. Ladle the soup into bowls, sprinkle with spring onions to garnish and serve immediately.

Puy lentils in smoked pancetta broth

This is a nod to my understanding of French cooking. The guys over the Channel cook with such love of the earth and the flavours that you get from it. Puy lentils are so tasty and take on the flavour of anything that you cook them with. This recipe is for a rustic farmhouse, Provençal-type soup that is both filling and delicious.

Serves 4

rapeseed oil
2 Toulouse sausages
100g butter, cubed
250g smoked pancetta in one piece, diced
4 sticks celery, finely chopped
3 garlic cloves, crushed
3 banana shallots, finely chopped
1 carrot, peeled and finely chopped
8 salted anchovy fillets, chopped
2 tablespoons dried herbes de Provence
300g Puy lentils
$\frac{1}{2}$ nutmeg, or to taste
750ml chicken stock
salt and pepper, to taste
handful of fresh flat-leaf parsley leaves, to serve

Heat a thin layer of rapeseed oil in a large frying pan over a medium heat. Add the sausages and fry, turning them occasionally, until they are cooked through and the skins are browned. Remove the sausages from the pan and leave to one side. Tip out any fat in the pan, then wipe out the pan with kitchen paper.

Melt the butter in the same pan over a medium heat. Add the pancetta to the pan and fry, stirring, for 2–3 minutes, until browned and the bacon fat has been rendered out. Add the celery, garlic, shallots and carrots and fry for a further 4–5 minutes so they take on the bacon flavour and start to soften. Add the anchovies and dried herbs and stir for a couple of minutes until the anchovies almost dissolve. This gives an underlying savoury flavour to the whole soup.

Add the Puy lentils and stir them around in the pan, giving them a covering of the bacon fat and flavour, a little like cooking a risotto. Grate the nutmeg on to the lentils, then pour in the stock and bring to the boil. Turn the heat down to low and leave the soup to simmer, uncovered, for 20–25 minutes until the lentils are tender.

Slice the Toulouse sausages, add to the lentil broth and leave for a few minutes to warm through. Stir in the parsley and season. Serve immediately.

Lamb and pearl barley broth

This is a bowl of rustic, winter warming loveliness. It is my version of Scotch broth, and it's lifted a little with the acidity that comes from the lemon zest, capers and yogurt.

This will keep for three to four days in the fridge, and tastes all the better for being left to mature for at least a day before serving.

Serves 4–6

4 tablespoons rapeseed oil
600g boneless lamb neck fillets, diced into
 4cm cubes
4 celery sticks, finely chopped
3 garlic cloves, crushed
2 carrots, peeled and diced
1 onion, finely chopped
8 salted anchovy fillets, chopped
2 tablespoons thyme leaves
1.5 litres lamb stock
100g pearl barley
1 lemon
2 tablespoons small capers in brine, drained
2 tablespoons chopped mint leaves
2 tablespoons chopped flat-leaf parsley leaves
1 tablespoon plain yogurt per serving
salt and pepper, to taste

Heat the rapeseed oil in a large saucepan over a medium-high heat. Add the lamb and fry, stirring, for about 10 minutes until caramelised and browned. Remove the meat from the pan but leave the fat.

Add the celery, garlic, carrots and onion and stir around to take on the flavour of the lamb. Add the anchovies and thyme to the pan, then return the lamb and stir everything together. Pour in the stock and bring to the boil. Reduce the heat to low and leave the soup to simmer, uncovered, for about $1\frac{1}{2}$ hours until the lamb is tender.

Stir in the pearl barley and continue simmering for a further 35–40 minutes until the barley is tender and the lamb is so tender it is starting to fall apart. You can carry on with the final flavouring and serve the soup now, but it really is best if you leave it to cool and chill it until the following day.

Reheat the soup, if necessary. Finely grate the lemon zest into the broth and stir in the capers, mint and parsley. Ladle the soup into bowls and drop a dollop of yogurt on top of each portion. Check for seasoning, but there are a lot of powerful flavours in here so you might not need any. Serve immediately.

Turnip and horseradish soup with crispy beef

I love this soup. It has those solid classic British flavours of turnip, horseradish and beef, but also a little sweet-and-sour hint from the vinegar. The beef is crispy, almost Chinese in style, and this gives a great texture and crunch to an otherwise smooth soup.

Serves 4–6

vegetable oil
1 onion, finely chopped
1 litre chicken stock
700g turnips, peeled and finely chopped
200ml double cream
3 tablespoons freshly grated horseradish
75ml white wine vinegar
50g caster sugar
250g beef bavette steak, thinly sliced
50g cornflour
2 green chillies, thinly sliced – with seeds and all
cayenne pepper, to taste
salt, to taste

Heat 3 tablespoons vegetable oil in a large saucepan over a low heat. Add the onion and a pinch of salt, cover the pan and leave the onion to sweat for 10–15 minutes until it is softened but not coloured. Add the chicken stock and turnips and bring to the boil. Reduce the heat to low and leave the soup to simmer, uncovered, for 10–15 minutes until the turnips are tender.

Stir in the double cream and return the soup to the boil, then stir in the horseradish. Transfer the soup to a blender and blend until smooth.

Put the white wine vinegar and caster sugar in another pan over a high heat and bring to the boil, stirring to dissolve the sugar. Pour this mixture into the blended soup to give a sweet acidity to the dish. Season and keep hot.

Dust the bavette steak strips with the cornflour, shaking off the excess. Heat 4–5 tablespoons vegetable oil in a large frying pan over a medium heat. Add the beef strips and fry for 6–8 minutes until very crispy. Remove the beef strips from the pan and drain them on kitchen paper. Sprinkle the green chillies over the beef and season with salt and cayenne pepper.

Ladle the soup into bowls and sprinkle the crispy beef and chilli mix over each portion. Serve immediately.

Frisée, poached egg and garlic croûton salad with roasted garlic dressing

A classic French salad with richness, acidity, salt, savoury and crunch – and so simple to make too.

The roast garlic adds an extra dimension to the classic French vinaigrette. Leftover dressing can be kept in a covered container in the fridge for 2–3 weeks. Add some crispy bacon to this salad if you want to make it super-amazing!

Serves 4

vegetable oil
2 tablespoons capers in brine, drained and patted dry
2 heads of frisée lettuce
2 tablespoons chopped flat-leaf parsley leaves
4 large free-range eggs – these must be really fresh
white wine vinegar for egg poaching
salt and pepper, to taste

For the roasted garlic dressing

1 head of garlic, cut in half through the equator
olive oil
2 egg yolks
1 tablespoon white wine vinegar
1 teaspoon Dijon mustard
1 teaspoon salt
250ml vegetable oil

For the garlic croûtons

16 slices of a thin French stick
olive oil
1 teaspoon dried herbes de Provence
cayenne pepper, taste
sea salt flakes, to taste
2 garlic cloves, halved

First, roast the garlic for the dressing. Preheat the oven to 180°C/Gas Mark 4. Place the garlic halves on a piece of kitchen foil large enough to wrap around them, drizzle with olive oil and wrap up tightly. Place the foil parcel in the oven and roast the garlic for 20 minutes, or until it is very tender, browned and it smells fantastic. Remove the garlic from the oven, open the foil and leave to cool. Do not turn the oven off.

To make the garlic croûtons, arrange the bread slices on a wire rack in a roasting tray. Drizzle with olive oil, then sprinkle with the dried herbs, cayenne and sea salt flakes. Place the tray in the oven and toast the croûtons for 5–8 minutes until crispy and dry. When you remove them from the oven immediately rub a garlic half over each one, pressing down, whilst they are still hot so they take on the maximum garlic flavour. Leave to one side until needed.

When the garlic is cool, squeeze out the soft cloves and put them in a small food processor. Add the egg yolks, white wine vinegar, Dijon mustard and the salt and blend. With the motor running, slowly add the vegetable oil until it emulsifies and thickens. Cover and keep in the fridge until needed.

To deep-fry the capers, heat about 5cm vegetable oil in a heavy-based saucepan over a high heat until it reaches 180°C. Add the capers and fry, stirring for 2–3 minutes until they are crispy and browned. Remove them with a slotted spoon and drain well on kitchen paper. Leave to one side until needed.

Separate the frisée leaves, discarding the dark green leaves as they are very bitter. Use only the yellow, light coloured leaves. Rinse the lettuce leaves and parsley leaves, then spin them dry in a salad spinner and keep in an airtight container until needed in the fridge.

Just before you are ready to serve, poach the eggs. Bring about 25cm water with a good splash of white wine vinegar to the boil in a deep frying pan or sauté pan over a high heat. The vinegar helps the egg keep its shape while it's cooking. Turn the heat down to low. One by one, crack the eggs into the pan and gently spoon the water over the eggs. Poach for 3–5 minutes until the whites are just set. Remove the eggs with a slotted spoon and drain on kitchen paper. Season.

When you are ready to serve, toss the frisée and parsley leaves with the roasted garlic dressing (you won't need all the dressing) and season. Divide among 4 plates, add the garlic croûtons and then the poached eggs and sprinkle with the deep-fried capers. Serve immediately whilst the eggs are still warm!

Fried duck egg, duck leg, spiced onion and pak choi salad

The sweet-and-sour balance of flavours in Chinese cookery is fantastic. I'm a huge fan of acidity in food; it helps cut through the richness of ingredients like duck or eggs. I know that this is not a 'British' dish, but my God, it tastes great and is a super salad for lunch or supper. The salad and spiced onions can also be served alongside plainly cooked pork, chicken or salmon.

Serves 4

2 duck legs, about 200g each
1 onion, thinly sliced
$1/4$ cucumber, deseeded and finely chopped
rapeseed oil
4 duck eggs
200g pak choi, quartered
sea salt flakes, to taste
1 orange, to finish
coriander leaves, to garnish

For the sweet chilli vinegar
150ml malt vinegar
2 tablespoons demerara sugar
2 fresh red chillies, thinly sliced – with seeds and all

For the soy dressing
4 teaspoons sesame seeds, toasted
1 tablespoon runny honey
1 tablespoon dark soy sauce
1 tablespoon rice wine vinegar
2 tablespoons rapeseed oil
1 tablespoon sesame oil

Prepare the individual components of this salad in advance so all you have to do is assemble it and fry the duck eggs at the last minute. First, cook the duck legs. Preheat the oven to 140°C/Gas Mark 1. Place the duck legs on a wire rack in a roasting tray. Place the tray in the oven and roast the duck legs for $1^{1}/_{2}$ hours, or until they are crispy and golden brown. Remove

them from the oven and leave to cool.

Meanwhile, put the onion and cucumber together in a non-metallic bowl. Stir in about 1 tablespoon of sea salt flakes and leave the vegetables to soften at room temperature for 20–25 minutes.

To make the sweet chilli vinegar, put the vinegar and sugar in a saucepan over a high heat and bring to the boil, stirring to dissolve the sugar. Stir in the chilli, then remove the pan and leave to cool.

Rinse the salt off the onion and cucumber, and place them in the washed bowl. Pour over the sweet chilli vinegar and leave to one side. It's best not to do this more than 2 hours before serving.

To make the dressing, mix the sesame seeds, honey, soy sauce and rice wine vinegar together in a non-metallic bowl. Whisk in the rapeseed oil and sesame oil until the dressing emulsifies and thickens. Leave to one side until needed.

Using tea towels to protect your fingers, remove the thigh bones from the duck legs by twisting them out. Tear the meat into large chunks, and do not worry if it falls apart when you take the bones out.

Heat 1–2 tablespoons of rapeseed oil in another frying pan at a medium-high heat. Carefully crack the duck eggs into the pan and fry for 2–3 minutes until the whites are set but the yolks are still runny. Season. If your pan isn't large enough and you don't have enough frying pans at this point, fry the duck eggs two at a time and keep them warm in a low oven until all four are fried.

To assemble the salad, toss the pak choi with the soy dressing, then mix in the duck leg meat and spiced onions and cucumber. Divide the salad among 4 bowls and place a fried egg on top of each. Finely grate over the zest of the orange to release the citrus oils and garnish with coriander leaves. Serve immediately.

Proper Pub Food

Blowtorched English lettuce, soft-boiled egg and salted anchovy salad with homemade salad cream

I love using a blowtorch, as it gives an extra dimension to dishes. It's great for adding colour, but most importantly it gives an amazing charred taste, almost as if ingredients have been cooked over a barbecue. In this case, it helps this solid British classic of boiled eggs and salad cream to a new level. Buy one! You won't regret it. Also, when you've finished cooking you can do a bit of plumbing... ha-ha!

Serves 4

4 Little Gem lettuces
4 large free-range eggs
4 best-quality salted anchovy fillets
rapeseed oil
handful of flat-leaf parsley leaves
salt and pepper, to taste

For the homemade salad cream
1 tablespoon plain white flour
4 tablespoons caster sugar
1 tablespoon English mustard powder
2 large free-range eggs
100ml white wine vinegar
150ml double cream
freshly squeezed juice of $\frac{1}{2}$ lemon

Cut the lettuce into wedges lengthways, then rinse well to remove any dirt or grit. Spin the wedges dry in a salad spinner and leave in the fridge until needed.

We have a bit of multi-tasking here – you're going to soft-boil the eggs and make the salad cream using the same saucepan at the same time. To soft-boil the eggs, bring a saucepan of water to the boil over a high heat. Add the 4 whole eggs, turn the heat down and set a timer to $6\frac{1}{2}$ minutes. At the same time, to make the salad cream, mix the flour, sugar, English mustard powder and a pinch of salt together in a mixing bowl that will fit the pan without the bottom of the bowl touching the water. Whisk in the 2 whole eggs and white wine vinegar. Place the bowl over the gently bubbling water and whisk the ingredients in the bowl until the eggs thicken the mix.

Remove the bowl from the heat and add the double cream and lemon juice to the salad cream mix. Pass the salad cream through a fine sieve and keep to one side to cool completely. This salad cream will keep in the fridge for 3 days.

When the timer pings for $6\frac{1}{2}$ minutes, remove the eggs from the hot water and cool them in running cold water, then leave to one side.

Place the lettuce wedges on to a baking tray and drizzle with a little rapeseed oil. Blowtorch the lettuce until it is a little charred and blackened around the edges. This won't take long!

Peel the soft-boiled eggs and cut each in half. Season.

To serve, mix the charred lettuce with parsley and dress with the salad cream. Place in a bowl and put the salted anchovy fillets on top. Twist black pepper over the top and add the soft-boiled eggs. The salad is ready to serve.

Iceberg lettuce and hake with lemon oil

Hake is a fantastic alternative to cod with a wonderful meaty taste. It is quite a flaky fish, so salting it before cooking helps to firm up the flesh and give it a wonderful deep flavour. This salad can be served on its own, but also goes very well with braised white beans or crusty bread.

Serves 4

5 tablespoons dry white wine

4 tablespoons sea salt flakes

4 tablespoons demerara sugar

pinch of saffron threads

600g hake fillets, trimmed, skinned and pin bones removed

400ml extra virgin olive oil

50g caster sugar

thinly pared peel of 2 lemons

400ml everyday olive oil

1 head of Iceberg lettuce, finely shredded

Mix the white wine, sea salt flakes, demerara sugar and saffron threads together in a non-metallic bowl to form a paste. Rub the hake fillets with this paste and return them to the bowl. Cover the bowl with clingfilm and put it in the fridge for 2 hours.

Meanwhile, mix the extra virgin olive oil, caster sugar and lemon peel together in a saucepan over a low heat, stirring to dissolve the sugar. Leave to simmer over a very low heat for 20 minutes, or until the lemon peel is very soft. Remove the pan from the heat, cover with clingfilm and leave the oil to infuse at room temperature until it is cool.

When the oil is cool, transfer it and the lemon peel to a blender and blend until smooth. Pass it through a fine sieve, then keep it in the fridge in a covered container until needed. Make sure you give it a good stir before you use it.

When you are ready to cook the hake, preheat the oven to 130°C/Gas Mark $\frac{1}{2}$. Rinse the hake in running cold water and pat it dry. Place it in a roasting tray and pour over the everyday olive oil, then cover the roasting tray with kitchen foil. Place the roasting tray in the oven and cook the hake for 20 minutes, or until the flesh flakes easily. Leave the fish to cool in the oil for about 30 minutes.

Put the lettuce oil in a large bowl. Remove the hake from its cooking oil and gently break the flesh into large chunks. Mix it gently with the iceberg. Drizzle a little lemon oil over the fish and lettuce and serve immediately.

Tom's Tip
The extra virgin lemon oil made in this recipe will keep for up to one month in the fridge. Use it to flavour salad dressings and vinaigrettes.

Potato and leek salad with mussel dressing

This warm salad is rooted in the West Country. The use of cider in cooking in that part of the country adds so much depth to sauces and dressings – it is an excellent alternative to wine. Make the effort to search out some great ciders. The levels of sweetness or acidity vary greatly and can change the dish completely, so be sure to taste before you use.

Iceberg lettuce is underused and often viewed as a cheap flavourless salad leaf. When it's used correctly, however, the crisp freshness of this great leaf can enhance a dish and balance soft and rich textures.

Serves 4

500g baby new potatoes, scrubbed
2 large leeks
vegetable oil for deep-frying
500g mussels, debearded and barnacles removed
150ml strong scrumpy cider
200ml rapeseed oil, plus extra for frying the leeks
2 tablespoons chopped chives
1 Granny Smith apple
1 head of Iceberg lettuce, roughly chopped
50ml cider vinegar
salt and pepper, to taste

Bring a large saucepan of salted water to the boil over a high heat. Add the potatoes and cook for 8–10 minutes, until tender. Drain the potatoes through a colander in the sink and leave to steam-dry.

Meanwhile, bring a small saucepan of salted water to the boil. Top and tail the leeks, then cut off the bottom third, which is mostly all white. Cut this white part in half lengthways, rinse well and then thinly slice. Drop the leek slices into the boiling water, stir and remove immediately with a slotted spoon. Leave to cool and dry on kitchen paper.

Heat enough oil for deep-frying in a deep-fat fryer or a heavy-based saucepan until it reaches 140°C. Add the sliced leeks and deep-fry for 2–3 minutes until crispy and golden brown. Drain well on kitchen

paper and season with salt, then leave to one side.

Cut the remaining green parts of the leeks on a slant into lozenge shape. Rinse them in running cold water to remove any dirt and grit, but take care so they hold their shapes. Pat dry on kitchen paper and leave to one side until needed.

To cook the mussels, wash them in running cold water. Discard any mussels that float, any with cracked shells and any open ones that do not snap shut when tapped. Heat a large saucepan over a high heat. Add the mussels and the scrumpy, cover the pan and cook for 5–6 minutes, shaking the pan occasionally, until the shells have opened. Strain the mussels, reserving the cooking liquid. Discard any mussels that have not opened.

Pass the cooking liquid through a fine sieve lined with muslin into a small pan. Bring to the boil over a high heat and boil until the liquid reduces by half. When the mussels are cool enough to handle, remove them from the shells and set aside.

Heat 2 tablespoons of the rapeseed oil in a large frying pan over a medium heat. Add the lozenge-shaped leeks to the pan and fry for 3–5 minutes until coloured on one side. Turn them over and then add the cooked new potatoes to the pan to warm through. Add the cooked mussels and gently stir, trying not to break anything up. Stir in the chives.

Grate about half the unpeeled Granny Smith apple directly into the pan and stir. This adds a lovely acidity and is well matched with the cider. Mix the reduced cooking liquid, cider vinegar and remaining 200ml rapeseed oil together to make a dressing, then add it to the pan.

Place the Iceberg lettuce into a large bowl. Add the mussel dressing and gently toss together. Serve immediately, whilst still warm, in individual bowls, garnished with the crispy leeks.

Classic Caesar salad

This is a great salad from the States and probably the best-known salad in the world. You'll find it on the menu in many gastro pubs. It works so well on its own with plenty of salted anchovies, but can easily be matched with chargrilled chicken or tuna to make it more substantial. Making your own dressing is so much better than buying it ready-made in a shop – the fresh taste is amazing. Choose big, meaty anchovies that aren't too salted or cured from a deli or online shop for a proper salad.

Serves 4

150g white bread, torn into bite-sized chunks
vegetable oil
2 heads of cos lettuce or 4 heads of Little Gem
    lettuces
100g Parmesan cheese in one piece, to serve
salt, to taste

For the Caesar dressing
25 salted anchovy fillets
2 egg yolks
2 garlic cloves, crushed
1 tablespoon Dijon mustard
1 tablespoon white wine vinegar
300ml vegetable oil
100g Parmesan cheese, freshly grated
freshly squeezed juice of 1 lemon
cayenne pepper, to taste

First, make the Caesar dressing. Place 5 of the anchovy fillets, the egg yolks, garlic, Dijon mustard and white wine vinegar in a food processor and blend together. With the motor running, slowly add the vegetable oil until it emulsifies and thickens. Add the Parmesan and lemon juice and season with cayenne. Taste to see if it needs any salt – it probably won't because of the saltiness of the anchovies and the Parmesan. Transfer the dressing to a bowl, cover and store in the fridge until needed. This will keep for up to a week.

To toast the croûtons, preheat the oven to 180°C/Gas Mark 4. Place the bread cubes on a baking tray and drizzle with a little vegetable oil. Place the tray in the oven and toast the croutons, stirring once, for 5–10 minutes until crispy and lightly coloured. Season the croûtons with salt whilst they are still warm, then leave to one side to cool.

Tear the lettuce into separate leaves and wash. Spin dry in a salad spinner and keep to one side. If you're not assembling the salad straight away, store the lettuce leaves in the fridge.

When ready to assemble the salad, toss the lettuce leaves and as much of the dressing as you like together in a large bowl. Add the remaining anchovy fillets and the croûtons. Use a vegetable peeler to shave the Parmesan over. Mix together and serve in the middle of the table for all to share.

Proper Pub Food

Chicken liver and French bean salad in a shallot and white wine reduction

This is a great first course, lunch or brunch salad. The key to making this fantastic dish is caramelising the chicken livers properly, without letting them stew, so you get a lovely meaty flavour. Fast and quick is the way with these boys!

Any liver always has a rich taste so it needs good acidity to cut through and lift it. Capers, mustard and sherry vinegar provide that in this recipe, but you get an extra oomph from the shallot and white wine reduction.

Serves 4

300g French beans, topped and tailed
150g butter, softened
50g Dijon mustard
20g capers in brine, drained
2 teaspoons chopped flat-leaf parsley leaves
vegetable oil
400g chicken livers, defrosted if frozen, trimmed and patted dry
100ml sherry vinegar
4 slices of sourdough bread
salt and pepper, to taste

For the shallot and white wine reduction
4 banana shallots, finely chopped
200ml dry white wine, such as Chablis

First, make the shallot and white wine reduction. Place the shallots and white wine in a small saucepan over a high heat and bring to the boil. Turn the heat down to low and leave the wine to reduce until the shallots become translucent and look a little like a light chutney. Transfer the shallots to a mixing bowl and leave to one side.

Meanwhile, preheat the grill to high and bring another pan of salted water to the boil. Add the French beans to the boiling water and blanch for 3–5 minutes until tender. Drain the beans, then quickly slice them in half lengthways whilst they are still warm. Add them to the bowl with the shallots, mix together and season. The important thing here is that the beans are still warm, so they absorb the flavours. Keep to one side.

Beat 100g of the butter, the Dijon mustard, capers and parsley together in another bowl, then leave to one side.

Heat a thin layer of vegetable oil in a large frying pan over a high heat. Add the chicken livers, but do not shake the pan about as you want them to caramelise and take on a lovely meaty flavour. After 2–3 minutes, when they are browned and cooked through so they are just pink in the middle if you cut one open, flip them over and cook for a further 30 seconds. Add the sherry vinegar to the pan, then transfer the chicken livers to the bowl with the green beans, leaving the cooking juices in the pan, and season.

Add the remaining 50g butter to the sherry vinegar in the pan and bring to the boil, whisking, to make a rustic dressing.

Meanwhile, toast the sourdough bread under the hot grill until it is crispy and browned on both sides. Spread each slice with the Dijon-flavoured butter whilst they are still hot.

Place the buttered toast on plates and top with the liver, bean and shallot salad. Drizzle the sherry vinegar dressing from the pan around the plates and serve immediately.

Tom's Tip
Make extra shallot and white wine reduction, because it keeps in the fridge for up to a week and can be used in all other types of cooking to add acidity and balance, such as a rare beef salad.

Roasted green pepper salad in horseradish dressing served with roasted bone marrow

I was never a huge fan of green peppers until I was introduced to this flavour combination by Anthony Demetre at his fantastic restaurant, Arbutus, in Soho, London. The taste of dry-roasted peppers goes so well with the other ingredients.

Serves 4

2 tablespoons salt
8 pieces of marrow bone, each 5cm
2–3 tablespoons rapeseed oil
4 large green peppers, deseeded and cut into large chunks
4 thin slices of French stick
extra virgin olive oil for drizzling
2 green chillies, thinly sliced – with seeds and all
100g wild rocket, rinsed, spun dry and leaves and stalks roughly chopped
sea salt flakes, to taste

For the horseradish dressing
100g fresh horseradish, peeled
200ml double cream
2 tablespoons prepared English mustard
1 teaspoon Worcestershire sauce
freshly squeezed juice of 1 lemon

Twenty-four hours before you plan to cook, dissolve the salt in a large bowl of water. Add the marrow bones and more water, if necessary, so they are covered, then cover the bowl with clingfilm and place in the fridge for 24 hours for any impurities to be removed.

Up to a day before you plan to serve the salad, make the horseradish dressing. Finely grate the horseradish into a bowl. Add the double cream, English mustard, Worcestershire sauce and lemon juice and mix together with a spoon. Cover and chill until needed.

The next day, preheat the oven to 200°C/Gas Mark 6. Remove the marrow bones from the water and pat dry on kitchen paper. Heat the rapeseed oil in a frying pan over a high heat. Add the bones and sear them on the ends, then transfer them to a roasting tray. Place the roasting tray in the oven and roast the bones for 10 minutes, or until the marrow is softened. Meanwhile, preheat the grill to high.

Heat a large dry frying pan over a high heat. Add the green peppers and stir actively for 3–4 minutes until they start to scald and colour. Season with sea salt flakes.

Whilst the peppers are cooking, grill 4 pieces of French stick until crispy on both sides and golden brown. Drizzle with a good glug of olive oil and season with sea salt flakes whilst they are still warm. Leave to one side until needed.

Add the chillies and wild rocket to the peppers and mix together. Pour over the horseradish dressing and mix again. Serve the salad with the roasted marrow bones and toasted French bread.

Tom's Tip
Mixed all together and then spread on toast works very well, as in this recipe, but this salad can also be served alongside roast beef if you want to add a super twist to your Sunday lunch.

Mixed beans and bacon salad in a bacon dripping dressing

I am a massive fan of pulses and grains, but there is always an issue of their mild flavour. Here, bacon and the bacon fat provide a wonderfully salty, meaty flavour boost that works so well with the beans and tomato purée.

Once heated through, so all the flavours marry, this salad is chilled to serve cold, but you could serve it straight away as a hot salad or side dish. Cabernet Sauvignon vinegar has a delicious sweet acidity that is a little more complex than balsamic, and adds more depth of flavour to any dressing, which is why I often use it in my recipes.

A classic vinaigrette dressing consists of a fat and an acid, such as olive oil and lemon juice or rapeseed oil and cider vinegar, so the use of bacon fat in this recipe is just a different fat flavour.

Serves 4

200g French beans, topped and tailed
150g podded broad beans
1 tablespoon cumin seeds
200g smoked streaky bacon in one piece, diced
100g butter, cubed
1 onion, diced
2 garlic cloves, crushed
1 tablespoon tomato purée
150g canned kidney beans, drained and rinsed
150g canned white beans, such as haricot, drained and rinsed
150g canned chickpeas, drained and rinsed
100ml chicken stock
1 tablespoon oregano
a handful of basil leaves
3 tablespoons Cabernet Sauvignon vinegar
salt and pepper, to taste

Bring a saucepan of salted water to the boil and place a bowl of iced water in the sink. Add the French beans to the boiling water and blanch for 3–5 minutes until tender. Add the broad beans to the pan and cook for a further 30 seconds. Drain well, then immediately plunge them into the iced water to stop the cooking and set the colours. Leave both beans to cool, then drain them.

Pop the broad beans out of their grey outer skins and cut the French beans into $1/2$cm pieces. Put both beans in a large bowl and leave to one side until needed.

Heat a large dry frying pan over a high heat. Add the cumin seeds, and toast, stirring constantly, for 1–2 minutes until aromatic. Add the bacon and butter and continue frying and stirring until the bacon is crispy and golden brown. Strain the bacon and cumin seeds through a fine sieve, reserving the butter and bacon fat.

Pour a little of the fat back into the pan over a medium heat. Add the onion, and fry, stirring, for 3–5 minutes until softened. Add the garlic and stir for a further 1–2 minutes. Add the tomato purée and stir for a further minute.

Add the blanched beans and canned pulses to the pan and stir over a high heat for a further 1–2 minutes. Pour in the chicken stock and toss the beans around. Add the oregano and basil – you can just tear in the basil leaves, there isn't any need to chop them. Tip in the bacon and cumin and mix, then transfer the salad to serving bowl.

Whisk the reserved bacon fat with the Cabernet Sauvignon vinegar and season. Pour over the bean salad and serve or leave to cool completely. When it's cool, cover and chill until about 10 minutes before you're ready to serve.

Tom's Tip
This bean salad is particularly good served with fish, such as mackerel or tuna. Basically, you can use any oily or meaty fish.

Warm tomato, onion and bread salad with beef dripping dressing

This makes great use of leftover beef dripping, a flavour that takes me right back to my childhood. Tomatoes and beef are a classic combination, and this is a British version of the great Italian salad, panzanella, intended to use up stale bread. Here, I add a beef flavour from the dripping to give this blokey salad a super-meaty taste without having any meat.

This is a tomato salad that has all the flavours that everybody knows, but every element has been enhanced to lift it to a new level. It's a great light summer lunch or side for a barbecue – I like to serve it with my Barbecued Short Rib of Beef, British Style on page 166.

Serves 4

2 red onions, peeled
rapeseed oil
$1/2$ loaf of sourdough bread, torn into bite-sized
   chunks
150g beef dripping, melted
1kg mixed heritage tomatoes, all roughly chopped
   the same size
1 white onion, very thinly sliced
2 tablespoons lemon thyme leaves
2 tablespoons sea salt flakes
2 tablespoons onion seeds, toasted
salt and pepper, to taste

For the beef dripping dressing
150g beef dripping
4 tablespoons chopped chives
4 tablespoons chopped spring onion,
   green parts only
rapeseed oil
3 tablespoons Cabernet Sauvignon vinegar

Preheat the oven at 180°C/Gas Mark 4. Trim the root ends of the red onions, then cut them into $1/2$cm wedges, but keep them attached at the root ends so they don't fall apart. Drizzle them with a little rapeseed oil and place in a small roasting tray. Place the tray in the oven and roast the onions for 10–15 minutes, until tender and caramelised.

Place the bread in another roasting tray and drizzle with 150g of the beef dripping. Add the tray to the oven and toast the bread for 6–8 minutes until crispy and lightly browned. Season straight away when the croûtons come out of the oven so they absorb the flavour as they cool. You can toast the bread while you are roasting the red onions. Do not turn the oven off.

Meanwhile, place the tomatoes, white onion and lemon thyme leaves in a large non-metallic bowl. Add the sea salt flakes and mix thoroughly. Leave to one side for 15 minutes, or until the tomatoes start to break down and you see a lot of water in the bowl. Drain the tomato mix in a colander, then tip the tomatoes and onion seeds into a baking tray. Place the tray in the oven and roast the tomato mix for 1–2 minutes just to warm through.

To make the beef dripping dressing, melt 150g beef dripping in a frying pan over a low heat. Add the chives and spring onion and stir for just 30 seconds to warm through. Stir in the vinegar, then taste and season with salt and pepper.

Tip the warm tomato mix into a large bowl. Add the onion seeds, crusty beef-flavoured croûtons and the roasted red onions. Add the beef dripping dressing, gently toss together and serve immediately.

Tom's Tip

The beef dripping can be left over from roast beef, or make your own from beef trimmings and beef fat from the butchers and a little butter. Dry-fry the trimmings in a heavy-based saucepan over a high heat until dark brown, but watch closely so they don't burn. Add beef fat and butter, turn the heat down to low and leave to cook for 30–45 minutes until the fat and butter take on the flavour of the beef trimmings. Pass the fat through a fine sieve into a bowl and leave to cool completely. You can now cover and store in the fridge almost indefinitely.

Baby spinach and fried sausage salad with English dressing

Sausages are by the far the best invention of the culinary world! I love them, and this is a way to serve them with a salad-like twist. My favourite sandwich when I was a child was cold sausage and English mustard and this is a more grown-up riff on that. The English dressing is the same as French dressing, or vinaigrette, but made with English mustard and rapeseed oil. That powerful pungent kick that comes from English mustard is one of life's delights. Be careful though, as too much and it can bring tears to your eyes! Poaching the sausages first is a chef's technique that allows you to fry them without them curling up.

Serves 4

8 good-quality pork sausages
rapeseed oil
500g baby spinach leaves, rinsed and dried in a salad
   spinner

For the English dressing
3 tablespoons prepared English mustard
4 teaspoons caster sugar
100ml white wine vinegar
400ml rapeseed oil
salt and cayenne pepper, to taste

Put the sausages and enough water to cover in a large frying pan over a high heat and bring to the boil. Reduce the heat to low and simmer for 15 minutes, or until all the water has evaporated, but the sausages have taken on no colour. Remove them from the pan and set to one side to cool.

To make the English dressing, whisk the mustard, sugar and white wine vinegar together in a non-metallic bowl. Slowly whisk in the rapeseed oil until it emulsifies and thickens into a dressing. Season with salt and cayenne pepper. This can stay in the fridge until needed, then just give it a whisk or shake before you use it.

When you are ready to fry the sausages, heat a thin layer of rapeseed oil in the frying pan over a medium-high heat. Add the sausages to the pan and fry, turning them over occasionally, for 3–5 minutes until the skins are crispy and browned. Remove the sausages from the pan and drain on kitchen paper, then thickly slice them.

Place the hot sausages and spinach leaves in a large bowl, add enough of the English dressing to coat all the ingredients and toss together. Serve immediately. Any leftover dressing will keep in the fridge indefinitely.

Crispy pork skin, mustard leaf and frankfurter salad with smoked garlic vinaigrette

Hello you! This is my idea of a great salad. It's got spicy mustard, a smoky garlic dressing and crispy, crunchy crackling. The method I use here is a great way to get super crackling. Try it one Sunday and serve it alongside your roast – then just sit back and bask in the compliments. Mustard leaf is a very spicy, tasty leaf and goes well with pork, which make it a natural for this salad.

Frankfurters are a great childhood memory for me, regarded as a cheap and cheerful ingredient. Used as in this recipe, however, they add a delightful contrast to the big flavours of the rest of the dish.

Serves 4

300g pork skin, preferably from the loin, in one piece – ask your butcher for this
vegetable oil
8 good-quality frankfurters, cut into bite-sized pieces
500g mustard leaves, rinsed and dried in a salad spinner
sea salt flakes

For the smoked garlic vinaigrette
1 bulb of smoked garlic, separated into cloves and peeled
50g Dijon mustard
1 teaspoon smoked paprika
1 teaspoon salt
2 tablespoons dry white wine
freshly squeezed juice of $1/2$ lemon
300ml peppery extra virgin olive oil

Preheat the oven to 110°C/Gas Mark $1/4$. Bring a roasting tray of water to the boil on the hob, then add the pork skin. Cover the tray with kitchen foil, shiny side down, then place it in the oven and braise the pork skin for 4 hours, or until it is very tender. Remove the skin from the water and transfer to a wire rack to cool and dry. Turn the oven temperature up to 200°C/Gas Mark 6.

When the pork skin is cool, place the wire rack with the skin into a roasting tray. Rub a little vegetable oil on to the pork skin, then rub in about 1 tablespoon sea salt flakes. Place the tray in the oven and roast the skin for about 20 minutes until the crackling is crunchy. Remove the crackling from the oven and break into chunks, then leave to one side.

Meanwhile, make the smoked garlic vinaigrette. Use a Microplane grater to very finely grate the smoked garlic into a bowl. Whisk in the Dijon mustard, smoked paprika, salt, the white wine and lemon juice. Slowly whisk in the olive oil until the mix emulsifies. Transfer to a bowl, cover and leave to one side until needed.

Heat 2 tablespoons vegetable oil in a large frying pan over a high heat. Add the frankfurters and fry, stirring occasionally, until they have nice tasty brown bits on them. Drain them well on kitchen paper, then place them in a large salad bowl. Add the pork crackling, mustard leaves and as much of the smoked garlic vinaigrette as you need to dress the salad. Serve immediately. Any leftover dressing will keep in a sealed container in the fridge for up to a week.

PROPER STARTERS & SNACKS

Asparagus with duck egg yolk dressing and parsley

English asparagus in season is one of the joys of being a chef! As a bunch, we look forward to this time of year more than most as it represents a change to warmer weather and shows summer is on its way! Farm shop asparagus is the best – peel it to get a fresher flavour without the bitterness of the skin.

I serve the asparagus here with a delicious dressing that's like a mix of hollandaise sauce, salad cream and mayonnaise rolled into one. The duck eggs give a lovely richness to the dressing and are a special touch for a celebratory meal.

Serves 4

300ml water
100g butter, cubed
20 asparagus spears, peeled and the woody ends
  of the stalks broken off
salt, to taste

For the duck egg yolk dressing
4 duck egg yolks
100ml white wine vinegar
50ml water
1 teaspoon English mustard powder
1 teaspoon sugar
$1/2$ teaspoon salt
$1/4$ teaspoon smoked paprika
2 hard-boiled duck eggs, shelled and finely grated
100ml double cream
2 tablespoons capers in brine, drained and chopped
2 tablespoons finely chopped flat-leaf parsley leaves,
  plus extra leaves, to garnish

Pour a couple centimetres of water into a saucepan over a high heat and bring to the boil. To make the dressing, whisk the egg yolks, white wine vinegar, water, mustard powder, sugar, salt and smoked paprika together in a heatproof bowl that will sit on top of the pan of boiling without touching the water. Place the bowl on top of the boiling water and whisk until the mix is creamy and doubles in volume.

Fold the hard-boiled eggs into the dressing, then add the double cream and then the capers and parsley. Remove the pan from the heat and keep to one side.

To cook the asparagus, bring the water and butter to the boil in a frying pan over a high heat, stirring to dissolve the butter. Add a pinch of salt and then place the asparagus in the pan and simmer for 3–4 minutes until tender. Remove the asparagus from the pan and drain on kitchen pepper.

Divide among 4 plates, drizzle the dressing over and garnish each plate with parsley leaves. Serve immediately, with the extra dressing on the side.

Scrambled eggs with English truffle

If you can get hold of fresh English truffles, they are truly amazing. Every day that a truffle is out of the ground the more it deteriorates, so the quicker they go from ground to the plate, the better they taste.

Slowly cooking the eggs takes time, but they become super-rich and smooth this way.

Serves 2–4

6 free-range eggs
1 fresh English truffle
150g button mushrooms, trimmed and very thinly sliced
1 tablespoon truffle oil
75g butter
100ml double cream
75g crème fraîche
2 tablespoons chopped chives
salt and pepper, to taste

At least 48 hours before you plan to cook, place the eggs and the truffle together in a bowl and cover with clingfilm. Place in the fridge and leave until needed. Infusing the eggs with the truffles this way boosts the flavour.

When you are ready to cook, season the button mushrooms and leave to one side.

Break and whisk the eggs with the truffle oil. Melt the butter in a saucepan over a medium heat. Add the eggs and whisk very slowly. When they are just about cooked whisk in the double cream and continue whisking until cooked as you like. Fold in the raw mushrooms, crème fraîche and chives. Season.

Spoon on to plates and then grate the truffle over the top. This is a very decadent touch but fantastic!

"**Slowly cooking the eggs takes time, but they become super-rich and smooth this way.**"

Braised leeks, blue cheese and toasted oats

This is a great vegetarian dish to serve as a first course (substitute the chicken stock with a good vegetable stock). It's also perfect on its own as a lunch dish. As a starter, however, it's good before roast meat and the super-tasty, crunchy topping adds a bit of texture.

Serves 4

50g butter
4 leeks, halved lengthways, rinsed and sliced
100ml chicken stock
175ml double cream
175g blue cheese
2 teaspoons thyme leaves
50g fresh breadcrumbs
50g oats
25g pine nuts
25g demerara sugar
25g sunflower seeds
75g butter, melted
salt and pepper, to taste

Preheat the oven to 200°C/Gas Mark 6.

Melt the butter in a flameproof dish on the hob. Add the leeks to the melted butter and season. Pour in the chicken stock and bring to the boil, then leave to bubble until the chicken stock reduces to a glaze. Add the double cream and bring back to the boil and reduce again by one-third. Crumble in the blue cheese and mix it in with the leeks. Stir in 1 teaspoon of the thyme leaves, then remove the dish from the heat.

Mix the remaining thyme leaves, breadcrumbs, oats, pine nuts, sugar and sunflower seeds together in a bowl. Pour in the melted butter and mix thoroughly. Spoon the oat mix over the top of the leeks. Place the dish in the oven and bake the leeks for 15–20 minutes until the toping is toasted and golden brown. Serve immediately.

St George's mushrooms, garlic and parsley on sourdough toast

Mushrooms on toast is a real favourite of mine. It was one of the first 'dishes' that I learnt to cook at home with my mum.

This version is right in time for the spring season, using St George's mushrooms and wild garlic, but you can vary the ingredients, depending on the season's available wild mushrooms. Or just use the always-dependable and very tasty button mushrooms with sorrel or spinach instead of wild garlic. The Parmesan cheese has a wonderful dairy acidity that cuts through the richness of this dish.

I like to toast my sourdough bread on a cast-iron grill pan for that appetizing 'burnt' bar marking flavour, but use the grill if you don't have the pan.

Serves 4

75g butter
2 tablespoons rapeseed oil
4 garlic cloves, crushed
1 banana shallot, finely chopped
400g St George's mushrooms, wiped and trimmed –
    nice small ones are best but if you can only get
    large ones, halve them
truffle oil, to taste
100ml double cream
100g wild garlic leaves
3 tablespoons very finely chopped parsley leaves
2 tablespoons finely chopped chives
lemon juice, to taste
salt and pepper, to taste
4 pieces of sourdough bread, toasted, to serve
100g Parmesan cheese, to serve

Melt the butter with the rapeseed oil in a large frying pan over a medium heat. Add the garlic and shallot and fry, stirring, for 2–3 minutes until the shallot is just softened. Add the St George's mushrooms, increase the heat to high and fry, stirring, for 3–4 minutes until they are just tender. Add the double cream and a splash of truffle oil and leave the cream to bubble until the mushrooms are glazed and creamy.

Stir in the wild garlic leaves, parsley and chives. Season and add lemon juice to taste. Spoon the mushroom mix on top of the hot pieces of toast. Grate the Parmesan cheese over the tops and serve immediately.

Spring onions, onion seeds and shallot dressing

This is a particularly flexible, all-round recipe. It's great as a first-course salad, like I suggest here, but I also sometimes serve it alongside main courses, such as cooked ham, cured meats or white fish. The different types of onion give layer after layer of taste and texture. Onion seeds are really fragrant and add great depth to the dish.

Serves 4

4 banana shallots
150ml milk
2 tablespoons onion seeds
200ml rapeseed oil
4 tablespoons Cabernet Sauvignon vinegar
2 tablespoons chopped chives
100g butter, cubed
300ml water
2–3 bunches of spring onions, trimmed
100g plain white flour
vegetable oil for deep-frying
salt and pepper, to taste

Slice 2 of the shallots into thin rings, then put in a bowl and pour over the milk. Leave on one side until needed. Finely chop the remaining shallots and leave on one side in a separate bowl.

Place the onion seeds in a dry frying pan over a medium-high heat and toast, stirring, for 2–3 minutes until aromatic. Immediately tip them into a bowl. Add the rapeseed oil and vinegar to the bowl, then stir in the finely chopped shallots and chives. Season with salt and pepper and leave to one side until needed.

Melt the butter with the water in a frying pan over a high heat and bring to the boil, stirring to dissolve the butter. Add the spring onions and a pinch of salt and simmer for 1–2 minutes until they are tender but still have a bite to them. Remove the spring onions from the pan and pat dry.

Drain the shallots from the milk and pat dry. Dust them in the flour, shaking off any excess. Heat enough oil for deep-frying in a deep-fat fryer until it reaches 180°C. Add the shallot rings and fry for 2–3 minutes until crispy and golden brown. Drain on kitchen paper and season.

Serve the spring onions with the dressing spooned over and covered with the crispy shallots.

Salmon tartare and chopped eggs with soda bread

I love the taste of smoked and raw salmon together. The balance of this dish is very important. There are many strong flavours all fighting for priority, so tasting as you make it is a must! The oyster leaves are a real find if you can get hold of them. They taste of oysters and are a great addition to this dish.

Serves 4

300g salmon fillet, skinned, pin bones removed and cut into 1cm dice
100g smoked salmon, whole not sliced, cut into 1cm dice
4 salted anchovy fillets, finely chopped
2 banana shallots, finely chopped
2 tablespoons chopped chives
1 tablespoon capers in brine, drained
1 tablespoon chopped cornichons
finely grated zest of 1 lemon
2 top-quality free-range egg yolks
2 hard-boiled eggs, shelled
2–3 tablespoons rapeseed oil, to taste
4 tablespoons mayonnaise
4 oyster leaves (optional) – look for these online if your greengrocer doesn't have any
4 dill sprigs
salt and cayenne pepper, to taste
smoked paprika, to garnish
1 loaf of freshly baked Soda Bread (see page 242), still warm, to serve

Mix the salmon and smoked salmon together in a non-metallic bowl. Add the anchovies, shallots, chives, capers, cornichons, lemon zest and salt and cayenne and mix. Add the egg yolks and mix again. Divide the salmon mix into 4 equal portions and put on plates.

Finely grate the hard-boiled eggs into a bowl and season. Mix with the rapeseed oil to make a 'loose' mix, then spread it on top of the salmon. Top with a spoonful of mayonnaise and dust with a little smoked paprika. Stick on an oyster leaf and a sprig of dill in each portion and serve with the warm soda bread.

Gin-cured salmon with buttermilk pancakes

This salmon is very similar to Scandinavian gravadlax and needs a couple of days to cure. You can play around with the flavour combinations in the cure to suit – try vodka and dill or whisky and coriander seeds.

The buttermilk pancakes are dead easy to make and go well with many different ingredients – I especially like them with fish, fruit and cured meats.

Serves 4

175g soft brown sugar
165g sea salt flakes
1 teaspoon fennel seeds
2 tablespoons juniper berries
2 salmon fillets, about 300g each, pin bones removed
150ml gin
crème fraîche, to serve
maple syrup, to serve
1 tablespoon juniper berries, crushed, to serve
4 shots of frozen gin, to serve

For the buttermilk pancakes
125g plain white flour
40g caster sugar
1 teaspoon salt
1 teaspoon bicarbonate of soda
300ml buttermilk
50g butter, melted
1 egg, beaten
rapeseed oil

Two days in advance, line a roasting pan or deep dish large enough to hold the salmon fillets with clingfilm, leaving enough over-hang to wrap around the fillets. Mix the brown sugar, sea salt flakes, fennel seeds and juniper berries together in a bowl. Spread a layer of this mix over the clingfilm. Place a salmon fillet, skin side down, on top. Spread half the remaining mix onto the salmon. Pour over the gin and then place the other salmon fillet on top, skin side up, so the two flesh sides are facing each other. Put the remaining cure mix on top of the salmon, then wrap very tightly with the clingfilm. Place this parcel in a non-metallic deep dish and place a weight on top. A large milk container will do. Leave this in the fridge for 48 hours, turning the salmon over after 24 hours. After 48 hours, rinse the salmon fillets and pat them dry.

To make the buttermilk pancakes, mix the flour, sugar, salt and bicarbonate of soda together in a large bowl and make a well in the centre. Mix the buttermilk, butter and egg together. Add about half the wet ingredients to the dry ingredients and give the mixture a quick whisk, but not too much. Gently stir in the rest of the wet ingredients. The mixture should be quite thick and a little lumpy. Leave it to rest at room temperature for 5–10 minutes before cooking.

When ready to cook the pancakes, heat a little oil in a non-stick frying pan over a low heat. Working in batches, depending on the size of your pan, add spoonfuls of the pancake mix and fry for $1\frac{1}{2}$–2 minutes on each side until bubbly on the surface and golden brown. You should get 12–16 pancakes. Transfer them to a low oven to keep warm while you cook the rest of the batter.

When you're ready to serve, very thinly slice the salmon and divide among the plates. Serve with the pancakes with a little crème fraîche, a spoonful of maple syrup and juniper berries sprinkled over. A shot of frozen gin goes really well with these, too!

Blowtorched mackerel with buckwheat blinis and pickled beetroot

I love classic buckwheat blinis. I serve them here with mackerel, but they go so well with any smoked or oily fish. The pickled beetroot is the true garnish for these little lovelies!

Serves 4

200g crème fraîche
2 tablespoons chopped chives
4 mackerel, about 350g each, filleted, pin bones removed and each fillet halved lengthways
rapeseed oil
2 banana shallots, thinly sliced
sea salt flakes and pepper, to taste
30g canned Avruga caviar (herring roe), to garnish

For the pickled beetroot
250g redcurrant jelly
250ml red wine vinegar
4 cloves
2 large cooked beetroots, peeled and cut into 1cm dice
75g Dijon mustard
salt and pepper, to taste

For the buckwheat blinis
150g plain white flour
75g buckwheat flour
2 teaspoons sugar
10g fresh yeast, crumbled
300ml milk
1 egg, separated
2 egg whites
vegetable oil

First, make the pickled beetroot. Put the redcurrant jelly, red wine vinegar and cloves in a saucepan over a high heat and bring to the boil, stirring to dissolve the jelly. Continue boiling until the mix is reduced to a glaze. Pass this glaze through a fine sieve into a clean bowl. Stir in the beetroot and Dijon mustard. Leave to one side to cool completely. Taste and see if it needs any seasoning, then cover and chill until required.

To make the blinis, mix the white flour, buckwheat flour, sugar and yeast together in a large mixing bowl and make a well in the centre. Warm the milk in a saucepan on the hob until it is blood heat. Make sure it is not too hot or it will kill the yeast. Pour the milk and egg yolk into the flour mix and whisk together to form a thick paste.

In a separate bowl, whisk the egg whites until they form stiff peaks, then fold them into the batter mix. Cover the bowl with clingfilm and leave in a warm place for about 30 minutes until frothy.

Meanwhile, whisk the crème fraîche until thick, then add the chives and season to taste. Cover and chill until needed.

When the blini batter is frothy, heat a thin layer of vegetable oil in a large non-stick frying pan over a medium heat. Drop small spoonfuls of the blini mix into the pan and fry for 3–4 minutes on each side until bubbly and golden brown. Continue making blinis until all the batter is used. You should get about 20. Keep the cooked blinis warm in a low oven while you cook the rest of the batter.

Rub each mackerel fillet with a little rapeseed oil. Place them in a roasting tray and use a blowtorch to cook them until they are just cooked, but still a little pink in the centre. They will have a fantastic charred flavour.

Divide the blinis among 4 plates and top with the pickled beetroot and the thinly sliced shallots. Serve the mackerel fillets alongside, with a spoonful of Avruga caviar on top.

Soused mackerel with dill-pickled vegetables

This is a pub classic that has been on our menus for many years, and has been done with so many variants of skill. Here, a dill-flavoured pickle mix gives the dish a Scandinavian feel. I use my blowtorch on the fish first to give a further charred dimension that adds a lovely bitter taste.

You could also use other oily fish, such as sardines or herring, and serve the fish with a little soured cream alongside, if you like.

Serves 4

2 large mackerel, about 550g each, filleted, pin bones
  removed and each fillet halved lengthways
rapeseed oil
1 lemon
a good country-style bread, such as sourdough,
  to serve

For the dill pickled vegetables
2 carrots, peeled and thinly sliced
2 garlic cloves, sliced
2 banana shallots, finely chopped
$1/4$ cucumber, deseeded and cut into
  bite-sized pieces
2 tablespoons sea salt flakes
1 bunch of dill
300ml Pickle Mix (see page 241)
200ml water
1 tablespoon dried chilli flakes

At least $6^1/_2$ hours before you want to serve, begin the dill-pickled vegetables. Mix the carrots, garlic, shallots and cucumber together in a large non-metallic bowl. Stir in the salt and leave the vegetables to cure at room temperature for 20–25 minutes.

Wash off the salt thoroughly in cold running water, then return the vegetables to the rinsed bowl. Set aside a few sprigs of dill to garnish, then put the remainder in a blender. Add the pickle mix and blend to make a green dill-flavoured vinegar mix. Pass this mixture through a fine sieve on to the vegetables. Add the water and sprinkle with the chilli flakes. Cover and chill until needed.

Rub each mackerel fillet with a little rapeseed oil. Place them into a roasting tray and use a blowtorch to cook them until they are just cooked, but still a little pink in the centre and charred on the outside. Grate the lemon zest over the top of the warm mackerel to release the citrus oils, then leave them to one side to cool a little.

Place the mackerel fillets into the pickling mix with the vegetables, then cover and place into the fridge for 6 hours.

To serve, remove the fillets from the mixture, sprinkle with the remaining dill leaves and serve with the pickled vegetables and bread.

Mussels cooked in ale

The French call this moules marinières and cook the mussels with white wine. Here, I use ale and call them 'mussels cooked in ale' – so very English, don't you think! The bitter flavour that comes from the mussels goes so well with beer or stout, this seems more of a natural combination than the French original.

Serves 4

75g butter
100g carrots, peeled and finely diced
100g celeriac, peeled and finely diced
4 banana shallots, finely chopped
3 bay leaves
150ml dark ale
2kg mussels, debearded and barnacles removed
4 tablespoons crème fraîche
1 tablespoon chopped chervil
1 tablespoon chopped parsley
1$\frac{1}{2}$ teaspoons chopped tarragon
salt and pepper, to taste
warm crusty bread, to serve (optional)

Melt the butter in a saucepan over a medium heat. Add the carrot, celeriac, shallots and bay leaves and fry, stirring, for 5–8 minutes until softened. Pour in the ale and bring to the boil. Remove the pan from the heat and leave to one side.

Wash the mussels in running cold water. Discard any mussels that float, any with cracked shells and any open ones that do not snap shut when tapped. Heat a large saucepan over a high heat. Add the mussels and the vegetable and ale mix, cover and cook, shaking the pan occasionally, for 4–5 minutes until the shells have opened. Discard any mussels that remain closed. Strain the mussels through a colander, reserving the cooking liquid.

Place the cooking liquid into a large pan over a high heat and bring to the boil. Continue boiling until it reduces down to one-third. Stir in the crème fraîche and the chopped herbs. Check the seasoning, but you probably won't need any. Pour this mix back over the mussels, then serve with warm crusty bread, if you like. And, a glass of ale alongside isn't bad, either.

Crab, broad beans and marjoram

This really does have a taste of summer about it. Make sure the crabmeat you buy is super-fresh – or even better still, cook the crab and pick the meat yourself! I love broad beans with marjoram; they work so well together, just like a proper marriage. Once the crab has been picked, this dish is very easy to assemble and has so much flavour.

Serves 4

100g podded broad beans
4 plum tomatoes, with a small X cut in the top of each
3 tablespoons rapeseed oil
4 banana shallots, finely chopped
2 garlic cloves, thinly sliced
250g white crab meat, well picked over
finely grated zest of 1 lemon
75g brown crab meat
2 tablespoons marjoram leaves
$1^{1}/_{2}$ tablespoons Cabernet Sauvignon vinegar
salt and pepper, to taste

Bring a saucepan of salted water to the boil and place a bowl of iced water in the sink. Add the broad beans to the boiling water and blanch for 3–5 minutes until tender. Drain well, then immediately plunge them into the iced water to stop the cooking and set the colour. Leave to cool, then drain well and pop them out of their grey outer skins. Leave on one side until needed.

Meanwhile, bring another large pan of water to the boil and set another bowl of iced water in the sink. Add the tomatoes to the boiling water and boil for 10 seconds, them immediately drain them and put in the iced water to stop the cooking. Drain the tomatoes again, then use a small knife to peel off the skins. Cut the tomatoes in half, scoop out the seeds and finely dice the flesh. Leave to one side until needed.

Heat 3 tablespoons of rapeseed oil in a deep frying pan or sauté pan over a medium heat. Add the shallots and garlic and season with salt and pepper. Cover the pan, turn the heat to low and leave the shallots to sweat, stirring occasionally, for 10–12 minutes until softened.

Add the white crab meat and gently heat through. Add the broad beans and lemon zest. When all the ingredients are warm, stir in the brown crab meat, marjoram and diced tomatoes. Add 150ml rapeseed oil and the vinegar, season and gently mix everything together. It's now ready to serve.

Tom's Tip

I serve this as a starter at the pub, but you can also serve it as a pasta dressing or simply on top of hot toast, or leave it to cool and make it into a salad.
If, for example, you have any leftovers, toss them with wild rocket for an unbeatable summer salad.

Warm crayfish and watercress salad in potato skins

This recipe is a great way to utilise the potato skins leftover after you've scooped out the flesh to mash or use in other recipes. If you leave this dish to cool, it is really good for outdoor eating using your hands. The earthiness of the potato goes so well with the river fish taste of trout and crayfish. The natural garnish for this salad is watercress and it tastes delicious with the acidity of the apple.

Serves 4

50g butter
250g cooked crayfish tails
100g smoked trout fillets, skinned
2 bunches of watercress, picked over
1 Granny Smith apple, peeled, cored and finely
   chopped
1 teaspoon cracked black pepper
100g thick Greek yogurt
salt, to taste

For the potato skins
2 baking potatoes
4 strips of pancetta
100g mature Cheddar cheese, freshly grated
rapeseed oil

To prepare the potato skins, preheat the oven to 180°C/Gas Mark 4. Place the potatoes in the oven and bake for $1^1/_2$ hours, or until they are cooked through and tender. Remove them from the oven and leave to cool. Do not turn off the oven.

When the potatoes are cool enough to handle, cut them in half lengthways and scoop out the flesh, taking care not to pierce the potato skins. Place a piece of pancetta into the bottom of each potato skin and add a sprinkling of the grated cheese. Drizzle a little rapeseed oil over the top of each, place them on a baking sheet and put back into the oven at 180°C/Gas Mark 4 for 8–10 minutes until crispy and the cheese has melted.

Meanwhile, cook the crayfish filling. Melt the butter in a large frying pan over a medium heat. Throw in the crayfish tails and gently warm them through. Do not have the heat too high or they will become tough. Add the smoked trout fillets and remove the pan from the heat. Stir in the watercress and apple, stirring just until the leaves wilt. Season with the cracked black pepper, then stir in the yogurt.

Spoon the salad into the crisp potato skins and serve.

Tom's Tip
The scooped out potato flesh can be used for mash or to make gnocchi. It will keep, covered, in the fridge for up to 2 days.

Smoked haddock, Parmesan and crème fraîche omelette

We have had a version of omelette Arnold Bennett in one form or another on the menu at The Hand & Flowers since we opened in 2005. If I am ever in the pub, I always order this as a starter. This is a larger version, however, intended for sticking in the middle of the table for everybody to dig into and help themselves.

At the pub we use hollandaise sauce, but here I suggest using crème fraîche. This just makes the recipe a little more accessible and a lot quicker to knock up for a first course or a lunch. I specify free-range eggs here because this really is a dish that is all about the eggs.

Serves 6–8

600ml milk
2 sides of good-quality smoked haddock, about 300g
  each – not that artificially dyed stuff!
60g butter
30g plain white flour
10 large free-range eggs
150g Parmesan cheese, freshly grated
3 tablespoons finely chopped chives
150g crème fraîche
2 extra large free-range egg yolks
salt and pepper, to taste

Put the milk in a large saucepan over a high heat and bring to the boil. Place the smoked haddock into the milk and turn off the heat. Place a lid on the pan and leave the smoked haddock to gently poach in the milk for 8–10 minutes until the fish is cooked through and the flesh flakes easily.

Remove the haddock from the pan and reserve the poaching milk. When the smoked haddock is cool enough to handle, remove all bones and the skin and discard. Flake the flesh into large pieces and leave to one side until needed.

Melt 30g of the butter in a saucepan over a medium heat. Add the flour and stir for 2–3 minutes to cook out the raw flavour. Slowly strain the poaching milk through a fine sieve on to the flour and butter, stirring to make a smooth sauce. Press a piece of clingfilm on the surface to prevent a skin forming and leave to one side until needed.

Preheat the grill to high if you don't have a blowtorch. Whisk the 10 whole eggs in a large bowl and season. Melt the remaining 30g butter in a 30cm non-stick frying pan with a flameproof handle over a low heat. Pour in the whisked eggs and cook the omelette nice and slowly for 4–5 minutes until it is just set. Remove the pan from the heat and cover the surface with the Parmesan. Add the chives and then place the flaked smoked haddock over the top.

Mix the crème fraîche, extra egg yolks and 6 tablespoons of the haddock-flavoured white sauce together. Spoon this mixture over the top of the omelette, then use a blowtorch to make a lovely glaze, or cook under a preheated grill. Serve in the middle of the table for everybody to help themselves.

Tom's Tip
You end up with more white sauce than the 6 tablespoons you need for this recipe. Use the leftovers to flavour a fish lasagne or fish pie. You can't go wrong.

Steak tartare on chargrilled sourdough with roasted beef marrow and watercress

I love steak tartare and I love bone marrow on toast, so I've combined both in my version of the classic steak tartare recipe. The better the quality of the beef marrow you buy, the better flavour you will get. The spicy peppery taste from watercress is a great match for beef, and when it is dressed with good-quality rapeseed oil you have the ultimate beef salad.

Serves 4

2 tablespoons salt
8 pieces of beef marrow bone, each 2½cm thick
rapeseed oil
100g English watercress sprigs
4 thick slices of sourdough bread
olive oil
250g raw beef fillet, very finely chopped
2 banana shallots, finely chopped
1 tablespoon small capers in brine, drained
1 tablespoon chopped cornichons
1 tablespoon finely chopped flat-leaf parsley leaves
Tabasco sauce, to taste
Worcestershire sauce, to taste
cracked black pepper, to taste
2 raw egg yolks
2 tablespoons rapeseed oil
freshly squeezed juice of 1 lemon
sea salt flakes, to taste

Twenty-four hours in advance, dissolve the salt in a large bowl of water. Add the marrow bones and more water, if necessary, so they are covered, then cover the bowl with clingfilm and place in the fridge for 24 hours for any impurities to be removed.

The next day, preheat the oven to 180°C/Gas Mark 4. Remove the marrow bones from the water and pat dry on kitchen paper. Heat 2–3 tablespoons oil in a frying pan over a high heat. Add the bones and sear them on the ends, then transfer them to a roasting tray. Place the roasting tray in the oven and roast the bones for 10 minutes, or until the marrow is softened.

Meanwhile, wash the watercress in cold running water, then spin dry in a salad spinner. Store in a covered container in the fridge until needed.

Just before you are ready to serve, heat a ridged grill pan over a high heat until it is very hot. If you don't have one, heat the grill to high. Drizzle the slices of bread with olive oil, then toast on the pan or under the grill. Make sure the grill pan is really hot so the bread gets the dark bar markings, which is where loads of flavour will be.

While the bread is toasting, mix the chopped beef, shallots, capers, cornichons and parsley together in a large bowl. Season with the Tabasco sauce, Worcestershire sauce, table salt and cracked pepper. Stir in the raw egg yolks.

Toss the watercress in a non-metallic bowl with the rapeseed oil, lemon juice and sea salt flakes.

Spread the steak tartare on top of the hot toasts. Serve immediately with the roasted marrow bone alongside and the watercress salad on top.

Crispy pig's cheeks and deep-fried shallots with taramasalata and flat breads

Think of this as a homemade kebab with a chilli kick. This dish takes time, but the result really is worth it. Braised pork cheeks are such a good and inexpensive ingredient, and you might be surprised what a great match they make with the fishy, garlicky taramasalata.

Serves 4

3 tablespoons rapeseed oil
2 celery sticks, finely chopped
1 carrot, peeled and finely chopped
$\frac{1}{2}$ onion, finely chopped
6 star anise
1 tablespoon white peppercorns
4 pig's cheeks
500ml chicken stock
4 banana shallots, sliced into rings
250ml milk
vegetable oil for deep-frying
plain white flour for dusting
3 tablespoons olive oil, plus extra for drizzling
1 green chilli, chopped – with seeds and all
salt and pepper, to taste

For the flat breads
250g strong white flour, plus extra for kneading and rolling
$\frac{1}{2}$ teaspoon salt
4 tablespoons olive oil
100ml warm water

For the taramasalata
4 medium slices of white bread, crusts removed
200ml milk
200g smoked cod's roe, skinned
3 garlic cloves, crushed
200ml mild olive oil or vegetable oil
freshly squeezed juice of $\frac{1}{2}$ lemon

Heat the rapeseed oil in a saucepan over a medium heat. Add the celery, carrot, onion, star anise and white peppercorns, cover the pan and leave the vegetables to sweat for at least 5 minutes until softened. Add the pig's cheeks and chicken stock. Increase the heat to high and bring to the boil, skimming any fat that rises to the surface. Turn the heat down to low, cover the pan and braise the cheeks for about $2\frac{1}{2}$ hours until tender. Remove the cheeks from the stock and leave them to cool.

Meanwhile, make the taramasalata. Put the bread in a food processor and pulse to form breadcrumbs. Tip these into a bowl and cover with the milk. Put the cod's roe and garlic into the processor and blend until smooth. Add the soaked bread and milk and blend again. With the motor running, slowly add the olive oil. Add the lemon juice and season. Transfer the taramasalata to a serving bowl, cover and chill until needed.

To make the flat breads, mix the flour and salt together in a bowl and make a well in the centre. Add the olive oil, then slowly add the warm water, bringing the paste together to form a dough. Knead into a tight ball and leave to rest, covered with clingfilm, for 30 minutes.

Meanwhile, put the shallots into a bowl, cover with the milk and leave to soak for 10 minutes. When ready to deep-fry the shallot rings, heat enough oil for deep frying in a deep-fat fryer or heavy-based frying pan to 180°C. Drain the shallots, then dust them in flour, shaking off the excess. Deep-fry the shallot rings for 3–5 minutes until crispy and golden brown. Drain on kitchen paper and season with salt and pepper whilst still hot. Leave these to one side until you are ready to serve. They don't need to be kept warm – they are added to the dish for their texture. Just make sure you don't cover them, because that will cause them to soften.

After the dough has rested, lightly flour the surface and divide the dough into 4 equal portions. Roll each portion into an oval shape about $\frac{1}{2}$cm thick. Heat a large non-stick frying pan over a medium heat. Add as many flat breads as will fit and dry-fry for 2–3 minutes on each side until lightly toasted and crisp. Transfer the breads to a low oven to keep warm until they are all cooked and until you are ready to serve.

Just before you're ready to serve, heat the olive oil in the pan over a high heat and throw in the braised pig's cheeks. Use 2 forks to shred the meat and cook, stirring, for 8–10 minutes until crispy. Season and sprinkle with the chopped green chilli.

Spread the flat breads with taramasalata, and then add the crispy pigs' cheeks and then the shallot rings. Drizzle with a little more olive oil and serve.

Tom's Tip

Don't throw away the liquid the pig's cheeks are braised in – it's packed with flavour. Leave it to cool completely, then strain and chill or freeze until you want to add it to soups, stews and gravies.

Braised pearl barley, smoked chicken and wild garlic

This is a version of risotto made with pearl barley rather than short-grained rice. Smoked chicken is so underused, but I like to include it in stocks, risottos and stews to give a rich smokiness. The powerful kick of wild garlic goes so well with chicken, so add a little more if you want a stronger flavour.

Serves 4–6

$1/2$ smoked chicken
1.5 litres chicken stock, plus a little extra, if needed
100g butter
50ml rapeseed oil
1 onion, finely chopped
350g pearl barley
100g Parmesan cheese, freshly grated
juice of 1 lemon
100g wild garlic leaves
2 tablespoons chopped chives
salt and pepper, to taste

Remove all the meat from the smoked chicken carcass so you have about 350g, then flake it and leave to one side. Put the bones and skin in a saucepan, add the chicken stock and bring to the boil, skimming the surface, as necessary. Reduce the heat to very low and leave to simmer for 15–20 minutes.

Melt 25g of the butter with the oil in another large saucepan over a low heat. Add the onion and fry, stirring, for at least 5 minutes until softened, but not coloured.

Stir in the pearl barley and continue cooking for 3–4 minutes until it is toasted. Pass about one-quarter of the hot chicken stock through a strainer on to the barley and continue stirring until the liquid has been absorbed. Repeat this process until all the barley is tender and most, if not all, of the stock has been absorbed. This should take about 40 minutes.

Stir in the smoked chicken, Parmesan cheese and the remaining butter. Remove the pan from the heat and leave the barley to rest for 2–3 minutes. Add the lemon juice and season. Stir in the wild garlic leaves and chives. If the mix needs loosening a little, just use any remaining stock or hot water. Serve immediately.

Baked egg custards, crispy ham and brown bread croûtons

I think of these individual custards as cheese and ham quiches without the pastry. This is a super-rich first course, so the custards don't need to be very big.

The different layers of flavours here are from the same two main ingredients, ham and cheese, but the contrast in textures makes a complex overall dish.

Makes 6

600ml double cream
3 sprigs of thyme
100g crusty brown bread, cut into $1/2$cm dice
rapeseed oil
200g cooked ham, finely chopped
3 eggs
3 extra egg yolks
1 teaspoon salt
$1/2$ teaspoon smoked paprika
$1/4$ teaspoon cayenne pepper
200g Gruyère cheese, freshly grated
$1/2$ nutmeg
50g Parmesan cheese, freshly grated
2 tablespoons finely chopped chives
6 slices of Parma ham
salt and pepper, to taste

Preheat the oven to 160°C/Gas Mark 3. Put the double cream and thyme in a saucepan over a high heat and bring to the boil. Remove from the heat and leave to one side to cool a little.

Meanwhile, put the brown bread cubes in a roasting tray, drizzle with about 3 tablespoons rapeseed oil and place in the oven for about 5 minutes until crispy. Remove the croûtons from the oven, season and leave to one side. Turn the oven temperature down to 130°C/Gas Mark $1/2$.

Heat 2 tablespoons rapeseed oil in a frying pan over a medium heat. Add the cooked ham and fry, stirring, for 3–4 minutes until crispy. Drain on kitchen paper and leave to one side until needed.

Whisk the eggs, yolks, salt, smoked paprika and cayenne together in a bowl. Return the cream to the boil, then pass it through a strainer on to the eggs, whisking. Add the Gruyère cheese and grate in the nutmeg

Bring a kettle of water to the boil. Divide the crispy cooked ham between six 150ml ramekins. Ladle the custard into each ramekin. Place the ramekins in a roasting tray and pour in enough boiling water to come half way up their sides. Place the tray in the oven and bake the custards for 15–20 minutes until they are just set. Remove the ramekins from the tray and sprinkle over the Parmesan cheese and chives while the custards are still warm.

Preheat the grill to high. Place the Parma ham on the grill rack and grill for 2–3 minutes until crispy. Drain on kitchen paper, then break into small pieces and serve on top of the custards with the brown bread croûtons. Serve immediately.

Warm buttered ham, English broccoli stalks and fried capers

This is a super-quick and light first course or lunchtime dish that uses up any leftover broccoli stalks. Personally, I prefer the stalks to the florets, as they have a better flavour and such a good texture.

Like with most cooking, the better the produce that you buy, the better it will taste. Get good ham....

Serves 4

vegetable oil
2 tablespoons capers in brine, drained and patted dry
2 broccoli stalks
75g butter, cubed
200ml water
pinch of salt
4 pieces of ham, about 150g each
2 tablespoons finely chopped flat-leaf parsley leaves
cracked black pepper, to taste

Heat about 5cm vegetable oil in a deep frying pan or heavy-based saucepan until it reaches 180°C. Add the capers and fry, stirring, for 2–3 minutes until they are crispy and browned. Remove them with a slotted spoon, and drain on kitchen paper. Season and leave to one side.

Cut the broccoli stalks lengthways into quarters and trim any woody bits. Melt the butter with the water in a saucepan over a medium heat. Add the broccoli stalks and salt and leave to simmer, uncovered, until the stalks are tender and coated in a nice butter glaze. Remove the stalks from the pan and keep hot.

Add the ham slices to the buttery glaze and warm through for about 1 minute on each side. Add extra water to the pan, if necessary.

Remove the ham from the glaze and place on 4 plates. Arrange the broccoli stalks on top. Stir the parsley into the glaze, then pour over the ham and broccoli stalks. Sprinkle over the capers, season with cracked black pepper and serve immediately.

Double Gloucester cheese scones and Old Spot bacon with sage butter

I'm from the West Country, and this is my tribute to the region – it's a savoury 'cream tea', from the great town of Gloucester. This makes a great breakfast, too!

Makes 8 scones

8 rashers of the best-quality Gloucester Old Spot bacon

For the sage butter
250g butter, softened
30 sage leaves, finely chopped
2 banana shallots, finely chopped
$1/2$ teaspoon salt
$1/4$ teaspoon cayenne pepper

For the double Gloucester cheese scones
225g self-raising white flour, plus extra for kneading
  and cutting out the scones
pinch of salt
50g butter
75g Double Gloucester cheese, freshly grated
150ml milk, plus a little extra for brushing

First, make the sage butter. Place the butter in a mixing bowl. Add sage leaves, shallots, salt and cayenne pepper and mix together. Shape into a log about $2^1/2$ cm thick and wrap tightly in greaseproof paper or clingfilm. Chill for at least an hour or up to a week, or freeze it for up to 3 months.

To make the scones, preheat the oven to 220°C/ Gas Mark 7. Mix the flour and the salt together in a large bowl, then rub in the butter with your fingers until the mixture resembles coarse crumbs. Add 50g of the cheese, then add the milk and mix to form a soft dough.

Roll the dough out on a lightly floured surface until it is about 2cm thick. Use a floured 5cm round cutter to cut out 8 scones, re-rolling the trimmings as necessary, but try to handle the dough as little as possible.

Place the scones on a baking sheet. Brush the tops with a little milk and sprinkle them with the remaining grated cheese. Place the baking sheet in the oven and bake the scones for 12–15 minutes until they are risen and golden brown. Transfer them to a wire rack to cool.

Meanwhile, preheat the grill to high. Place the bacon on the grill rack and grill for 3–5 minutes until cooked through and as tender or crisp as you like.

Cut the scones in half and toast them under the grill. Spread with the sage butter, add the bacon and serve.

Potted ham hock, mustard seeds and tarragon jelly

Toasted mustard seeds give a slightly different texture to this classic combination, and the addition of tarragon gives a herbal lift to the richness of the meat and jelly. These will keep for two to three days in the fridge, and are also great to pack for picnics, if that's your thing.

Makes 4

1 ham hock, about 1kg
10 white peppercorns
2 bay leaves
2 celery sticks, halved
1 carrot, peeled
$\frac{1}{2}$ onion, studded with 3 cloves
2 tablespoons white wine vinegar
2 leaves of gelatine
2 tablespoons yellow mustard seeds, toasted
2 tablespoons finely chopped tarragon leaves
4 slices of sourdough bread, toasted, to serve
a selection of pickles, ideally home-made –
    try the Pickled Beetroot (see page 66) or Piccalilli
    (see page 90)

Place the ham hock in a large saucepan, cover with water and bring to the boil, then drain. Repeat this process 2 more times to remove any impurities.

Return the ham hock to the pan. Add the white peppercorns, bay leaves, celery, carrot, onion, white wine vinegar and water to cover and bring to the boil Reduce the heat to very low and leave to simmer, uncovered, for $2\frac{1}{2}$–3 hours until the ham is tender. Remove the ham from the stock and leave it to one side to cool.

Pass the stock through a sieve lined with muslin or a tea towel and keep 300ml warm to use in this recipe; the remainder can be used in other recipes.

When the ham is cool enough to handle, flake the meat away from the bone and remove and discard as much fat as possible. Try to keep some big chunks of meat! Put the meat in a large mixing bowl and leave to one side.

Soak the gelatine leaves in cold water for about 5 minutes until softened. Squeeze out the water, then add them to the warm stock and stir until the gelatine has dissolved.

Add the toasted mustard seeds and tarragon to the ham. Pour over the jellied stock and gently mix through. Place the mix into four 150ml ramekins and leave to cool completely. Cover and place in the fridge for at least 1–2 hours until set.

Serve with hot sourdough toast and homemade pickles.

Tom's Tip
You will end up with more poaching stock than you need for this recipe, but don't throw out the extra. It's packed with flavours and is ideal for using in other recipes, such as the pork pie on page 90.

Crispy pig's ears with truffle oil mayonnaise

This is proper party food. Pig's ears are so easily disregarded, but they really are lush! The use of truffle oil gives a wonderful taste of the expensive to this cheap-and-cheerful cut of meat.

Serves 4

2 pig's ears
100ml white wine vinegar
8 star anise
2 celery sticks, chopped
1 carrot, peeled and chopped
1 onion, chopped
1 tablespoon white peppercorns
150g plain white flour
2 eggs, beaten
150g panko breadcrumbs
vegetable oil for deep-frying
fresh truffle (optional)

For the truffle oil mayonnaise
2 large egg yolks
2 tablespoons Dijon mustard
2 tablespoons white wine vinegar
300ml vegetable oil
3 tablespoons truffle oil
lemon juice, to taste
salt and cayenne pepper, to taste

Make room in your fridge for 2 baking sheets with a large carton of milk or other 1kg weight lying on them. Firstly, trim the pig's ears and use a blowtorch to remove any hairs. Place them in a large saucepan and add the white wine vinegar, star anise, celery, carrot, onion and white peppercorns. Cover with water and bring to the boil, skimming the surface as necessary. Reduce the heat to low and leave to gently braise for 2 hours. Turn the heat off and leave the ears to cool in the stock.

Remove the pig's ears from the stock and place on a baking sheet lined with clingfilm. Put another layer of clingfilm on top and then place another baking sheet on top. Put a weight of about 1kg, such as a large carton of milk, on top of the tray, then put the ears and trays in the fridge for 12 hours.

Meanwhile, make the truffle oil mayonnaise. Place the eggs, Dijon mustard and white wine vinegar into a food processor and blend until smooth. With the motor running, slowly add the vegetable oil until it emulsifies and thickens. Blend in the truffle oil, then add a good squeeze of lemon juice and season with salt and cayenne. Transfer to a bowl, cover and chill until needed.

Remove the ears from the fridge and cut into strips. Place the flour, egg wash and breadcrumbs in separate bowls in a row on the work surface and 'pane' the ear strips. In non-cheffy English, that means simply to dip the strips into the flour, tapping off any excess, then dipping them into the eggs, letting the excess drip back into the bowl, and then finally into the panko breadcrumbs. Leave on one side.

Heat enough oil for deep-frying in a deep-fat fryer or heavy-based saucepan to 180°C. Add the pig's ears, in batches if necessary, and fry for 4–5 minutes until crispy. Drain well on kitchen paper and season. Reheat the oil between batches, if necessary.

Serve the fried pig's ears with the truffle-oil mayonnaise to dip them in. Grate fresh truffle over the top, if you have any. It's decadent, but amazing!

Pig's trotters and bacon on toast

Please don't turn your nose up at the thought of these – just try them! You'll find the trotters are so tasty and full of flavour. This is the best-ever version of 'meat paste', something I remember from when I was a kid. This mix is also a great stuffing for roast pork

Serves 4–6

2 large pig's trotters, about 600g each
1.2 litres Brown Chicken Stock (see page 240)
4 celery sticks, halved
1 carrot, peeled and halved
1 onion, quartered
8 star anise
2 tablespoons white peppercorns
100ml water
50g caster sugar
freshly squeezed juice of 1 lemon
75g butter
3 banana shallots, finely chopped
2 tablespoons rapeseed oil
175g smoked streaky bacon in one piece, cut into lardons
4 tablespoons finely chopped ready-to-eat dried apple
2 tablespoons prepared English mustard
2 tablespoons sherry vinegar
1 teaspoon ground mace
salt and pepper, to taste
2 Granny Smith apples, to serve
4 slices of sourdough bread, toasted, to serve

Singe the pig's trotters with a blowtorch to remove any hairs. Place them into a large saucepan, cover with water and bring to the boil, then drain. Repeat this process two more times to remove any impurities.

Return the trotters to the pan, add the brown chicken stock, celery, carrot, onion, star anise and white peppercorns and bring to the boil. Reduce the heat to very low and leave to simmer, uncovered, for $2^1/_2$–3 hours until the trotters are tender. Turn off the heat and leave the trotters to cool in the stock.

Meanwhile, put the water and sugar in saucepan and bring to the boil, stirring to dissolve the sugar. As soon as it boils, remove the pan from the heat and add the lemon juice. Leave to cool completely, then place in the fridge until needed.

When the trotters are cool, remove them from the stock and flake the meat and skin into a mixing bowl. Pass the stock through a fine sieve into the washed pan, place over a high heat and boil until the stock has reduced by half.

Melt the butter in a frying pan over a medium heat. Add the shallots and fry, stirring, for 3–5 minutes until softened. Tip them into the bowl with the trotter meat.

Heat the oil in the pan over a medium heat. Add the lardons and fry, stirring, for about 2–3 minutes until browned and crispy. Use a slotted spoon to transfer these to the bowl with the trotter meat. Add the dried apples, mustard, sherry vinegar, mace and salt and pepper. Shred together with a fork and season, adding a little of the cooking stock to make the mix moist. The trotter mixture can stay in the fridge until needed or be used straight away.

Just before you are ready to serve, slice the Granny Smith apples on a Japanese mandoline. Put them into the stock syrup mix you made earlier and leave for just a couple of seconds to prevent oxidising and to give them a sweet glaze.

Place the trotter mixture in a pan over medium heat and stir until warmed through. Divide it between the slices of toast. Place the Granny Smith slices on top and serve.

Game terrine glazed in port jelly with cranberry compôte

This recipe looks complicated, but I promise you the results are amazing. Cutting a terrine in half for the first time is one of the joys of being a chef! This makes a great dish for the Christmas period when you have plenty of people around to help you polish it off.

Serves 12

500g pork belly, skinned and chopped
850g game mix – ask your butcher for boneless, skinless mixed venison, pheasant, hare and so on
250g pork liver
50g butter
2 onions, finely chopped
3 garlic cloves, finely chopped
6 juniper berries
2 dried bay leaves
2 cloves
1$\frac{1}{2}$ teaspoons thyme leaves
1 teaspoon cracked black pepper
2 tablespoons brandy
2 tablespoons red wine
2 teaspoons salt
2g saltpetre (optional)
hot toast, to serve

For the cranberry compôte
200g demerara sugar
100ml freshly squeezed orange juice
2cm piece of fresh ginger, peeled and finely chopped
400g cranberries, defrosted if frozen
$\frac{1}{2}$ nutmeg
1 orange

For the port jelly
350ml port
50g caster sugar
3 leaves of gelatine

Preheat the oven to 130°C /Gas Mark $\frac{1}{2}$ and bring a kettle of water to the boil. Line 25 x 10cm terrine or a 1.2 litre ovenproof dish with clingfilm, then leave to one side. Mince the pork belly, game mix and pork liver together and put into a large bowl, then leave to one side.

Melt the butter in a frying pan over a low heat. Add the onion and garlic and fry, stirring, for at least 5 minutes until softened, but not coloured. Remove the pan from the heat and leave the onions and butter to cool, then add them to the bowl with the minced meats.

Grind the juniper berries, bay leaves, cloves, thyme and black pepper together in a spice grinder. Add this spice and herb mix to the minced meats. Add the brandy, red wine, salt and saltpetre, if using. Get your hands in and combine thoroughly. The salt will begin to break down the meat and you will find the mixture becomes a little tighter in your hands.

Push the meat mix into the lined terrine, trying not to have any air bubbles. Bring the clingfilm over the top to seal, then place the terrine's lid on top (if it has one). Place the terrine in a roasting tray and pour in enough boiling water to come halfway up the sides. Place the tray in the oven and cook the terrine for 1$\frac{1}{2}$–2 hours until the centre of the terrine has reached 70°C on an instant-read thermometer. Remove the terrine from the tray, take the lid off and put a heavy weight on the top to press the meat down. Leave to cool completely, then place in the fridge for 12 hours, still with the weight on top.

Meanwhile, make the cranberry compôte. Place the demerara sugar, orange juice and ginger in a saucepan over a high heat and bring to the boil, stirring to dissolve the sugar. Stir in the cranberries and grate in the nutmeg. Simmer the cranberries, stirring frequently, for about 15 minutes until they soften and form a chutney-like appearance. Grate in the orange zest, then transfer the compôte to a bowl and leave to cool.

To make the port jelly, place the port and caster sugar in a saucepan over a high heat and bring to the boil, stirring to dissolve the sugar. When the sugar has dissolved, remove the pan from the heat and leave to one side.

Soak the gelatine leaves in cold water for about 5 minutes until softened. Squeeze out the water, then add them to the warm port mix and stir until the gelatine has dissolved. Pass through a fine sieve into a bowl.

Remove the terrine from its mould and scrape off any excess fat or jelly. Use a ladle to pour the port jelly over the top of the terrine. Place the terrine back into the fridge for about 10 minutes until the jelly sets. You will need to do this 3 or 4 times to get a good layer of jelly.

After the jelly has set, use a long, thin knife to trim the sides of terrine so it looks smart, then slice and serve with the cranberry compôte and toast.

Tom's Tip

If you want to get ahead over the holiday period, the cranberry compôte will keep in a covered container in the fridge for up to a week.

Pork pie with piccalilli

I love traditional pork pies – they are one of the great British classics. And when you add a dollop of hot, sweet piccalilli everything feels right in the world. I try to recreate familiar British foods at my pub, but take them to a higher level. Just try and stop yourself from smiling when you try this lush pork pie.

Serves 16

1kg boneless pork shoulder, skinned and diced
250g smoked streaky bacon in once piece, diced
250g pork belly, skinned and minced
3 tablespoons chopped sage leaves
2 tablespoons thyme leaves
1 teaspoon cayenne pepper
1 teaspoon ground mace
1 teaspoon cracked black pepper
1 teaspoon cracked white pepper
1 teaspoon salt
2 eggs beaten with a splash of double cream, to glaze
300ml ham stock or chicken stock
3 leaves of gelatine

For the hot-water crust pastry
550g plain white flour, plus extra for rolling
$1\frac{1}{2}$ teaspoons salt
100g butter, cubed
100g lard, cubed, plus extra for greasing the tin
200ml water
2 eggs, beaten

For the piccalilli
150g French beans, topped and tailed and cut into 1cm dice
4 shallots, finely chopped
2 small onions, finely chopped
$\frac{1}{2}$ large head of cauliflower, broken into small florets
1 small cucumber, deseeded and cut into 1cm dice
3 tablespoons sea salt flakes
300ml white wine vinegar
125ml malt vinegar
$\frac{1}{4}$ teaspoon dried chilli flakes
350g caster sugar
2 tablespoons English mustard powder

2 tablespoons ground turmeric
$1\frac{1}{2}$ tablespoons cornflour

At least 24 hours in advance, start the piccalilli. Mix the French beans, shallots, onions, cauliflower, cucumber and sea salt together in a large non-metallic bowl. Cover the bowl with clingfilm and leave to stand at room temperature for 24 hours.

Meanwhile, put the white wine vinegar, malt vinegar and chilli flakes in a saucepan over a high heat and bring to the boil. Remove the pan from the heat and leave mix on one side to cool.

After the vegetables have been in the fridge for 24 hours, rinse them well to remove the salt, then return them to the washed bowl. Combine the caster sugar, mustard powder, turmeric and cornflour in a bowl. Stir in a little of the vinegar mixture until smooth, then add this thin paste to the remaining vinegar mixture in the pan. Bring to just below the boil, stirring, until it thickens slightly. Pour it over the vegetables and blend together well. Leave to one side to cool completely.

To make the hot-water crust pastry, mix the flour and salt together in a large bowl and make a well in the centre. Melt the butter and lard with the water in a saucepan over a medium heat. Pour this melted fat and the eggs into the well and mix with a wooden spoon to form a dough. Use your hand to knead the dough around the bowl until it is smooth and silky. Cover the bowl with clingfilm and leave the dough to rest for 1 hour, or until the dough becomes elastic and easy to work.

Meanwhile, make the filling. Mix the pork shoulder, bacon, pork belly, sage and thyme leaves, cayenne, mace, the black and white peppers and the salt together in a large bowl. Leave to one side until needed.

Preheat the oven to 180°C/Gas Mark 4. Generously grease a deep 25cm springform cake tin with lard. Cut off one-quarter of the dough, wrap in clingfilm and leave to one side to use later for the pie lid.

Roll the remaining dough out on a lightly floured surface into a 45cm circle about 1cm thick. Drape the pastry over the rolling pin and unroll it over the pan, then gently ease it down into the pan. Press it down on to the base, but leave the overhang.

Fill the pastry case with the filling, pressing it down against the base and side. Roll out the remaining pastry into a 25cm circle 1cm thick. Place it on top of the pie. Dampen the underneath edge and press to seal with the overhang. Use a fork to crimp all around the edge, then cut a steam hole in the centre.

Place the pie on a baking sheet and bake for 30 minutes. Reduce the heat to 160°C/Gas Mark 3 and bake for a further 1¼ hours. Remove the pie from the oven and brush the pastry with the egg glaze, then return it to the oven and bake for a further 15 minutes, or until the pastry is golden brown and the juices run clear when you stick a skewer into the filling. Transfer the pie to a wire rack and leave to cool completely.

When the pie is cool, warm the stock in a saucepan over a medium heat. Do not let it boil. Soak the gelatine leaves in cold water for about 5 minutes until softened. Squeeze out the water, then add them to the warm stock and stir until the gelatine has dissolved. Pour the stock in to the pie through the steam hole, then leave the gelatine to cool and set.

Serve the pie cut into wedges with the piccalilli.

Potted rabbit with carrot and carrot-top salad

This dish is full of beautiful woodland flavours. The lovely, delicate gamey flavour of rabbit is a classic match for the warm, piny sweetness of juniper and star anise. The tender baby carrots have a little kick of vinegar and cayenne and a soft note of caraway. Serve with slices of toasted sourdough.

Serves 4–6

150g sea salt flakes
8 juniper berries
4 bay leaves
4 star anise, lightly crushed
1 large rabbit, about 1.2kg, jointed into legs, shoulders and saddle
500g duck fat
150g smoked streaky bacon, cut into lardons
4 slices of sourdough bread, toasted, to serve

For the carrot top salad
1 bunch of young carrots with the tops still attached
100ml rapeseed oil
25ml cider vinegar
1 large handful of dandelion leaves (*pis en lit*), rinsed and spun dry
1 tablespoon caraway seeds, toasted
2 tablespoons finely chopped flat-leaf parsley leaves
salt and cayenne pepper, to taste

Mix the sea salt flakes, juniper berries, bay leaves and star anise together. Sprinkle a thin layer of this salt mix on to a non-metallic tray, then place the rabbit pieces on top. Cover with the remaining salt mix, then wrap in clingfilm. Place in the fridge and leave for 12 hours.

Rinse the salt from the rabbit pieces then put them in a large saucepan. Cover with the duck fat and the lardons and place over a medium heat until the duck fat melts. Reduce the heat to low and leave the rabbit and bacon to 'confit' for about 1$\frac{1}{2}$ hours until the meat is cooked through and tender. Turn off the heat and leave the rabbit pieces and bacon to cool a little in the pan.

When the rabbit is cool enough to handle, remove the meat from the bones and flake the flesh into a bowl. Add the lardons and use 2 forks to shed both meats. Reheat the duck fat to melt it, then strain it though a fine sieve. Add as much of the duck fat as necessary to make a pâté-like consistency. The amount of fat you need will depend on how succulent the rabbit was. Taste and add cayenne pepper and salt, if needed.

Divide the mix into 4 equal portions and pack it into 4 suitable serving bowls, a 25 x 10cm terrine or other suitable serving dish and leave to cool completely. Cover and chill until needed, but remember it should be removed from the fridge at least 20 minutes before you serve. Don't forget.

Meanwhile, make the carrot top salad. Bring a saucepan of water with a large pinch of salt to the boil. Pick the frilly green tops from the carrots and wash them well to remove any grit. Peel and cut the carrots into chunky strips.

Add the carrot strips to the boiling water and boil for 2–3 minutes until just tender. Drain well and transfer to a large mixing bowl. Whilst the carrots are still warm, drizzle them with the rapeseed oil and cider vinegar, then set aside to cool. They will take on more flavour when dressed warm like this.

When you're ready to serve, add the dandelion leaves and carrot tops, caraway seeds and parsley to the bowl with the carrots. Season with salt and cayenne and mix thoroughly. Serve with the potted rabbit and some toasted sourdough bread.

Deep-fried 'popcorn' cockles with chilli vinegar

This is a great beachside-style snack, based on the jars of pickled cockles you get at the seafront, but I've added a hot chilli vinegar kick. The polenta and cornflour that coat the cockles give them a light crunchy chew, a bit like when you eat popcorn.

Serves 8 as a snack

2kg cockles
500ml milk
300g plain white flour
150g cornflour
100g fine polenta
rapeseed oil for deep-frying
4 fresh red chillies, finely chopped – with seeds
    and all
sea salt flakes, to taste

For the chilli vinegar
300ml malt vinegar
75g demerara sugar
4 dried red chillies – you want hot ones!

First, make the chilli vinegar. Mix the malt vinegar, sugar and chillies together in a saucepan over a high heat and bring to the boil, stirring to dissolve the sugar. Remove the pan from the heat, pour the mixture into a vinegar dispenser, including the chillies, and leave to cool completely. Keep this in the fridge until needed, where it will last for ages.

At least $2^1/_2$ hours before you plan to serve, discard any cockles with broken shells or any open ones that don't snap shut when tapped. Wash the cockles under running cold water to remove any grit or dirt (don't cut corners here: run the water long enough to clean them properly).

Heat a large saucepan over a high heat until very hot and pour in the cockles. Add a splash of water and put a lid on the pan. Steam the cockles, shaking the pan occasionally, for 5–6 minutes until all the shells have opened. Discard any cockles that remain closed. Drain through a colander and leave the cockles to cool.

Pour the milk into a large bowl. When the cockles are cool enough to handle, remove them from the shells and add them to the milk. Discard the shells. Cover the bowl with clingfilm and transfer to the fridge for at least 2 hours.

When you are ready to fry the cockles, mix the flour, cornflour and polenta together. Heat enough oil for deep-frying in a deep-fat fryer or heavy-based saucepan until it reaches 180°C.

Working in batches, dust the cockles in the flour mix, shaking off any excess, then deep-fry a few at a time, so you don't get big clumps, for 3–5 minutes until they float to the surface and are golden brown. Use a slotted spoon to remove them from the oil and drain well on kitchen paper. Season the cockles with sea salt flakes and the finely chopped red chilli. Reheat the oil to the correct temperature between batches, if necessary.

Serve the cockles in rolled baking parchment or newspaper and with the chilli vinegar for sprinkling over.

Oyster fritters with seaweed mayonnaise

If you're not a fan of raw oysters and hate the thought of that 'snot' texture, this is the oyster dish for you! Here the oysters are deep-fried until crispy and cooked through. Think of them as chicken nuggets that taste of the sea! Serve these with a dipping mayonnaise that tastes of seaweed and has a little kick from wasabi.

Serves 4

250g plain white flour, plus extra for dusting
20g fresh yeast, crumbled
500ml milk, blood heat
vegetable oil for deep-frying
24 large rock oysters
lemon wedges, to serve

For the seaweed salt
1 sheet nori seaweed
4 teaspoons sea salt flakes

For the seaweed mayonnaise
50g fresh gutweed
120ml rice wine vinegar
2 egg yolks
1 teaspoon wasabi paste
250ml vegetable oil

Mix the flour and yeast together in a large bowl and make a well in the centre. Gradually whisk in the milk to form a batter. Cover with clingfilm and leave for 1 hour at room temperature until slightly bubbly and aerated.

Meanwhile, make the seaweed salt. Break the seaweed sheet into a food processor and pulse a couple of times. Add the sea salt and pulse a few more times until well blended together. Leave to one side until needed.

To make the seaweed mayonnaise, first pick over the gutweed and rinse it well, making sure you get rid of all dirt and any grit, then squeeze it dry. Place it in a food processor with the rice wine vinegar, egg yolks and wasabi paste and blend. With the motor running, slowly add the oil until it emulsifies and thickens. Transfer to a bowl, cover and chill until needed.

Open the oysters and strain off the liquid.

When you are ready to deep-fry the oyster fritters, heat enough oil for deep-frying in a deep-fat fryer or a heavy-based saucepan until it reaches 180°C. One at a time, dust the oysters in flour and shake off the excess, then dip them into the batter, letting the excess drip off. Deep-fry the oysters for about 2 minutes until golden brown. Use a slotted spoon to remove them from the oil, drain well on kitchen paper, then season with the seaweed salt.

Serve immediately with the mayonnaise and lemon wedges for squeezing over.

Tom's Tip
Don't waste the oyster liquid. Stir it into the mayonnaise to enhance the flavour.

Deep-fried whitebait with Marie Rose sauce

This classic crunchy fish snack instantly makes me think of sitting in the sunshine in a pub garden by the seaside.

Serves 4

500g whitebait
1.2 litres milk
vegetable oil for deep-frying
400g plain white flour
2 teaspoons cayenne pepper

For the Marie Rose sauce
2 egg yolks
2 tablespoons white wine vinegar
1 tablespoon Dijon mustard
300ml vegetable oil
200g tomato ketchup
1 tablespoon brandy
1 tablespoon Worcestershire sauce
1 teaspoon Tabasco sauce
salt and cayenne pepper, to taste

Place the whitebait into a plastic container, pour over the milk, cover and leave in the fridge for 2–3 hours.

Meanwhile, make the Marie Rose sauce. Place the egg yolks, white wine vinegar and Dijon mustard into a food processor and blend together until smooth. With the motor running, slowly add the oil until it emulsifies and thickens. Transfer to a bowl and stir in the tomato ketchup, brandy, Worcestershire sauce and Tabasco sauce and season with salt and cayenne. Pass through a fine sieve, then cover and chill until needed.

When ready to fry the whitebait, heat enough oil for deep-frying in a deep-fat fryer or heavy-based saucepan to 180°C. Mix the flour with the cayenne in a shallow bowl. Drain the whitebait. Working with a handful at a time, toss the whitebait in the flour mix and shake off the excess. Add handfuls of whitebait to the fryer and fry for 5-6 minutes, until crispy. Drain on kitchen paper and season. Reheat the oil between handfuls, if necessary.

Serve immediately with the Marie Rose sauce.

Pickled quail's eggs with curried onion sauce

These delicious bite-sized eggs make gorgeous mouthfuls when dunked in my fantastic curried onion sauce. Quail's eggs taste similar to chicken's eggs, but they have a higher yolk to white ratio and are a great small snack.

Makes 12

100ml Pickle Mix (see page 241)
100ml water
12 quail's eggs

For the curried onion sauce
3 tablespoons vegetable oil
2 tablespoons Curry Powder (see page 241)
1 tablespoon tomato purée
2 red onions, finely chopped
2 Spanish onions, finely chopped
2 plum tomatoes, roughly chopped
1 teaspoon salt
2 tablespoons chopped chives
2 tablespoons onion seeds, toasted

At least 4 hours before you plan to serve, mix all the ingredients for the pickle mix and water together in a large non-metallic bowl and set aside.

Bring a saucepan of water to the boil over a high heat and place a bowl of iced water next to the hob. Add the quail's eggs to the boiling water and set a timer for 2 minutes. After 2 minutes use a slotted spoon to immediately transfer them to the iced water and leave them to cool. When the eggs are cool, peel them and put them in the pickle mix. Leave for at least 4 hours or up to 3 days.

Meanwhile, make the curried onion sauce. Heat the vegetable oil in a large saucepan over a medium heat. Add the curry powder and stir for 1–2 minutes to cook out the raw flavour. Add the tomato purée and continue stirring for a further 2 minutes. Stir in the red onions, Spanish onions, tomatoes and salt. Reduce the heat to low, cover the pan and leave the vegetables to simmer for 20 minutes, or until the onion has softened.

Transfer the mixture to a blender and purée until smooth, then pass through a fine sieve. Stir in the chives and onion seeds. You can keep this hot, or leave it to cool completely and chill until needed.

Serve the pickled eggs with the sauce.
(See picture, page 103.)

" These delicious bite-sized eggs make gorgeous mouthfuls when dunked in my fantastic curried onion sauce."

Salt cod Scotch eggs with red pepper sauce

I like to play around with making different varieties of Scotch eggs and this version is one of my favourites – dried salt cod wrapped around a runny quail's egg. Serve hot with the red pepper sauce and a slice of grilled chorizo.

Makes 12

150g sea salt flakes
500ml olive oil, plus 4 tablespoons
2 tablespoons Pernod
2 tablespoons dry white wine
1 teaspoon saffron threads
750g cod fillets, skinned
2 or 3 baking potatoes – you are going to need 300g baked flesh
2 garlic cloves, crushed
12 quail's eggs
150g plain white flour, for dusting
2 eggs, beaten
150g fine dry breadcrumbs (use panko breadcrumbs whenever possible), for coating
vegetable oil for deep-frying
salt, to taste

For the red pepper sauce
4 tablespoons olive oil
3 red peppers, deseeded and sliced
2 banana shallots, sliced
1 fresh red chilli, sliced – with seeds and all
$1/2$ teaspoon saffron threads
100ml dry white wine
50g sugar
50ml white wine vinegar
100g butter, cubed

At least 24 hours ahead, mix the sea salt flakes, 4 tablespoons olive oil, the Pernod, white wine and saffron threads together in a large non-metallic bowl until it forms a paste. Add the cod and rub it all over with the paste, then cover the bowl with clingfilm and put in the fridge for 24 hours.

When ready to cook the cod, preheat the oven to 140°C/Gas Mark 1. Remove the cod from the salt paste and rinse thoroughly in cold running water for 5 minutes. Place it in a roasting tray, pour over 500ml olive oil and cover the tray with kitchen foil. Place the tray in the oven and roast the cod for 25 minutes. Remove the tray from the oven and leave the cod to cool completely in the olive oil. When the fish is cool enough to handle, remove any pin bones and flake the flesh.

As soon as the cod comes out of the oven, increase the oven temperature to 180°C/Gas Mark 4. When it reaches the correct temperature, place the potatoes in the oven and bake for $1^1/_2$ hours, or until cooked through and tender. When cool enough to handle, peel them and put them through a potato ricer into a large bowl or use a masher. Add the garlic cloves and flaked cod to 300g mashed potatoes and beat together, then leave to one side.

Meanwhile, bring a saucepan of water to the boil over a high heat and place a bowl of iced water next to the hob. Add the quail's eggs to the boiling water and set a timer for 2 minutes. After 2 minutes, use a slotted spoon to immediately transfer them to the iced water and leave them to cool. When the eggs are cool, peel them, but be careful not to break the eggs!

Shape the cod and potato mix around the eggs to form 12 mini Scotch eggs. Place the flour, egg wash and breadcrumbs in separate bowls in a row on the work surface. One by one, dip the Scotch eggs into the flour, tapping off any excess, then into the eggs, letting the excess drip back into the bowl, and then into the breadcrumbs. Place each Scotch egg on kitchen roll as it is coated and keep in the fridge until you are ready to fry them. They can be kept for up to 2 days in the fridge at this stage.

To make the red pepper sauce, heat the olive oil in a saucepan over a medium heat. Add the peppers, shallots and chilli and fry, stirring, for 3–5 minutes until softened. Add the saffron, reduce the heat to low and leave to slowly cook for 20–25 minutes until the peppers and shallots are very tender.

Stir in the wine, sugar and white wine vinegar, increase the heat to medium and leave to simmer, uncovered, until almost all the liquid has evaporated. Transfer the sauce to a blender and purée. Add the butter, which will give the sauce a shine, and blend again. Season, then pass the sauce through a sieve. Leave to one side to cool until needed.

When ready to deep-fry the Scotch eggs, heat enough oil for deep-frying in a deep-fat fryer or heavy-based saucepan to 180°C. Working in batches, if necessary, add the eggs to the oil and deep-fry for 3–4 minutes until they are nice and golden brown. Drain well on kitchen paper and sprinkle with salt. Reheat the oil between batches, if necessary. Serve the eggs immediately while they are still hot with the red pepper sauce.

Spicy roasted nuts

Spicy roasted peanuts are the country's quintessential pub snack. By now, it won't surprise you that I give it my own special twist! This recipe is so easy and quick, and well worth the extra effort before your mates come round.

Serves 4

1 tablespoon Curry Powder (see page 241)
2 teaspoons table salt
1 teaspoon cayenne pepper
1 teaspoon ground cumin
$\frac{1}{2}$ teaspoon ground turmeric
4–6 teaspoons water
500g peeled peanuts

Preheat the oven to 180°C/Gas Mark 4. Mix the curry powder, salt, cayenne, cumin and turmeric together in a bowl. Stir in the water until a paste forms. Add the peanuts and make sure they get a good coating.

Transfer the peanuts to a roasting tray. Place the tray in the oven and roast the peanuts for 5 minutes. Give them a good stir, then return the tray to the oven and roast the peanuts for a further 5 minutes. Repeat this process 4 or 5 times until the paste has dried and the nuts have a lovely toasted flavour and aroma. Leave to cool, then enjoy with a good beer.

(See picture, page 103.)

Smoky bacon crisps

You can't beat home-cooked crisps and these crunchy bacon beauties win my vote every time.

Serves 4–6

10 slices of pancetta
1 teaspoon smoked paprika
1 teaspoon table salt, plus extra for the boiling water
5 large chipping potatoes
vegetable oil for deep-frying

Preheat the oven to 80°C/Gas Mark at its lowest and the grill to high. Place the pancetta strips on the grill rack and grill until crispy and golden. Transfer the pancetta to a roasting tray lined with greaseproof paper and place in the oven for about 2 hours until dry and very crisp. Set aside and leave to cool, then grind in a pestle and mortar. Transfer to a bowl, add the smoked paprika and salt and set aside until needed.

Bring a large pan of salted water to the boil. Peel the potatoes, then use the crinkle cutter on a mandoline to slice them about 0.2cm thick. Working in batches, if necessary, add the potato slices to the boiling water and stir, then immediately remove them with a slotted spoon and leave them to dry on a tea towel. Bring the water back to the boil before adding another batch.

When the potatoes are completely dry, heat enough vegetable oil for deep-frying in a deep-fat fryer or heavy-based saucepan to 180°C. Working in batches, if necessary, add the potato slices and deep-fry for 2–3 minutes until crispy and golden brown. Remove them with a slotted spoon and drain well on kitchen paper. Season immediately with the smoky bacon powder and serve.

Pork scratchings

This snack needs no introduction! This recipe will make enough for a whole gang of your mates. Wash them down with a good pint of ale.

1kg pork skin from a pork loin – ask your butcher for the skin
1 tablespoon salt
200ml white wine vinegar

Preheat the oven to 180°C/Gas Mark 4. Cut the pork skin into 7½cm pieces. Don't worry, they don't need to be exact. Place them in a large non-metallic bowl, add the salt and vinegar, mix together thoroughly and leave to stand for 1–2 minutes.

Transfer the pork skin pieces to a wire rack in a roasting tray. Place the tray in the oven and roast the pieces of pork skin for 10–15 minutes until crispy and crunchy. Watch them closely, as they might even take longer. The better the quality of the pork skin, the quicker they will cook. Leave to cool completely, then serve. These will keep crispy for 2–3 days in an airtight container.

Opposite (left to right): Spicy roasted nuts (page 101); Pork scratchings (above); Pickled quail's eggs with curried onion sauce (page 99).

PROPER
FISH

Fish and chips with pea purée and tartare sauce

Sometimes the simple classics are the best. Take your time to get this right and you will have a world-class dish! Halibut is the ideal fish to use, but any good quality white flat fish will be fine. You need the best quality brand of frozen petis pois for this recipe. Anything else will give a grainy texture – so don't skimp on your peas! At my pub we always serve our fish and chips with round chips simply because they look more interesting.

Serves 4

4 halibut fillets, about 180g each
sea salt flakes, to taste
table salt, to taste
lemon wedges, to serve – wrap them in muslin if you
    want to posh this up

For the chips
4 large potatoes for chipping, such as Maris piper
vegetable oil for deep-frying

For the tartare sauce
3 egg yolks
1 tablespoon Dijon mustard
4 teaspoons white wine vinegar
500ml vegetable oil
2 hard-boiled eggs, shelled and grated
1 shallot, finely chopped
2 tablespoons finely chopped gherkins
2 tablespoons capers in brine, drained and finely
    chopped
2 tablespoons finely chopped parsley leaves

For the beer batter
2 egg whites
240ml beer or sparkling water
350g self-raising white flour
large pinch of bicarbonate of soda

For the pea purée
25g butter
1 shallot, finely chopped
1/2 teaspoon sea salt flakes
100ml chicken stock
1 tablespoon finely chopped mint leaves
350g frozen peas, defrosted
4 teaspoons caster sugar

To make thick chips, top and tail each potato, then use an apple corer to cut out the centres. Remember, we are making round chips here. Bring a large saucepan of salted water to the boil over a high heat. Add the potatoes, return the water to the boil and boil for about 5 minutes until tender, but still holding their shapes. Use a slotted spoon to remove them from the water and leave them to drain. Dry well on a wire rack.

When the potatoes are completely dry, heat enough oil for deep-frying in a deep-fat fryer or heavy-based saucepan until it reaches 140°C. Add the potatoes and fry for 8–10 minutes until the oil stops bubbling, which means all the moisture has been removed. Use a slotted spoon to remove the potatoes from the oil, return them to the wire rack and leave to cool completely.

Meanwhile, make the tartare sauce. Place the egg yolks, Dijon mustard and white wine vinegar in a food processor and blend until smooth. With the motor still running, slowly add the oil until the mixture emulsifies and thickens. Stir in the remaining ingredients and season. Cover and keep in the fridge until needed.

To make the pea purée, melt the butter in a saucepan over a low heat. Add the shallots and sea salt and fry, stirring occasionally, for at least 5 minutes until softened, but not coloured. Add the chicken stock and mint and bring to the boil. Add the peas and sugar, return the stock to the boil and boil for 5–6 minutes until the peas are tender. Strain the peas and shallots over a bowl to catch the liquid, then transfer them to a blender. Add 2 tablespoons of

(continued on page 108)

(continued from page 106)

the cooking liquid and blend until smooth, but not too thin. Adjust the seasoning with table salt, if necessary, then set aside and keep hot.

To make the batter, mix the egg whites and beer together until fluffy. Mix the flour and bicarbonate of soda together in a large bowl and add the egg-white mix.

Just before you are ready to fry the fish, fry the potatoes for a second time. Reheat the oil to 180°C. Add the potatoes to the fryer again and fry for 2–3 minutes until crispy and golden brown. Drain well on kitchen paper, sprinkle with salt and keep hot in a low oven.

Reheat the oil to 180°C, if necessary. Dip the fish into the batter, letting any excess drip back into the bowl, then add to the oil and fry for 3–5 minutes until crispy and golden brown. Drain on kitchen paper. Keep the fried fillets warm in the low oven until they are all fried, but do not cover them with kitchen paper. Sprinkle with sea salt flakes and serve immediately with the chips, pea purée and tartare sauce and lemon wedges for squeezing over.

"Sometimes the simple classics are the best. Take your time to get this right and you will have a world-class dish!"

Lattice-topped fish pie

I use salmon, smoked haddock and prawns in this pie, but you can swap them about for whichever fish you fancy. The puff pastry gives a nice crust with a contrasting texture. I prefer this to the more usual mashed potato topping, which I think gives a fish pie the same consistency all the way through.

Serves 4

140g butter, softened
2 leeks, slit lengthways, rinsed and thinly sliced
400ml chicken stock, fish stock or vegetable stock
200ml milk
40g plain white flour, plus extra for rolling out the puff pastry
finely grated zest of 1 lemon
freshly grated nutmeg, to taste
2 tablespoons chopped flat-leaf parsley leaves
1 tablespoon chopped tarragon
300g skinless salmon fillet, chopped
250g boneless, skinless smoked haddock, chopped
200g raw prawns, peeled
500g all-butter puff pastry, defrosted if frozen
2 egg yolks beaten with a splash of double cream for sealing and glazing
salt and pepper, to taste

Rub the insides of a 1.5-litre pie dish with 50g of the butter, then set aside.

Melt 50g of the remaining butter in a saucepan over a low heat. Add the leeks and a pinch of salt and fry, stirring occasionally, for at least 5 minutes until softened, but not coloured. Tip the leeks into the bottom of the pie dish and leave to one side.

Mix the stock of your choice and the milk together in the washed pan and bring to the boil. In a separate pan, melt the remaining 40g butter over a medium heat. Add the flour and stir for 2–3 minutes to cook out the raw flavour. Slowly add the boiling stock and milk mix, whisking constantly, to make a thick sauce. Season with the lemon zest, nutmeg and salt and pepper, then set aside and leave to cool completely. When the sauce is cool, stir in the parsley and tarragon.

Scatter the salmon and smoked haddock over the leeks in the pie dish, then top with the prawns. Pour the cooled sauce over the top.

Roll out the puff pastry on a lightly floured surface until it is $\frac{1}{2}$cm thick. Cut into strips long enough to reach from each side of the pie dish, each about 1cm wide. Brush the rim of the pie dish with the egg mix and arrange evenly spaced strips of puff pastry in one direction. Next, interweave more strips through the already stuck-down strips, going under and over to create a lattice pattern. Take your time, because this can be quite tricky. Brush pastry strips with the remaining egg glaze, then place the pie in the fridge for at least 30 minutes or up to 6 hours.

When you're ready to bake, preheat the oven to 200°C/Gas Mark 6 and place the fish pie on a baking sheet. Place the baking sheet in the oven and bake the pie for 25–30 minutes until the fish is cooked through and flakes easily, the pastry is golden brown and the sauce is bubbling. Serve straight away. With salad or peas? Try both!

Proper Pub Food

Pot-roasted pollock, chickpeas and chorizo

This dish tastes amazing. It is a bit of a 'campfire' dish, perfect for feeding friends, that leaves you feeling content and happy. It has a Spanish feel to it, but you can use different pulses and different flavoured sausages, if you like – try butter beans and Toulouse sausages or white haricot beans and merguez sausages.

Serves 4–6

150g dried chickpeas
4 tablespoons sea salt flakes
a pinch of saffron
1 fillet of pollock, about 500g, skinned and pin bones removed
100ml olive oil
2 garlic cloves, grated
2 fresh red chillies, chopped – with seeds and all
2 onions, finely chopped
4 cooking chorizos, cut into bite-sized chunks
2 dried bay leaves
1 cinnamon stick
1 teaspoon ground cumin
1 teaspoon smoked paprika
1 x 400g can chopped tomatoes
200ml chicken stock
400g spinach leaves
salt and pepper, to taste

A day ahead, place the chickpeas in a large bowl with water to cover and leave to soak overnight.

The next day, drain the chickpeas and place them in a saucepan with fresh water to cover. Bring to the boil, skimming the surface as necessary. Reduce the heat to very low and leave them to simmer, uncovered, for 2 hours, or until the chickpeas are tender. Remove the pan from the heat and leave the chickpeas to cool in the water in the uncovered pan. They will expand in size.

Meanwhile, mix together the sea salt flakes and saffron. Place of piece of clingfilm large enough to wrap around the pollock on the work surface. Sprinkle half the salt mix on to the clingfilm and place the pollock on top, then sprinkle the remaining salt mix over the fish and wrap in the clingfilm tightly. Place this parcel into the fridge for $1^1/_2$ hours.

Heat the olive oil in a large flameproof casserole over a medium heat. Add garlic, red chillies and onions and fry, stirring occasionally, for 6–8 minutes until the onion has softened.

Add the chorizo to the pot and continue frying for a further 5 minutes so the red paprika-soaked oil comes out from the sausage. Stir in the bay leaves, cinnamon stick, cumin and paprika and fry, stirring, for a further 3–4 minutes.

Preheat the oven to 170°C/Gas Mark 3. Drain the chickpeas and add them to the pot, then add the canned tomatoes and pour in the stock. Bring to the boil and put it in the oven for 45 minutes.

Remove the pan from the oven and taste the chickpeas. The sauce should have reduced a little and thickened. Add salt, if necessary.

Rinse the pollock thoroughly in running cold water. Pat it dry and place on top of the chickpeas. Place the pot back into the oven for a further 15 minutes, or until the fish is cooked through and the flesh flakes easily.

Remove the pot from the oven. Gently take the fish from the pot and place it onto a large serving plate. Stir the spinach into the hot chickpeas until it just wilts. Spoon this mix over and around the fish and serve immediately. Remember to take out the bay leaves and the cinnamon.

Halibut, wild rice and sorrel baked in puff pastry with lime cream

Here's an all-in-one dinner, wrapped in puff pastry, a bit like a giant fish pasty. This is a perfect Sunday lunch dish, served whole in the centre of the table. When I serve it at home, I just let everyone cut their own slice.

There is a bit of work to get to the final point, but it is so worth it – you get lots of flavours, textures and smells all wrapped up in pastry. To avoid a last-minute rush, quite a bit of the work can be done in advance and the final dish can be assembled up to two hours before baking.

Serves 4

2 tablespoons olive oil
2 garlic cloves, crushed
1 onion, finely chopped
150g button mushrooms, wiped, trimmed and quartered
150g wild rice
400ml vegetable stock
finely grated zest of 1 lemon
1 ball of mozzarella, 250g, drained and finely diced
2 tablespoons chopped dill
large handful of spinach leaves
large handful of sorrel leaves
500g halibut fillets, trimmed and skinned
500g all-butter puff pastry, defrosted if frozen
plain white flour for rolling out the pastry
2 egg yolks beaten with a splash of double cream for sealing and glazing
salt and pepper, to taste

For the lime cream
200ml double cream
1 lime
1 tablespoon cracked black pepper

Heat the olive oil in a large saucepan over a medium heat. Add the garlic and onion and fry, stirring occasionally, for at least 5 minutes until softened, but not coloured. Add the mushrooms and fry for a further 2–3 minutes until they are just softened.

Stir in the wild rice, then add the vegetable stock and bring to the boil. Reduce the heat to medium, cover the pan and leave to simmer for about 45 minutes until the rice is tender and all the stock has been absorbed.

Remove the pan from the heat, stir in the lemon zest and season. Leave the wild rice mix to cool completely. When it's cool, add the mozzarella and dill and gently stir them though the wild rice, then leave to one side until needed.

Meanwhile, bring a saucepan of salted water to the boil and place a bowl of iced water in the sink. Put the spinach and the sorrel into the boiling water and blanch for about 2 seconds to just soften. Drain them well, then immediately plunge them into the iced water to stop the cooking and set the colour. Drain again. Lay the spinach and sorrel leaves out on a dry clean tea towel to soak up any water.

Place a large sheet of clingfilm over your work surface and arrange a layer of the dry spinach and sorrel on top, then season. Put a large spoonful or two of the rice mix on top of the spinach, then place the fish on top of the rice. Cover the fish with the remaining rice mix, then wrap over the remaining spinach and sorrel. You are looking for a green parcel. Wrap this parcel in the clingfilm tightly and leave to rest for 1–2 hours in the fridge.

After the halibut has rested, roll out the puff pastry on a lightly floured surface into a rectangle $\frac{1}{2}$cm thick. Cut out the corners to make it look like a cross. Remove the clingfilm from the halibut parcel and place the parcel in the centre of the cross. Wrap the fish up in the puff pastry and use the egg glaze to seal the edges. Place it seam-side down on a piece of baking parchment on a thick baking sheet and place in the fridge for at least 1 hour or up to 2 hours.

Meanwhile, make the lime cream. Pour the double cream into a bowl. Grate the zest of the lime on top and then squeeze the juice through a fine sieve into the cream. Whisk until the cream thickens. Add the cracked black pepper and a pinch of salt. Cover and chill until needed.

When you are ready to bake, preheat the oven to 200°C/Gas Mark 6 and glaze the pastry with the egg wash. Put the baking sheet in the oven and roast the halibut parcel for 25–30 minutes until the pastry is golden brown. Remove from the oven and leave the parcel to rest for 5–10 minutes before slicing. Serve with the lime cream.

Proper Pub Food

Fish burgers with herb mayonnaise

Try these as a great alternative to the classic beef burger. The trick to this recipe is salting the fish and prawns first to remove the excess moisture, which then helps them to bind together. Once you shape these they will keep in the fridge for up to two days before cooking, and they are robust enough to cook on a barbecue.

Makes 4

350g pollock fillet, skinned and pin bones removed
200g mackerel fillet, skinned and pin bones removed
100g raw prawns, peeled
2 tablespoons sea salt flakes
2 garlic cloves, crushed
2 tablespoons capers in brine, drained and chopped
1 teaspoon bicarbonate of soda
1 tablespoon chopped dill
1 teaspoon English mustard powder
1 beef tomato, cut into 4 slices
1 Spanish onion, thinly sliced
4 soft buns, halved
4 tablespoons rapeseed oil
4 thick slices of pancetta
1 Little Gem lettuce, separated into leaves, rinsed
    and dried
salt and pepper, to taste

For the herb mayonnaise
leaves from 1 small bunch of chervil
leaves from 1 small bunch of flat-leaf parsley
leaves from $1/4$ bunch of tarragon
3 egg yolks
2 tablespoons white wine vinegar
1 tablespoon Dijon mustard
500ml vegetable oil

Place the fish fillets and prawns on a rimmed, non-metallic plate. Sprinkle over the sea salt flakes, then place the fish in the fridge for $1^1/_2$–2 hours until the textures become firm.

After the fish has become firm, rinse it thoroughly under running cold water, drain well on a tea towel and pat dry.

If you have a mincer, mince the fish into a bowl. If not, very finely chop the fish with a sharp knife. Add the garlic, capers, bicarbonate of soda, dill and mustard powder and mix together. Shape into 4 large burgers, cover with clingfilm and leave in the fridge for at least 1 hour before cooking.

Meanwhile, make the herb mayonnaise. Bring a saucepan of salted water to the boil and place a bowl of iced water in the sink. Add the chervil, parsley and tarragon into the boiling water and blanch for about 2 minutes until the herbs are soft. Drain well, then immediately plunge them into the iced water to stop the cooking and set the colours. Leave to cool completely, then squeeze them to remove any excess liquid.

Place the herbs, egg yolks, white wine vinegar and Dijon mustard into a food processor and blend. With the motor still running, slowly add the oil until it emulsifies and thickens. Season, cover and keep in the fridge until needed.

Place the tomato and onion slices on a plate and season. Leave for about 10 minutes to draw out some moisture.

When ready to cook, preheat the grill to high and toast the buns. Heat the rapeseed oil in a large non-stick frying pan over a medium heat. Add the fish burgers and fry for 2–3 minutes on each side until cooked through and lightly coloured. Remove them from the pan and cover with foil to keep hot.

Add the pancetta to the pan and fry for about 4 minutes on each side until they are crispy and browned. Divide the tomato slices between the buns and then add the fish burgers, wilted onion and lettuce. Top with the pancetta and finish with the herb mayonnaise. Serve immediately.

Proper Paella

There are so many versions of paella, and I'm not going to claim this is the definitive one, but it does taste great and can be cooked outside over hot coals, which makes it very cool and authentic!

Serves 4–6

250g tomatoes, with a small X cut in the top of each
100ml olive oil
6 chicken thighs
150g cooking chorizo sausage, sliced
1 Spanish onion, finely chopped
1 green pepper, deseeded and finely chopped
1 red pepper, deseeded and finely chopped
2 garlic cloves, crushed
$1^{1}/_{2}$ teaspoons sweet paprika
$^{1}/_{2}$ teaspoon cayenne pepper
large pinch of saffron threads
350g paella rice
1.2 litres chicken stock, plus a little extra, if needed
75g shelled fresh peas
12 tiger prawns
3 tablespoons chopped flat-leaf parsley leaves
finely grated zest and freshly squeezed juice of
    1 lemon
salt and pepper, to taste
1 lemon, cut in half, to garnish

Bring a saucepan of water to the boil over a high heat and put a bowl of iced water in the sink. Add the tomatoes to the water and boil for 10 seconds, then immediately drain and put them in the iced water to stop the cooking. Drain them again and use a small knife to peel off the skins. Cut the tomatoes in half, scoop out the seeds and finely dice the flesh. Leave to one side until needed.

Meanwhile, heat the olive oil in a paella pan or very large frying pan over a medium heat. Add the chicken thighs, skin side down, and fry for 5–8 minutes until the skin is caramelised and brown all over. Remove them from the pan, drain on kitchen paper and leave to one side.

Add the chorizo to the pan and fry, stirring occasionally, until a little tinged. Remove the chorizo from the pan, drain on kitchen paper and leave to one side. Add the onion, the green and red peppers and the garlic to the pan and fry, stirring, for 2–3 minutes. Stir in the sweet paprika, cayenne and saffron. Add the paella rice and stir around so it is well coated. Pour in the stock and bring to the boil. Add the tomatoes.

Turn the heat down to low and simmer, uncovered and without stirring, for 15–20 minutes. Gently stir in the peas, lay the tiger prawns on top and return the chicken thighs and chorizo sausage to the pan. Continue simmering for a further 15 minutes, turning the prawns over once halfway through to make sure they cook all the way through, or until the rice is tender. You may need to add a little more stock. Stir in the parsley and lemon zest and juice. Check to see if it needs any salt and pepper. Garnish with a lemon in the middle of the pan and serve immediately.

Salmon fishcakes with watercress soup

This is a dish that we had on The Hand & Flowers' menu when we first opened. It's a firm favourite of mine – and in pubs up and down the country. Although someone did complain once that it had too much fish in it?! The use of the smoked salmon here gives the fishcakes extra depth of flavour.

Makes 4

3 or 4 baking potatoes, depending on their size – in the end you are going to need 350g of the baked potato flesh
350g salmon fillet, skinned
2 tablespoons capers in brine, drained
2 tablespoons chopped dill
2 tablespoons chopped flat-leaf parsley leaves
1 tablespoon English mustard powder
$1/2$ teaspoon cayenne pepper
$1/2$ teaspoon salt
finely grated zest of 1 lemon
100g smoked salmon, chopped
150g plain white flour
3 eggs, beaten
150g panko breadcrumbs
4 tablespoons rapeseed oil
salt and pepper, to taste

For the watercress soup
30g butter
2 banana shallots, finely chopped
100ml chicken stock
200ml double cream
200g watercress leaves, picked over and chopped

Preheat the oven to 180°C/Gas Mark 4. Place the potatoes in the oven and bake for $1 1/2$ hours, or until they are baked through and tender. Remove them from the oven, but do not turn off the oven. When they are cool enough to handle, cut them in half lengthways and scoop out the flesh, then put it though a potato ricer into a bowl or use a masher. Season the salmon, wrap it in kitchen foil and place it on a baking sheet. Place the baking sheet in the oven and roast the salmon for 8–10 minutes until just cooked through and the flesh flakes easily.

Weigh out 350g of the baked potatoes and put in a large bowl. Mix in the capers, dill, parsley, mustard powder, cayenne, salt and lemon zest, then mix in the smoked salmon. Gently break the salmon pieces into large chunks and fold them into the mix. Divide the mix into four equal balls and shape into fishcakes. Cover with clingfilm, place in the fridge and leave to rest for at least 1 hour or up to 6 hours.

Meanwhile, make the watercress soup. Melt the butter in a saucepan over a low heat. Add the shallots and fry, stirring occasionally, for at least 5 minutes until softened, but not coloured. Add the chicken stock and bring to the boil, then continue boiling until it reduces by half. Pour in the double cream and return the liquid to the boil. Add the watercress, then immediately pour into a blender and season. Blend the soup until smooth, then pass it through a fine sieve. Leave to one side until needed.

To coat the fishcakes with breadcrumbs, put the flour, eggs and panko breadcrumbs into separate bowls in a row on the work surface. One by one, dip the fishcakes first into the flour, tapping off any excess, then into the eggs, letting the excess drip back into the bowl, and then into the breadcrumbs, patting them on. Place each fishcake on kitchen paper as it is coated and leave to one side until ready to fry.

When ready to fry the fishcakes, heat the rapeseed oil in a large frying pan over a medium heat. Add the fishcakes and fry for about 5 minutes on each side until golden brown, crispy and hot all the way through. Drain on kitchen paper. Meanwhile, reheat the soup, if necessary.

Serve each of the fishcakes with a bowl of soup on the side.

Tom's Tip
Use the baked potato skins from the Warm Crayfish and Watercress Salad in Potato Skins (see page 71).

Smoked haddock fishcakes with fried egg and cheese sauce

This is a change to the pub classic of smoked haddock and poached egg. It has a little more crunch and texture here from the breadcrumbs and the fried egg. This goes very well with a crisp salad or wilted spinach.

Makes 4

3 or 4 baking potatoes, depending on their size – in the end you are going to need 350g of the baked potato flesh
300ml milk
400g undyed smoked haddock fillet
1 ball mozzarella, 250g, drained and cut into $1/2$ cm dice
3 tablespoons chopped chives, plus extra, to garnish
1 teaspoon cracked black pepper
$1/2$ teaspoon salt
150g plain white flour
3 eggs, beaten
150g panko breadcrumbs
rapeseed oil
4 eggs
salt and pepper, to taste

For the cheese sauce
15g butter
1 tablespoon plain white flour
125g Gruyère cheese, freshly grated
75g Parmesan cheese, freshly grated
2 tablespoons crème fraîche
1 tablespoon wholegrain Dijon mustard

Preheat the oven to 180°C/Gas Mark 4. Place the potatoes in the oven and bake for $1 1/2$ hours, or until they are baked through and tender. Remove them from the oven, but do not turn off the oven. When they are cool enough to handle, cut them in half lengthways and scoop out the flesh, then put it though a potato ricer into a bowl or use a masher. Weight out 350g of the baked potatoes, put it in a large bowl and leave to one side until needed.
Put the milk in a large saucepan over a high heat and bring to the boil. Place the smoked haddock into the milk and turn off the heat. Cover the pan and leave the smoked haddock to gently poach in the residual heat for 8–10 minutes until the fish is cooked through and the flesh flakes easily.

Remove the haddock from the pan and reserve the poaching milk. When the smoked haddock is cool enough to handle, remove all bones and the skin and discard. Flake the flesh into large pieces and leave to one side until needed.

To make the cheese sauce, melt the butter in a saucepan over a medium heat. Add the flour and stir for 2–3 minutes to cook out the raw flavour. Slowly whisk in the haddock poaching milk, whisking constantly, to make a thick white sauce. Remove the pan from the heat. Whilst the sauce is still hot, add the Gruyère cheese and Parmesan cheese, stirring until they have melted. Stir in the the crème fraîche and Dijon mustard and season. Keep on one side.

Add the mozzarella, chives, black pepper and salt to the mashed potatoes, then gently fold in the smoked haddock. Divide the mix into four equal balls and shape into fishcakes. Cover with clingfilm, place in the fridge and leave to rest for at least 1 hour or up to 6 hours.

To coat the fishcakes with breadcrumbs, put the flour, eggs and panko breadcrumbs into separate bowls in a row on the work surface. One by one, dip the fishcakes first into the flour, tapping off any excess, then into the eggs, letting the excess drip back into the bowl, and then into the breadcrumbs, patting them on. Place each fishcake on kitchen roll as it is coated and leave until ready to fry.

When ready to fry the fishcakes, heat 4 tablespoons rapeseed oil in a large frying pan over a medium heat. Add the fishcakes and fry for about 5 minutes on each side until golden brown, crispy and hot all the way through. Drain on kitchen paper and keep hot. Wipe out the pan with kitchen paper.

To fry the eggs, heat a thin layer of rapeseed oil in the pan over a medium heat. One by one, crack the eggs into the pan and fry for about 3 minutes until the whites are just set. Season.

To serve, reheat the sauce, if necessary. Pour a little sauce into the bottom of 4 bowls, then add a fishcake into each and top each with a fried egg. Garnish the eggs with chopped chives and serve immediately.

"It has a little more crunch and texture here from the breadcrumbs and the fried egg..."

Tomato and olive tart with Cornish gurnard

Served as a whole tart, this is a real centrepiece, full of flavour and colour. Gurnard is a great alternative for red mullet and is, perhaps, more plentiful and offers greater value. This tart can also be made without any fish – just add more olives and basil.

Serves 4

500g all-butter puff pastry, defrosted if frozen
plain white flour for rolling out the pastry and dusting the fish
6–8 plum tomatoes, with a small X cut in the top of each
2 teaspoons thyme leaves
1 teaspoon sugar
$\frac{1}{2}$ teaspoon sea salt flakes, plus extra for sprinkling
handful of basil leaves
olive oil
4 large gurnard fillets, or 8 smaller ones, total weight about 800g

For the tapenade
115g stoned black olives
25g salted anchovy fillets
2 tablespoons capers in brine, drained
3 tablespoons freshly grated Parmesan cheese
2 garlic cloves, crushed
130ml extra virgin olive oil

Roll the puff pastry out on a lightly floured surface into a rectangle about 25 x 12cm. Transfer the pastry to a sheet of baking parchment on a baking sheet. Cover with clingfilm and leave in the fridge for at least 1 hour or up to 6 hours.

Meanwhile, make the tapenade. Put the black olives, anchovies, capers, Parmesan cheese and garlic in a food processor and process to break down. Add the olive oil and blend again to make a thick purée. Leave to one side until needed.

When ready to bake the tart, preheat the oven to 200°C/Gas Mark 6. Place the baking sheet in the oven and bake the pastry for 15–20 minutes until it is crisp and golden brown. Remove the baking sheet from the oven and carefully transfer the pastry to a wire rack to cool.

Meanwhile, bring a saucepan of water to the boil and put a bowl of iced water in the sink. Add the tomatoes and boil for 10 seconds, then immediately drain and put them in the iced water to stop the cooking. Drain the tomatoes again and use a small knife to peel off the skins.

Cut the tomatoes into $\frac{1}{2}$cm slices and lay them on a non-metallic tray. Season with the thyme leaves, sugar and sea salt flakes, then leave for 15–20 minutes, until they soften. Transfer to a clean tea towel and leave to dry.

Reheat the oven to 190°C/Gas Mark 5. Spread a layer of tapenade over the base of the puff pastry tart case, leaving a border on all sides. Layer the tomatoes on top, placing a basil leaf between each slice. Drizzle the tart with olive oil and return to the oven for 5–8 minutes to warm through

While the tart is in the oven, heat 4 tablespoons olive oil in a large non-stick frying pan over a medium heat. Dust the gurnard fillets in flour, shaking off the excess. Place them in the oil, skin sides down, and fry for 7–8 minutes until not quite cooked through.

Remove the tart from the oven and place the gurnard fillets on top. Sprinkle with sea salt flakes, then return to the oven for a further 1–2 minutes until the fish is cooked through, the flesh flakes easily and the pastry is hot.

Remove the tart from the oven, drizzle with a little more olive oil and add a few fresh basil leaves. Sprinkle with sea salt flakes and it's ready to serve.

Steamed trout and courgette flowers with Parmesan tuiles and horseradish mayonnaise

This is a very light seasonal dish, using the best of British summer vegetables. The horseradish gives the dish the acidity that marries all of the flavours together and lifts the taste of the trout. This recipe also works well with salmon, lemon sole or plaice.

Serves 2

70g butter
4 small courgettes with flowers attached
2 tablespoons podded broad beans
2 tablespoons shelled fresh peas
4 trout fillets, 70–100g each
10 basil leaves, shredded
1 tablespoon chopped flat-leaf parsley leaves
1 tablespoon chopped mint leaves
handful of wild rocket leaves, rinsed and spun dry
salt and pepper, to taste

For the Parmesan tuiles
100g Parmesan cheese, freshly grated

For the horseradish mayonnaise
2 egg yolks
40g horseradish, peeled and freshly grated
2 tablespoons white wine vinegar
1 tablespoon Dijon mustard
1 teaspoon horseradish cream
500ml vegetable oil
cayenne pepper, to taste
freshly squeezed lemon juice, to taste

To make the Parmesan tuiles, preheat the oven to 180°C/Gas Mark 4 and line a baking sheet with baking parchment. Place an ungreased biscuit cutter in a shape you like on a baking sheet and sprinkle in one-sixth of the cheese. Lift off the cutter and repeat to make a total of 6 tuiles. Place the baking sheet in the oven and bake the tuiles for 2–3 minutes until the cheese melts into the desired shape. Remove the baking sheet from the oven and leave the tuiles to cool and become crisp before you take them off the baking sheet. They can be stored in an airtight container for up to 2 days.

To make the horseradish mayonnaise, place the egg yolks, fresh horseradish, white wine vinegar, mustard and horseradish cream in a food processor and blend. With the motor still running, slowly add the vegetable oil until it emulsifies and thickens. Season with cayenne, lemon juice and salt. Transfer the mayonnaise to a bowl, cover and put in the fridge until needed.

Melt the butter in a large deep frying pan over a medium heat and add a big splash of water. Remove the flowers from the courgettes and keep to one side. Thickly slice the courgettes, add them to the pan and cook for 1–2 minutes, then add the broad beans and peas, season and continue cooking for a further 2 minutes.

Place the trout fillets on top of the vegetables and cover with a piece of kitchen foil, which will effectively steam the fillets. Leave them to steam for 2–3 minutes, then remove them from the pan. Stir the herbs, rocket leaves and courgette flowers into the vegetables and season. They will wilt in the heat.

Spread each plate with horseradish mayonnaise and spoon the vegetables on top. Place the trout on top of the vegetables and serve immediately with crispy Parmesan tuiles on each plate.

Steamed orange and thyme rainbow trout

Freshly steamed rainbow trout is a great fish. Rainbow trout is farmed, sustainable and good value for money. I serve it here with a potato salad, but the real stars of this dish are the toasted fennel seeds, orange zest and thyme leaves. Perhaps not your normal fish garnishes, but they give the mild trout flavour a massive lift.

Serves 2

200g baby new potatoes, scrubbed
2–3 tablespoons Greek yogurt, to taste
2 tablespoons chopped mint
1 cos lettuce, rinsed and shredded
4 rainbow trout fillets, pin-bones removed, but skin left on
75g butter, melted
1 tablespoon fennel seeds, toasted
1 tablespoon lemon thyme leaves
freshly grated zest of 1 orange
sea salt flakes, to taste
rapeseed oil, to serve

Bring a saucepan of salted water to the boil over a high heat. Add the new potatoes and return the water to the boil, then boil for 8–10 minutes until tender. Drain well, then leave them in the colander to steam dry for 3–4 minutes.

Transfer the potatoes to a bowl. Whilst they are still hot, stir in the yogurt and mint, then add the lettuce and season. Keep to one side until needed.

Select a pan that your steamer fits over and bring about 5cm water to the boil over a high heat. Cut out a sheet of baking parchment that fits the base of your steamer basket.

Place the trout fillets, skin side up, on the baking parchment and steam for 3–4 minutes. The fish should be still a little raw at this point. Gently peel the skin from the fillets and drizzle the flesh with some of the melted butter. Discard the skin. Season the fillets with the fennel seeds, thyme leaves and orange zest. Sprinkle over sea salt flakes to taste, then re-cover the steamer and steam the fillets for a further 1–2 minutes until the flesh flakes easily.

Place 2 fillets on each plate and add the potato salad. Drizzle each plate with rapeseed oil and serve.

Proper Pub Food

Turbot, toasted cucumber, mushrooms and radishes

Turbot is the king of fish, but other meaty fish, such as halibut and monkfish, work with this dish. You don't have to save cucumbers just for salads and sandwiches. I know cooking cucumber might sound odd, but it is lovely. The seeds give off a great toasted flavour.

Serves 2

75g butter
rapeseed oil
2 banana shallots, finely chopped
150g girolles or other wild mushrooms, wiped and trimmed
Cabernet Sauvignon vinegar, to taste
2 turbot fillets, 180–200g each, skinned
$1/4$ cucumber, halved lengthways with the edges just trimmed
6–8 large breakfast radishes with the leaves still attached, halved lengthways
sea salt flakes and pepper, to taste

Melt 30g of the butter with about 2 tablespoons rapeseed oil in a frying pan over a low heat. Add the shallots and fry, stirring occasionally, for at least 5 minutes until softened, but not coloured. Add the girolle mushrooms and continue stirring for a further 1–2 minutes until they are just tender. Add a splash of Cabernet Sauvignon vinegar and a pinch of salt. Remove the pan from the heat and leave the mushrooms to one side to cool.

Meanwhile, preheat the oven to 180°C/Gas Mark 4 and line a roasting tray with a piece of kitchen foil large enough to wrap around the fillets and mushrooms. Place the cooked mushrooms in the middle of the foil and put the turbot fillets on top. Season with sea salt flakes, then dot the remaining butter on top of the fish. Bring the edges of the foil up to seal the fish in a bag-like ball. This doesn't need to look neat!

Place the tray into the oven and roast the fish for 10–12 minutes until the fillets are firm to the touch when you open the foil bag.

Whilst the fish is cooking, heat 1 tablespoon rapeseed oil in a frying pan over a medium heat. Place the cucumber, seed side down, into the pan and place another pan or light weight on top. Cook the cucumbers until they are browned on the seed side. They will taste a little like cucumber popcorn!

When the cucumbers are browned, turn them over and throw the radishes into the pan. Drizzle over a little more rapeseed oil and toss them all around in the pan for 1–2 minutes until just tender. Season with sea salt flakes.

Remove the turbot from the oven and open the foil bag. Divide the mushrooms between 2 plates and put a fillet on top of each, but pour the juices into a bowl and season with Cabernet Sauvignon vinegar and salt and pepper. Garnish the plates with the radishes and cucumber and spoon over some of the cooking sauce and serve immediately.

Grey mullet, Swiss chard and butter sauce

I love this dish. Both the main ingredients are underused and offer great value for money. This is what I call clean and tidy food – it's simple and lets the produce speak for itself. Grey mullet is like a poor man's sea bass and should be treated the same way for fantastic results. Swiss chard has a fresh sour taste – a little like a cross between spinach and sorrel – that provides a good balance to the rich sauce.

Serves 2

2 banana shallots, finely chopped
75ml white wine vinegar
75ml dry white wine
75ml double cream
6 sprigs of rosemary, 3 tied together
200g butter, 100g of which is very cold and diced, plus an extra knob to finish the fish
2 very large Swiss chard leaves and stalks
150ml water
freshly squeezed juice of 1 lemon, plus extra for seasoning the sauce
$\frac{1}{2}$ teaspoon salt
2 tablespoons rapeseed oil
2 grey mullet fillets, about 180g each, pin bones removed, but unskinned
plain white flour for dusting
salt and pepper, to taste

Mix the shallots, white wine vinegar and wine together in a saucepan over a medium heat and bring to the boil. Continue boiling until the liquid reduces down to a glaze. Add the cream and return the liquid to the boil. Add the rosemary sprigs and continue boiling until the liquid is reduced by about one-third.

Turn the heat to very low and slowly whisk in 100g diced butter, whisking constantly until it emulsifies into a sauce. Season with lemon juice, salt and pepper. Remove the rosemary sprigs and leave the sauce to one side, covered with clingfilm to keep it warm.

Trim the Swiss chard by removing the leaves from the stalks. Thinly shred the leaves, then peel and trim the stalks into pieces 10 x 3cm. Set both aside until needed.

Combine the water, remaining 100g butter, the freshly squeezed lemon juice and the $\frac{1}{2}$ teaspoon salt in a deep frying pan over a high heat, stirring to melt the butter. Bring to the boil, then add the Swiss chard leaves and stalks, reduce the heat to low and leave to simmer, uncovered, while you cook the fish.

Heat the rapeseed oil in a non-stick frying pan over a low heat. Dust the skin side of the grey mullet fillets with flour, shaking off the excess, then gently place in the pan, skin side down, and cook slowly until almost cooked through, but the top side still looks raw. If the pan is over a low heat the fish will cook perfectly.

Add the chard leaves and stalks and continue cooking for 30 seconds – 1 minute until they are tender. Season.

Gently flip the fish over and add a knob of butter and a squeeze of lemon juice to the pan. This will steam the fish to finish the cooking and give a lovely flavour and colour.

To serve, divide the butter sauce between 2 plates and add the chard leaves and stalks. Top each portion with a grey mullet fillet and serve immediately.

Proper Pub Food

Plaice poached in red wine, slow-roasted onions and salt-baked carrots

Fish is normally associated with white wine, but poaching it in red wine gives it a fantastic taste. Here, I treat these tender fillets more like a piece of meat, serving them with substantial and robust vegetables. You must be careful when cooking plaice, as it can go a bit like cotton wool and become dry if you overcook it.

Serves 2

3 Spanish onions, unpeeled and cut in half through
   the equator
4 tablespoons rapeseed oil, plus extra for drizzling
leaves from 1/2 bunch of thyme
2 tablespoons soft dark brown sugar
4 tablespoons balsamic vinegar
2 tablespoons onion seeds, toasted
1 tablespoon chopped chives
1 strong white onion, thinly sliced into rings
150ml milk
6 tablespoons sea salt flakes
2 tablespoons demerara sugar
4 carrots, unpeeled
plain white flour for dusting
250ml red wine
100ml beef stock
1 teaspoon Marmite
2 thick fillets of plaice, 180–200g each, skinned
40g butter
salt and pepper, to taste

A day ahead, preheat the oven to 110°C/Gas Mark 1/4. Place the Spanish onions in a roasting tray, give them a little drizzle of rapeseed oil and add a sprinkling of thyme leaves. Place the tray into the oven and roast the onions for 8 hours.

Remove the tray from the oven and leave the onions to cool a little. Scoop out the roasted onion flesh and chop it to form a rough onion paste. Place this into a colander or fine sieve and leave to drain for 3–4 hours.

Place the soft brown sugar in a saucepan over a high heat and stir until it starts to melt. Add the balsamic vinegar, bring to the boil and boil for 1–2 minutes, without stirring, until a caramel forms. Add the drained onion paste and heat through. Stir in the onion seeds and the chives. Season. Remove the pan from the heat and leave to one side until needed.

Meanwhile, place the white onion rings in a bowl and pour over the milk and leave to one side.

Preheat the oven to 190°/Gas Mark 5. Mix the sea salt flakes, demerara sugar and remaining thyme leaves together, then sprinkle a thin layer of this mix on the base of a roasting tray. Place the carrots on top then cover with the rest of the salt mix. Place the tray in the oven and roast the carrots for 45 minutes, or until they are tender. Remove the tray from the oven and leave the carrots to cool a little.

When the carrots are cool enough to handle, scrape the salt mix off them. With a sharp knife scrape the skin from the carrots and keep them hot in the turned-off oven.

Remove the onion rings from the milk, pat dry and lightly dust them in the flour, shaking off any excess. Heat enough oil for deep-frying in a deep-fat fryer or heavy-based saucepan until it reaches 180°C. Add the onion rings and fry for about 2 minutes until crispy and golden brown. Drain on kitchen paper and season. Leave to one side and keep hot in the turned-off oven (but do not cover).

Place the wine, beef stock and Marmite together in a frying pan over a high heat and bring to the boil. Continue boiling until the liquid has reduced by one-third. Turn the heat down to very low and add the plaice fillets, then turn the heat off and leave them to poach in the residual heat for 4–5 minutes until they are firm to the touch.

Turn the fish over in the wine to finish cooking for 30 seconds. Remove the fillets from the wine and keep warm. Bring the wine back to the boil and boil until reduced by half. Pass this through a fine sieve into a clean pan and put back onto the heat. Gently stir in the butter.

Serve the poached plaice fillets with the slow-roasted onions and salt-baked carrots. Pour over a little sauce and then add the crispy onion rings. Serve immediately.

Sea bass, sea vegetables and mussels

This is a real taste of the seaside. While it's cooking the smells of the fish and sea vegetables fill the room with the nostalgia of being in a coastal town. Cooking the bass skin side down gives it a nice crispy texture, a good contrast to the soft sea vegetables.

Serves 2

450g mussels, debearded and barnacles removed
2 tablespoons rapeseed oil
2 line-caught sea bass fillets, 180–200g each, skin on, but pin bones removed
plain white flour for dusting
100g smoked streaky bacon in one piece, diced
40g butter
50g samphire, picked over and washed
50g sea aster, picked over and washed
50g sea beet, picked over and washed
50g sea purslane, picked over and washed
1 lemon, halved
salt, to taste

First, cook the mussels. Wash the mussels in running cold water. Discard any mussels that float, any with cracked shells and any open ones that do not snap shut when tapped. Heat a large saucepan over a high heat. Add the mussels and a splash or water, cover the pan and cook for 5–6 minutes, shaking the pan occasionally, until the shells have opened. Drain the mussels and discard any that have not opened. When the mussels are cool enough to handle, remove them from the shells and set aside.

Heat the rapeseed oil in a large frying pan over a low heat. Season the fish and dust the skin sides with flour, shaking off the excess. Then place the fillets into the pan, skin side down, and fry for about 8 minutes until the skin becomes crispy.

Meanwhile, heat another frying pan over a medium heat. Add the bacon and fry, stirring occasionally, for 4–5 minutes until it becomes crisp and renders out its fat and flavour.

Add 20g of the butter to the bacon and heat until it melts and becomes a lovely hazelnut-brown colour. Take the pan off the heat and stir in the sea vegetables with a small splash of water. Just let them gently wilt. Add the mussels to warm through.

Flip the fillets over when the skins are crispy, then throw in the remaining 20g butter. Squeeze over the juice of the lemon and baste the sea bass with the buttery pan juices.

Remove the sea vegetables and bacon from the pan and pat with kitchen paper. Divide them between 2 plates, place the fish on top and spoon a little of the cooking butter over the top. Serve immediately.

Flaked skate, dandelion leaves, charred lemon and anchovies

Skate is such a lush fish, but you don't see it often as it has a very short shelf life. When it is at its freshest it is simply stunning, meaty, moist and delicious, but after a couple of days it develops a very powerful smell of ammonia and must be thrown away. If you are on the coast and ever see this on the fishmonger's slab, buy it! The dandelion salad is really bitter and works very well with fish. This is a great lunch dish.

Serves 2

rapeseed oil
2 tablespoons capers in brine, drained and patted dry
1 lemon
100ml olive oil
1 skate wing, about 700g, on the bone, but skinned and trimmed
150g dandelion leaves (*pis en lit*), rinsed and patted dry
leaves from $1/2$ bunch of flat-leaf parsley
10 salted anchovy fillets
salt and pepper, to taste

Heat enough rapeseed oil for deep-frying the capers in a heavy-based saucepan until it reaches 180°C. Add the capers and deep-fry for 2–3 minutes until crispy. Remove them with a slotted spoon, then drain well on kitchen paper and season. Leave to one side until needed.

Thinly peel the zest of the lemon and leave the flesh to one side. Over a medium heat pour the olive oil into a deep frying pan large enough for the whole skate wing. Add the lemon zest and heat until the oil shimmers.

Add the skate wing, thick side down, and gently poach in the oil for 5 minutes. Use a fish slice or two palette knives to gently turn the fish over and poach the other side for a further 4–5 minutes until the flesh flakes easily. Skate is a very meaty and moist fish and cooking it on the bone like this means it will remain juicy.

Transfer the fish to a plate, cover with foil to keep it hot and leave to one side. Don't worry if it breaks up a bit because you are going to flake it for serving. Turn the heat off and leave the oil to cool.

Meanwhile, mix the dandelion leaves and parsley leaves together in a non-metallic bowl. Segment the lemon and squeeze the juice from the membrane on to the salad. Place the lemon segments on a baking tray and use a blowtorch to char them. Add them to the salad, then add a couple of tablespoons of the skate cooking oil and toss together. Season.

Flake big chunks of the skate wing from the bone and divide between 2 plates. They will come away from the bones very easily. Add a few salted anchovy fillets on top and scatter with the deep-fried capers. Stick a handful of the dandelion salad on top and garnish the plate with a little drizzle of the skate-cooking oil. Serve immediately.

Gilthead bream and oyster mushrooms

There is no doubt about it – gilthead bream is a fantastic fish. It is normally farmed in the Mediterranean sea, making it sustainable, and it travels very well. The skin crisps beautifully when it's cooked, and in this recipe its super taste is well balanced with the powerful flavours of the soy sauce and honey.

Serves 2

vegetable oil
2 garlic cloves, crushed
2 banana shallots, finely chopped
2½cm piece of fresh ginger, peeled and finely chopped
200g oyster mushrooms, wiped, trimmed and pulled apart
2 sprigs of rosemary
2 gilthead bream fillets, about 220g each, pin bones removed
plain white flour for dusting
40g butter
1 lemon, halved
2 bunches of spring onions, cut into 3cm pieces
2 tablespoons sesame seeds, plus more to garnish
1 tablespoon sesame oil
2 tablespoons runny honey
1 tablespoon dark soy sauce
salt, to taste

Heat 2 tablespoons vegetable oil in a large frying pan over a high heat. Add the garlic, shallots and ginger and fry, stirring, for 3–4 minutes until lightly browned. Add the oyster mushrooms and season with a pinch of salt. Stir-fry for 1–2 minutes until they just start to soften. Remove the pan from the heat and set aside.

Heat another 2 tablespoons vegetable oil in a non-stick frying pan over a medium heat. Place a sprig of rosemary into the flesh side of each bream fillet, where the pin bones were. Dust the skin sides in the flour, shaking off any excess, then gently add them to the frying pan. Press the fillets down until they don't want to curl up anymore. Turn the heat to low and leave for about 8 minutes, until the skin gets very crispy and the flesh is almost cooked through. Flip the fillets over and add the butter. Leave the butter to melt until it starts foaming and turns a hazelnut brown, then squeeze the juice of the lemon into the pan and baste the fish with the buttery pan juices.

Meanwhile, return the pan with the mushrooms to a medium heat. Add the spring onions and sesame seeds and toss around in the pan for 1–2 minutes until the spring onions are just tender. Drizzle the sesame oil over the mushrooms and transfer them to a hot serving bowl. Check the seasoning – you may not need any more salt.

Remove the fish from the pan and remove the rosemary stalks. Add the runny honey to the foaming butter and cook until the honey caramelises and turns an amber colour. Pour in the dark soy sauce and stir well. Remove from the heat.

Divide the mushrooms between 2 plates and place the fish on top. Spoon the honey and soy sauce over each fillet, sprinkle with sesame seeds and serve immediately.

Whole lemon soles, mustard leaves and turnips cooked in cider

Cooking fish on the bone, as I do in this wonderful winter dish, is the perfect way to keep the fish moist and it stops shrinking, too. Lemon sole is a flat fish, which means there are no fiddly little pin bones to worry about and the central spine makes it easy to remove the fillets when the fish is cooked. You can't go wrong with this recipe.

Serves 2

110g butter
4 large turnips, peeled and cut into 1cm dice
200ml scrumpy cider
2 tablespoons cider vinegar
1 tablespoon yellow mustard seeds, toasted
2 teaspoons thyme leaves
2 lemon soles on the bone, dark skin removed, but the white skin left on and the sides trimmed
plain white flour for dusting
4 tablespoons vegetable oil
freshly squeezed juice of $1/2$ lemon
200g mustard leaves, rinsed and spun dry in a salad spinner
salt and pepper, to taste

Melt 20g of the butter in a frying pan over a medium-high heat until the butter begins to foam. Add the turnips and fry, stirring occasionally, for about 5 minutes, until they start to colour all over.

Stir in the cider, turn the heat up and bring to the boil. Add the cider vinegar and continue boiling until the turnips are tender and most of the liquid has evaporated. Stir in 50g of the remaining butter, the mustard seeds and the thyme leaves. Turn the heat off and whisk until the butter emulsifies. Season and leave to one side until needed.

Lightly dust the white-skinned side of the lemon soles with flour, shaking off the excess. Heat the vegetable oil in another frying pan over a medium heat. Add the fish and fry for about 6 minutes, until it is three-quarters of the way cooked through. Gently turn the soles over, add 25g of the remaining butter and the lemon juice and cook for a further 2 minutes, or until the fish is cooked through and the flesh flakes easily.

Melt the remaining 15g butter in a saucepan over a high heat. Add the mustard leaves and stir, as if you were cooking spinach, just until they wilt. They will cook very quickly, so this should be done at the last moment. Season with salt.

Divide the fish between 2 plates and spoon the mustard leaves on top. Spoon the turnips and cider sauce over the top and serve immediately.

Tom's Tip

If you don't have a frying pan large enough to fry both lemon soles at once, use 2 pans. It's better to fry both fish at the same time and serve straight away, than to fry one after the other, keeping one warm.

Spiced monkfish and aubergine purée with green olive dressing

Whenever you cook monkfish, you should treat it like a piece of meat and allow it to rest and relax before cutting and serving, as this helps it retain its moisture. Cooking aubergine like I do in this recipe and then leaving it to drain removes the excess water that it contains. The remaining aubergine flesh works like a sponge, absorbing all the lovely flavours that you put with it.

Serves 2

2 large aubergines
2 tablespoons cumin seeds
2 tablespoons coriander seeds
olive oil
100ml double cream
finely grated zest and freshly squeezed juice of
    1 lemon
2 monkfish fillets, about 220g each, skinned and the
    thin grey membrane rubbed off
butter, for cooking
salt and pepper, to taste
celery leaves, to garnish

For the green olive dressing
100g green olives, stoned and chopped
6 salted anchovy fillets, chopped
1 tablespoon capers in brine, drained
1 fresh red chilli, chopped – with seeds and all
75ml extra virgin olive oil
juice of $\frac{1}{2}$ lemon
1 tablespoon chopped flat-leaf parsely leaves

A day in advance, preheat the oven to 180°C/Gas Mark 4.

Use a blow torch or a gas flame on the hob to char the aubergine skins all over. When they are charred, put them in a roasting tray, place the tray in the oven and roast them for 35–45 minutes until they are very soft. Take the aubergines out of the oven and leave to cool. Do not turn the oven off.

Mix the cumin and coriander seeds together in a roasting tray. Place the tray in the oven and toast the seeds, taking the tray out once or twice and stirring, for 8–10 minutes until they are aromatic. Immediately remove the seeds from the tray and leave to one side until needed the next day.

When the aubergines are cool enough to handle, cut them in half lengthways and scoop out the flesh, avoiding any of the charred skin. Chop the flesh until it forms a rough purée. Scrape the purée into a colander over a bowl and leave it to drain overnight.

The next day, put the cumin and coriander into a spice grinder and grid to form a powder, then pass through a fine sieve to remove any bigger pieces.

Heat 4 tablespoons of olive oil in a saucepan over a medium heat. Add $1\frac{1}{2}$ tablespoons of the toasted spice powder and fry, stirring, for 2–3 minutes. Add the drained aubergine purée and stir until it is warmed through. Add the double cream and lemon zest and juice and season. Cover with foil and keep hot until needed. Or you can leave this to cool and reheat it gently just before serving. It will keep for 2–3 days in a covered container in the fridge.

Dust the monkfish fillets in the remaining spice mix. Heat 4 tablespoons olive oil and some butter in a large non-stick frying pan over a medium heat. Add the monkfish and fry, turning the fillets all the time so the spices don't burn, for 6–8 minutes until cooked through and the flesh flakes easily. Remove them from the pan and baste in the warm butter and a squeeze of lemon juice. Leave to rest, as though they were pieces of meat.

While the monkfish is resting, make the green olive dressing. Mix the green olives, anchovies, capers and red chilli together in a non-metallic bowl. Stir in the olive oil, the rest of the lemon juice and parsley and season, although it might not need much seasoning because there are lots of bold flavours here.

To serve, reheat the aubergine purée, if necessary. Place a spoonful of the purée on each plate. Slice the monkfish and place on top of the purée, then spoon the green olive dressing over the top, garnish with celery leaves and serve immediately.

Salmon barbecued in pine with pine nut and Parmesan pesto

This is a super-tasty dish, and you can use other good meaty fish instead of the salmon.

Using pine to marinate the salmon in and cook it over gives a real earthy, outdoor taste. Covering the fish in pine whilst cooking works in two ways – it both steams and smokes the fish for extra flavour.

Serves 4

2kg small pine branches
4 salmon fillets, about 200g each
2 tablespoons sea salt flakes
250ml peppery extra virgin olive oil

For the pine nut and Parmesan pesto
2 garlic cloves
1 tablespoon thyme leaves
finely grated zest of 1 lemon
75g pine nuts, toasted
50g Parmesan cheese, freshly grated
170ml extra virgin olive oil
salt and pepper, to taste

The day before cooking, remove about 400g of pine leaves from the branches, then put half of them in a plastic container with a lid. Put the salmon fillets on top and sprinkle with the sea salt flakes. Pour over the olive oil, then add the remaining pine leaves. Put the lid on and give the box a gentle shake. Place the box in the fridge and leave the salmon to marinate for 24 hours.

To make the pine nut and parmesan pesto, grind the garlic, thyme and lemon zest together with a pestle and mortar. Add the pine nuts and crush, then mix in the Parmesan. Slowly add the olive oil, season and mix all ingredients together. Set aside at room temperature.

Before you plan to cook, light a barbecue and leave the coals to become glowing.

Put 1kg of the remaining pine branches on to the coals and then put the grate on top of the branches. Remove the salmon fillets from the marinade and put them straight on to the hot grate. Place the remaining pine leaves on top of the fillets and grill, for 3 minutes. Halfway through the cooking time, brush off the top pine leaves, turn the fillets over and brush with the pine nut and Parmesan pesto and continue grilling for a further 2–3 minutes until the salmon is cooked through and the flesh flakes easily.

Remove the fillets from the grate, spread with more pine nut and Parmesan pesto and serve.

Barbecued sardines with salt-cured onion salad

I love this barbecue dish; the onions taste so fresh and really complement the oily rich fish. This is the ultimate in finger food — pulling the toasted fish apart in chunks is one of life's joys. Really simple but so good!

The salad is like a coleslaw without mayonnaise, and a good splash of chilli vinegar gives the whole dish a proper zing.

Serves 4–6

8–12 sardines, gutted and scaled
rapeseed oil
sea salt flakes, to taste

For the salt-cured onion salad
10–15 baby onions, halved from top to bottom
2 green chillies, chopped – with seeds and all
1 white onion, thinly sliced
1 red onion, thinly sliced
1 Spanish onion, thinly sliced
1 banana shallot, sliced
$1/4$ white cabbage, cored and finely shredded
1 tablespoon onion seeds, toasted
2 tablespoons sea salt flakes
6 spring onions, thinly sliced
$1/2$ bunch chives, chopped
1 bunch of mint leaves, chopped

For the chilli malt vinegar
150ml malt vinegar
75g demerara sugar
2–3 teaspoons dried chilli flakes, to taste

First, make the salt-cured onion salad. Mix the baby onions, chillies, white, red and Spanish onions, shallot, cabbage and onion seeds together in a large non-metallic bowl. Add the sea salt flakes, toss together and leave the salad to cure for 30 minutes.

Meanwhile, light a barbecue and leave the coals to become glowing.

To make the chilli malt vinegar, mix the vinegar, sugar and chilli flakes together in a saucepan over a high heat and bring to the boil, stirring to dissolve the sugar. Remove the pan from the heat and set aside for the mix to cool.

When the coals are at the correct temperature for barbecuing, place the sardines into a mesh barbecue cage and drizzle with rapeseed oil. Place over the hot coals and grill for about 5 minutes, turning once, until the sardine flesh flakes easily and the skins are charred. Sprinkle with sea salt flakes.

Wash the onion salad ingredients under running cold water to remove the salt. Pat them dry, then place them in a mixing bowl. Add the spring onions, chives and mint and rapeseed oil to taste, then toss everything together.

Serve the fish whole with the onion salad and the chilli malt vinegar for sprinkling over.

Chilli-hot grilled mackerel with shrimp kachumber

I owe the inspiration for this dish to my Goan kitchen porter, Ariston, who showed me how fish is cured with a red chilli paste to preserve it in the markets and beachside cafés in Goa, due to the lack of refrigeration. I serve the mackerel with a shrimp kachumber alongside. This dish is a fantastic celebration of the wondeful flavours of India.

Serves 2

2 large mackerel, about 550g each, gutted

For the red chilli marinade
6 dried red chillies, chopped – with seeds and all
250ml rice wine vinegar
2 garlic cloves, peeled
freshly squeezed juice of 1 lime
60g palm sugar
2 teaspoons chickpea flour
1 teaspoon ground chilli powder
1 teaspoon ground coriander
1 teaspoon ground cumin

For the shrimp kachumber
3 plum tomatoes, with a small 'X' cut in the top of each
1 Spanish onion, halved and thinly sliced
$1/4$ cucumber, halved lengthways, deseeded and sliced
1 tablespoon sea salt flakes, plus more for seasoning
2 tablespoons chopped coriander
1 tablespoon chopped mint
1 teaspoon coriander seeds, toasted and crushed
1 teaspoon cumin seeds
$1/2$ teaspoon ground turmeric
2 tablespoons vegetable oil
125g poached brown shrimps
2 tablespoons plain yogurt

Begin the red chilli marinade a week in advance. Place the dried chillies into a jam jar, cover with the rice wine vinegar, seal the jar and keep in the fridge for one week.

After one week, remove the chillies and place them in a small food processor or pestle and mortar. Reserve the rice vinegar. Add the garlic and the lime juice to the food processor and blend or pound. As the chillies and garlic start to break down, add the palm sugar, chickpea flour, chilli powder, ground coriander and ground cumin. Pour in a little of the rice wine vinegar and blend to make a paste-like consistency.

Cut 4 or 5 slits into the sides of each mackerel and rub in the red chilli marinade. Place the fish on a non-metallic plate in the fridge for at least one hour or up to 24 hours. The longer you leave the fish in the marinade, the stronger the chilli flavour will be.

Meanwhile, make the kachumber. To peel and deseed the tomatoes, bring a saucepan of water to the boil over a high heat and put a bowl of iced water in the sink. Add the tomatoes to the water and boil for 10 seconds, then immediately drain and put them in the iced water to stop the cooking. Drain them again and use a small knife to peel off the skins. Cut the tomatoes in half, scoop out the seeds and finely dice the flesh.

Place the diced tomatoes in a non-metallic bowl and add the onion and cucumber. Sprinkle with 1 tablespoon of the sea salt flakes and leave for 15 minutes.

After 15 minutes, tip the vegetables into a colander and rinse them quickly in cold running water, then pat them dry. Return the vegetables to the bowl and add the chopped coriander, mint and coriander seeds.

Preheat the grill to very hot – as hot as you can heat it!

While the grill is heating, mix the cumin seeds and turmeric together in a dry frying pan over a medium heat and toast, stirring, for 1–2 minutes until aromatic. Add the vegetable oil and the brown shrimps and heat through, stirring. Tip the contents of the pan on to the cucumber salad and mix together. Stir in the yogurt and season with sea salt flakes.

Place the mackerel on the grill rack and grill for about 5 minutes, turning them over once halfway through, until charred, cooked through and the flesh flakes easily. Immediately serve the mackerel whole with the kachumber alongside.

Tom's Tip
If you don't use all the red chilli paste it keeps very well in a covered container in the fridge for ages, and is also good for flavouring chicken or duck.

"This dish is a fantastic celebration of the wonderful flavours of India."

PROPER
MEAT

Hot pork buns with rhubarb sauce

I use rhubarb to replace apple in lots of recipes, as it works so well in both sweet and savoury dishes, and in this recipe it replaces the apple sauce you might expect with roast pork.
If you're not familiar with the hand of pork cut, it is the shoulder with the forearm still attached. You get loads of crackling when you roast it properly, which provides the crunch and texture in this dish.

The buns are steamed like Chinese buns, so they have that distinctive soft, chewy texture. The best pork buns ever are served at David Chang's Momofuku Ssäm restaurant, in New York City. These are a good alternative and save you the plane fare!

Serves 6; makes 12 buns

1 hand of pork, about $4\frac{1}{2}$kg
75g butter
150g smoked streaky bacon in one piece, diced
2 onions, finely chopped
100g fresh breadcrumbs
1 bunch of sage leaves, chopped
freshly grated nutmeg, to taste
salt and pepper, to taste

For the buns
565g strong white flour, plus extra for kneading
10g dried yeast
225ml water, blood heat
75g sugar
50ml vegetable oil
125ml boiling water

For the rhubarb sauce
100g butter, cubed
100g caster sugar
350g rhubarb, chopped
50ml grenadine

Preheat the oven to 150°C/Gas Mark 2. Place the hand of pork in a roasting tray and roast for $4\frac{1}{2}$–5 hours until the meat is tender.

Meanwhile, make the dough for the buns. Mix 125g of the strong white flour and yeast together in a bowl and make a well in the centre. Stir in the water, cover the bowl with clingfilm and leave to one side for 20–30 minutes until the yeast is frothy.

Mix the sugar and vegetable oil together in a large heatproof bowl and pour in the boiling water, stirring until the sugar dissolves. Leave to cool to blood heat. Add the yeast mix, then add the remaining strong white flour and mix together to form a dough. Tip out the dough on to a lightly floured surface and knead for 10–15 minutes until it is stretchy and elastic.

Place the dough into a bowl and cover with clingfilm. Leave the dough to rise at room temperature until at least doubled in size, which will take $1\frac{1}{2}$–2 hours. Knock the dough back, tip it out onto a lightly floured surface and roll it into a sausage shape, about 30cm long and 4cm thick. Cut into 12 equal pieces and roll into smooth balls. Line a baking sheet with baking parchment, place the dough balls on top, cover with clingfilm and leave to prove for 1 hour, or until they rise and increase in volume by about half. They won't double in size.

Meanwhile, make the rhubarb sauce. Melt the butter and sugar in a large frying pan over a medium heat, stirring to dissolve the sugar. Add the rhubarb and grenadine, turn the heat to low and leave the rhubarb to stew, uncovered and stirring frequently, for about 15 minutes until it breaks down completely. Transfer the rhubarb to a blender and blend until smooth, then pass it through a fine sieve. Transfer to a serving bowl and keep until needed. This can be served hot or cold.

Melt the 75g butter in a large frying pan. Add the smoked bacon and fry, stirring occasionally, for about 5 minutes, until the bacon is crisp and the fat has rendered out. Add the onions, reduce the heat to low and fry, stirring occasionally, for at least 5 minutes until they are softened, but not coloured. Stir in the breadcrumbs and sage and season with nutmeg and salt. Keep to one side.

When you are ready to steam the buns, put about 5cm of water in a saucepan and line the base of a Chinese steamer basket that fits over the pan with baking parchment. Place the buns in the steamer, a few at a time, and steam for 15 minutes.

When all the buns have been steamed, shred the pork from the bone. When ready to serve, cut each bun in half. Spoon in some sage and onion mix, followed by the rhubarb purée and then the pork.

Brined pork belly and Puy lentils with black cabbage salsa

The brine really helps to enhance the flavour and also helps to create really crisp crackling. This dish has been on the lunch menu at my pub on and off for a couple of years. The cabbage salsa is a more iron-rich version of a classic Italian salsa verde. It cuts through the richness of the lentils and fat content of the pork.

Serves 4–6

1kg pork belly
4 tablespoons rapeseed oil
70g smoked streaky bacon in one piece, rind removed and finely chopped
1 onion, finely chopped
1 tablespoon dried herbes de Provence
200g Puy lentils
175ml white wine
400ml chicken stock

For the brine
1 litre water
500g coarse sea salt
150g demerara sugar
1 tablespoon black peppercorns
2 cloves
1 bay leaf
1 sprig of thyme

For the black cabbage salsa
50g black cabbage leaves, tough stalks removed and the leaves chopped
25g parsley leaves
25g mint leaves
35g capers in brine, drained
2 salted anchovy fillets
2 garlic cloves
1 shallot, finely chopped
1 teaspoon salt
$\frac{1}{4}$ teaspoon cayenne pepper
1 lemon
150ml olive oil

About twenty-four hours before you plan to cook, make the brine. Mix all the ingredients together in a saucepan over a high heat and bring to the boil, stirring to dissolve the sugar and salt. Remove the pan from the heat and leave the brine to cool to room temperature. Place the pork belly in a non-metallic container and pour the brine over to cover. Cover the container and put into the fridge for 24 hours.

When ready to cook, preheat the oven to 150°C/Gas Mark 2. Remove the pork belly from the brine and pat it dry. Place the pork belly on a wire rack in a roasting tray. Place the tray in the oven and roast the pork belly for $2\frac{1}{2}$–3 hours until tender, crispy and golden brown. Remove the pork belly from the oven and leave it to rest, uncovered, for at least 45 minutes before carving.

Meanwhile, heat the rapeseed oil in a saucepan over a medium heat. Add the bacon and fry, stirring occasionally, for about 5 minutes until it is crispy. Add the onion, reduce the heat to low and continue frying until it is softened. Stir in the dried herbs and the lentils and stir for a further 1–2 minutes. Add the white wine and bring to the boil. Pour in the chicken stock and turn the heat down. Leave the lentils to simmer, uncovered, for 25–30 minutes until they are just soft.

As close to serving as possible, make the black cabbage salsa. Bring a saucepan of water to the boil and place a bowl of iced water in the sink. Add the black cabbage to the water and blanch for 2 minutes, or until just tender. Use a slotted spoon to remove the cabbage leaves and immediately plunge them into the iced water to stop the cooking and set the colour. Return the water to the boil, then add the parsley and mint and blanch for about 1 minute. Use a slotted spoon to remove and immediately add to the iced water. When all the leaves are cool, drain well and squeeze dry.

Chop the cabbage, mint, parsley, capers, anchovies and garlic together on a chopping board, then transfer to a bowl. Stir in the shallot, salt and cayenne, then grate in the lemon zest. Stir in the olive oil to make a rough salsa. Slice the pork and serve with the salsa and lentils.

Proper Pub Food

Pork faggots
in onion gravy

There used to be a proper butcher's shop at the bottom of Westgate Street, in my hometown of Gloucester, where they made their own faggots and took them out of the oven just in time for lunch. It was the ultimate fast food takeaway! Sadly the butchers are no longer there, but this is my version of their fantastic dish.

Makes 6–8 faggots

250g pig's caul
500g pork belly, skinned and coarsely minced
150g streaky smoked bacon in one piece, rind
    removed and coarsely minced
150g pig's liver, coarsely minced
100g pig's hearts, coarsely minced
150g coarse fresh breadcrumbs
1 teaspoon salt
1 teaspoon cracked black pepper
2 tablespoons rapeseed oil
1 onion, chopped
2 eggs, beaten
20 sage leaves, finely chopped
steamed cabbage, to serve
mashed potatoes, hot, to serve
prepared English mustard, to serve (optional)

For the onion gravy
rapeseed oil
3 or 4 whole onions, unpeeled and halved along the
    equator
2 tablespoons demerara sugar
$1/2$ bunch of thyme
30g butter
30g plain white flour
600ml Brown Chicken Stock (see page 240)

Wash the pig's caul in running cold water, then leave it in a bowl of water to soak for a couple of hours.

Mix the pork belly, bacon, liver and hearts together in a bowl. Add the breadcrumbs, salt and black pepper and stir with your hand for about 5 minutes until the mix firms up, then set aside.

Heat the rapeseed oil in a frying pan over a low heat. Add the onion and fry, stirring, for at least 5 minutes until softened, but not coloured. Remove the onion from the pan and leave to cool. Mix the eggs, sage and cold onions into the faggot mix. Shape the mix into 6 or 8 balls. Drain the pig's caul and use it to wrap around the faggots. Double wrap them so the mix doesn't leak out or to prevent them falling apart if the caul rips. Place the faggots into an ovenproof dish and then into the fridge for $1^{1}/_{2}$–2 hours to rest.

Meanwhile, start the onion gravy. Preheat the oven to 180°C/Gas Mark 4. Heat 2 tablespoons rapeseed oil in a large frying pan over a medium-high heat. Add the halved onions, cut sides down, and fry for 8–10 minutes until blackened. Transfer the onions to a roasting tray lined with a piece of kitchen foil large enough to wrap around them and sprinkle with the demerara sugar and thyme. Drizzle with a little oil and seal the foil up as a bag. Place the roasting tray in the oven and roast the onions for 2 hours until they are really caramelised and soft. When the onions are cool enough to handle, but still hot, scoop the flesh into a food processor and process until a rich brown pulp forms, then leave to one side.

Melt the butter in a saucepan over a medium heat. Add the flour and stir for 1–2 minutes to cook out the raw flavour and make a roux. Pour in the brown chicken stock and simmer, stirring occasionally, over a very low heat for 30–40 minutes, until it has reduced by about one-quarter.

When you are ready to cook the faggots, reheat the oven to 180°C/Gas Mark 4. Put the dish with the faggots on the middle shelf and roast for 15 minutes. Turn them over and roast for another 15 minutes. Pour the onion gravy over and continue roasting for a further 20 minutes, or until the gravy is bubbling and thickened around the edges of the dish. Serve with steamed cabbage, mashed potatoes and English mustard. This is proper lush.

Mustard-flavoured salt-baked pork knuckles and roasted cabbage

This is a very rustic-looking dish, but my God it tastes amazing! This is a real chef's dish, full of peasant-style cooking that is at the root of all gastronomic cooking. I wish all posh-looking food tasted as good as this! This goes very well with crushed swede or mash.

Food like this dish is one of the reasons the great British pub scene is looking very rosy these days.

Serves 4

1kg plain white flour, plus extra for rolling out the dough
300g salt
3 egg whites, beaten
300ml water
2 pork knuckles, about 1.2 kg each
4 tablespoons prepared English mustard, plus extra to serve
$\frac{1}{2}$ bunch of rosemary
100g butter, cubed
1 onion, thinly sliced
100g smoked streaky bacon, in one piece, horizontally cut into 4 slices
2 fresh bay leaves
1 carrot, peeled and sliced on an angle
$\frac{1}{2}$ bunch thyme
1 savoy cabbage, trimmed and quartered
350ml Brown Chicken Stock (see page 240) or duck stock

Mix the flour and salt together in a large mixing bowl. Add the egg whites, then gradually add the water and mix until a dough forms. You might not need all the water. Wrap the dough in clingfilm and transfer it to the fridge to rest for 1 hour.

Preheat the oven to 150°C/Gas Mark 2.

Roll the dough out on a lightly floured surface until about 1cm thick, then cut into 2 pieces. Place a pork knuckle on each piece of dough and brush each knuckle with mustard. Place a few sprigs of rosemary on top of each, then wrap the salt crust around and seal. Make sure it is well sealed. Just press the dough together and it should stick, but you can add a little water, if necessary.

Transfer the pork knuckles to a roasting tray. Place the roasting tray in the oven and bake the pork knuckles for $4\frac{1}{2}$ hours. Remove the tray from the oven and leave the pork knuckles to rest for at least 1 hour.

When you take the pork out of the oven, turn the temperature up to 190°C/Gas Mark 5. Melt the butter in a roasting tray over a medium heat. Add the onion and bacon and stir around until the onion has started to soften. Add the bay leaves, carrot and thyme. Place the cabbage quarters on top and pour over the stock. Bring to the boil, then cover the tray with kitchen foil. Transfer the tray to the oven and braise the cabbage for 25–30 minutes until it is tender.

When the cabbage is cooked, transfer it to a bowl and keep hot. Place the tray, with the bacon, carrot and onion still in it, on the hob over high heat and boil the cooking liquid until it reduces to a sauce consistency.

After the pork has rested for an hour, open the salt dough crusts and flake the meat from the bones. Divide the cabbage between 4 bowls and top each with the bacon, carrot and onion. Pass the sauce through a fine sieve and spoon it over the top, add the pork and serve.

Proper Pub Food

Honey-roasted bacon and malt-vinegar-mint sauce with pease pudding

This recipe gives you so many big, powerful flavours on the plate, all working together. Think of this as the best mushy peas and bacon you'll ever eat.

I think a whole piece of bacon is an overlooked alternative to a joint of meat for a Sunday roast, and it is very easy to cook. Plus, if you don't eat it all warm, it makes ace sandwiches.

Serves 4–6

750g smoked streaky bacon in one piece, rind removed
200g runny honey
150ml malt vinegar
150g caster sugar
1 teaspoon dried chilli flakes
2 tablespoons chopped mint
salt and pepper, to taste

For the pease pudding
200g dry split green peas
150g butter, cubed
1 onion, finely chopped
3 sprigs of rosemary
2 bay leaves
2 sprigs of thyme
100ml white wine vinegar
700ml ham stock or chicken stock, plus a little extra for blending, if necessary
4 tablespoons chopped mint leaves

Preheat the oven to 180°C/Gas Mark 4. Put the piece of bacon in a roasting tray and cover with the honey. Place the tray in the oven and set a timer for 10 minutes. After 10 minutes, baste the bacon with the honey, then return it to the oven and reset the timer for another 10 minutes. Repeat the basting and put back into the oven. Set the timer for 5 minutes and repeat the process. Keep basting and roasting for 45–50 minutes in total until the honey is thick and has glazed the bacon all over. Transfer the bacon to a chopping board and leave it to rest for 25 minutes.

Meanwhile, make the pease pudding. Place the dry split peas in a saucepan with enough cold water to cover and bring to the boil. Drain in a colander, then repeat the process.

Melt 75g of the butter in a pan over a low heat. Add the onion and fry, stirring occasionally, for at least 5 minutes until softened, but not coloured. Tie the rosemary, bay leaves and thyme together with string, then add this to the pan with the split peas and stir. Add the white wine vinegar, bring to the boil and continue boiling until the liquid reduces to a glaze. Add the ham stock or chicken stock and return to the boil, then reduce the heat to low and simmer, uncovered, for about 45 minutes until the peas are very soft.

While the bacon is roasting, mix the malt vinegar, sugar and chilli flakes together in a saucepan and bring to the boil, stirring to dissolve the sugar. Remove the pan from the heat and leave the liquid to cool, which will take at least 20 minutes.

To finish the pease pudding, remove the herbs from the split peas. Add the remaining butter and use a hand blender to blend the peas until they are smooth. If it is too thick, add a little more stock. Stir in the mint and season.

Add the 2 tablespoons chopped mint to the malt vinegar mix. Slice the warm bacon and serve with the malt-vinegar-mint sauce spooned over the top and the pease pudding alongside.

Tom's Tip
Don't forget to use the timer when you are roasting the bacon. The longer you cook the bacon for, the more chance you have of burning it. I have learnt this from experience!

Hot salt-beef bagels with pickled vegetables and black pepper cream cheese

The curing of meat is normally associated with pork, but brisket and other cheaper, slower-cooked pieces of beef really benefit from the brining process as well.

Once cooked, salt beef is great to have in the fridge. You get so many uses from it, hot or cold: serve it with mash, Pease Pudding (see page 153), lentils, in a sandwich with mustard or in these cream cheese bagels with pickled vegetables.

2.5kg beef brisket

For the brine
2 litres water
500g sea salt
400g demerara sugar
50g saltpetre
6 bay leaves
6 cloves
1 bunch of thyme
2 teaspoons black peppercorns

Braising vegetables
2 carrots, peeled and thickly chopped
1 onion, quartered
1 bulb of garlic, halved through the equator
4 celery sticks, halved
4 bay leaves
1 bunch of rosemary

Seven days before you plan to cook, make the brine. Mix all the brine ingredients together in a saucepan and bring to the boil, stirring to dissolve the salt, sugar and saltpetre. Boil for 5 minutes, then remove the pan from the heat and leave the brine to cool to room temperature.

Pierce the beef brisket all over with a skewer and then place it in a non-metallic container. Pour over the brine, making sure that the beef is completely covered. It may need weighing down. Cover the container and put in the fridge for 7 days.

After 7 days, remove the beef from the brine and rinse it in running cold water.

Place the beef in a large saucepan and add all the ingredients for the braising vegetables. Pour in enough cold water to cover the ingredients and bring to the boil, skimming the surface, as necessary. Turn the heat down to low and leave to simmer, uncovered, for 2 1/2–3 hours until the beef is tender. Remove the pan from the heat, and leave the beef to

cool completely in the stock, uncovered, which will take a couple of hours.

When cool, remove the salt beef from the liquid and pat dry. Cover and chill until needed, when it can be sliced and served hot or cold. Keep some of the cooking liquid to reheat the beef in if you're planning to serve it hot.

To make the bagels...

4 thick slices of salt beef, about 150g total weight (see salt beef recipe, left)
200ml water – or use beef braising stock if you made your own salt beef
4 bagels, halved horizontally
50g butter
1/2 bunch dill sprigs, to garnish
salt, to taste

For the pickled vegetables
8 button mushrooms, wiped, trimmed and quartered
2 baby carrots, trimmed, peeled and chopped
2 baby cucumbers, deseeded and chopped
2 baby radishes, trimmed and chopped
2 baby shallots, chopped
250ml Pickling Mix (see page 241)

For the black pepper cream cheese
150g cream cheese
2 teaspoons cracked black pepper

First, make the pickled vegetables. Combine the mushrooms, carrots, cucumbers, radishes and shallots in a large non-metallic bowl. Stir in the pickling mix, cover with clingfilm and leave for 2 hours at room temperature.

Meanwhile, make the black pepper cream cheese. Beat the cream cheese until it is soft, then add the cracked black pepper and a pinch of salt. Cover and chill until needed.

When you're ready to assemble the sandwiches, preheat the grill to high and bring the water or beef braising liquid to the boil. Place the bagels under the grill and toast both halves, then spread with the cream cheese.

Add the butter to the boiling liquid and stir until it melts. Drop the salt beef into the liquid and leave for 1–2 minutes to warm through. When the beef is warm, divide the slices between the bagel bottoms, sprinkle with fresh dill and top with the bagel tops. Serve with the pickled vegetables and enjoy!

Ginger-braised ox cheeks with spiced red lentils and watercress yogurt

Here's curry crossed with French braising. I love it! Spices have become widely used in British cuisine and, when handled properly, they really can give a huge lift to your cooking. The ginger in this recipe, for example, is so good with the beef, adding a real dark warmth to the dish. This is a proper winter warmer that will leave you feeling content, happy and ready for a good snooze!

Serves 4

300ml stout
4 star anise
2 teaspoons coriander seeds
2 teaspoons cumin seeds
1 teaspoon dried chilli flakes
1 teaspoon ground ginger
2 large ox cheeks, about 400g each, cut in half and trimmed
rapeseed oil
2 onions, finely chopped
6 garlic cloves, crushed
150g fresh root ginger, skin on and finely chopped
900ml beef stock
salt and pepper, to taste
1 onion, sliced, to serve
chopped coriander leaves, to serve

For the spiced red lentils
250g red lentils
4 tablespoons rapeseed oil
1 onion, finely chopped
4 garlic cloves, grated
2 teaspoons turmeric
1 teaspoon chilli powder
1 cinnamon stick
800ml chicken stock
freshly squeezed juice of 2 limes

For the watercress yogurt
leaves only from 1 bunch of watercress, finely chopped
200g plain yogurt
1 teaspoon cracked black pepper

One or two days before you plan to serve this, mix the stout, star anise, coriander and cumin seeds, chilli flakes and ground ginger together in a large bowl. Add the ox cheeks, cover with clingfilm and leave to marinate in the fridge for 24 hours.

The next day, preheat the oven to 140°C/Gas Mark 1. Remove the ox cheeks from the marinade and pat dry with a tea towel. Reserve the marinade. Heat about 4 tablespoons rapeseed oil in a flameproof casserole over a medium-high heat. Add the ox cheeks and sear on both sides until they turn a lovely brown caramelised colour. Remove the ox cheeks from the pan and set aside.

Add the onions to the fat remaining in the pot, reduce the heat to low and fry, stirring occasionally, for at least 5 minutes until softened, but not coloured. Add a little extra oil to the pot, if necessary, then add the garlic and ginger and fry, stirring, for 4–5 minutes until they are browned, but not burnt.

Return the ox cheeks to the pot, pour in the stout marinade and the beef stock and bring to the boil. Cover the pot and place it in the oven for about 3½ hours until the beef is very tender. Remove the pot from the oven and leave on one side for at least 1 hour. You can serve the dish at this point, but it really does taste even better if you leave the cheeks to cool in the covered pot for 24 hours. If you do decide to wait a day, once the beef and liquid are completely cool, transfer the pot to the fridge.

Meanwhile, make the spiced red lentils. Preheat the oven to 180°C/Gas Mark 4 and place the lentils into a roasting tray. Place the tray in the oven and toast the lentils for 10–15 minutes until they are just a little tinged. Remove the tray from the oven and set aside.

Heat the oil in a large saucepan over a low heat. Add the onion and garlic and fry, stirring occasionally, for at least 5 minutes until softened, but not coloured. Stir in the turmeric and chilli powder and stir for a further 1–2 minutes. Add the lentils and the cinnamon stick, then pour in the chicken stock and bring to the boil. Reduce the heat to low and leave the lentils to simmer, uncovered and stirring occasionally to make sure they don't catch on the base of the pan, for about 40 minutes until they fall apart and you have purée in the pan. Add the lime juice and season with salt and pepper.

Just before serving, mix the watercress, yogurt and black pepper together. Reheat the ox cheeks and their cooking juices.

Serve the ox cheeks with a little of the cooking juices, the red lentil purée, a good dollop of the watercress yogurt and garnished with the onion slices and coriander.

" This is a proper winter warmer that will leave you feeling content, happy and ready for a good snooze!"

Flash-fried sirloin steaks with mustard seed dressing

I love these steaks. The recipe goes against everything that you get told about resting meat before serving it, but these are so thin you just cook them very quickly and eat them straight out of the pan. This is my idea of a great lunch dish.

Serves 2

50g butter

4 tablespoons rapeseed oil

2 sirloin steaks, 150g each

2 tablespoons chopped chives

salt and pepper, to taste

100g croûtons, diced and toasted, to serve

2 large handfuls of wild rocket, tossed with a little rapeseed oil, to serve

For the mustard seed dressing

100ml rapeseed oil

2 tablespoons yellow mustard seeds, toasted

1 tablespoon Dijon mustard

1 tablespoon Cabernet Sauvignon vinegar

1 garlic clove, crushed

1 tablespoon capers in brine, drained and chopped

To make the mustard seed dressing, whisk the rapeseed oil, mustard seeds, Dijon mustard, vinegar, garlic and capers together in a non-metallic bowl and season with salt and pepper. Set aside until needed.

When ready to cook the steaks, melt the butter with the oil in a large frying pan over a medium-high heat. Add the steaks and fry for about 2 minutes until caramelised on one side. Flip the steaks over and fry for a further 1 minute. Take care not to over-cook – 'blue' is better than well done with these thin steaks.

Transfer the steaks to plates and cover liberally with the dressing. Sprinkle with the chives and the crisp croûtons. Place the wild rocket on top of the steaks and serve immediately.

Braised shin of beef in red wine

This is the best ever beef stew. I know that is quite a claim, but I stand by it! This has been on my menu in one form or another every winter since we opened. People come back just for the glazed carrots!

Serves 6

6 pieces of boneless beef shin, about 225g each
1 bottle (750ml) red wine
2 tablespoons salt
6 pieces of marrow bone, each about 2½ cm thick
rapeseed oil
2 carrots, peeled and finely chopped
2 celery sticks, finely chopped
1 onion, finely chopped
1.5 litres veal stock
5 dried bay leaves
1 clove
1 tablespoon white peppercorns
1 tablespoon salt
1 bunch of thyme, tied together
sea salt flakes, to serve

For the glazed carrots
6 carrots, topped and tailed
400ml water
250g butter, cubed
150g caster sugar
4 star anise
1 tablespoon salt
sea salt flakes, to taste

For the suet dumplings
225g fresh fine white breadcrumbs
225g self-raising white flour
225g grated suet
4 tablespoons chopped flat-leaf parsley leaves
pinch of salt
2 eggs, beaten
4 tablespoons milk
1 litre chicken stock

Up to 2 days before you plan to cook, put the beef in a large bowl and pour over the wine. Cover the bowl with clingfilm, place in the fridge and leave to marinate for at least 24 hours and up to 48 hours. The longer you leave the beef to marinate at this stage, the deeper the final flavour will be.

A day before you plan to cook, dissolve the salt in a large bowl of water. Add the marrow bones and more water, if necessary, so they are covered, then cover the bowl with clingfilm and place in the fridge for 24 hours for any impurities to be removed.

Strain the beef shins, then pat them dry. Reserve the marinade. Heat 3 tablespoons rapeseed oil in a flameproof casserole over a medium-high heat. Add the shins and fry, turning them until they are browned on both sides. Transfer them to a colander in the sink and leave for the excess fat to drain off, if there is any. Wipe out the pan with kitchen paper.

Add another 3 tablespoons rapeseed oil to the pot over a medium-high heat. Add the carrots, celery and onion and fry, stirring frequently, for 8–10 minutes until they are softened and browned. Watch closely that they don't burn though. At the same time, place the red wine from the marinade into a saucepan over a high heat and bring to the boil, skimming the surface as necessary.

Meanwhile, preheat the oven to 160°C/Gas Mark 3.

When the vegetables have browned, add the beef shins and pour over the boiling red wine. Stir in the veal stock, bay leaves, clove, white peppercorns, salt and thyme. Bring the liquid to a simmer and cover the pot. Place the pot in the oven and braise the beef shins for 2½ hours, or until they are very tender.

When the shins are tender, remove the pot from the oven and leave them to cool in the cooking liquid, uncovered. This will take about 3–4 hours.

When the shins are cool, remove them from the cooking liquid and leave to one side. Pass the cooking liquid through a sieve lined with muslin into a saucepan. Place the saucepan over a high heat and bring the liquid to the boil, skimming the surface as

(continued on page 162)

(continued from page 161)

necessary. Leave to boil until it reduces to a sauce consistency, then pass the liquid through a sieve lined with muslin again. Return the sauce to the washed flameproof casserole, cover and leave to one side until just before serving.

Meanwhile, make the glazed carrots. Peel the carrots and rub them down with a green scouring pad to make them very smooth and remove any marks from the peeler, then set aside. Place the water, butter, sugar, star anise and salt in a large saucepan over a high heat and bring to the boil, stirring to melt the butter and dissolve the sugar. Add the carrots, reduce the heat to medium-low and leave the carrots to simmer, uncovered, for 25–30 minutes until they are tender and the liquid has reduced by half.

To roast the marrow bones, reheat the oven to 200°C/ Gas Mark 6. Remove the marrow bones from the water and pat dry on kitchen paper. Heat 2–3 tablespoons of oil in a frying pan over a high heat. Add the bones and sear them on the ends, then transfer them to a roasting tray. Place the roasting tray in the oven and roast the bones for 10 minutes, or until the marrow is softened. Remove them from the oven and keep hot.

Reduce the oven temperature to 180°C/Gas Mark 4.

To make the suet dumplings, mix the breadcrumbs, flour, suet, parsley and salt together in a mixing bowl and make a well in the centre. Whisk the eggs and milk together, then add to the dry ingredients and mix until a soft dough forms. Shape into 6 dumplings.

Place the chicken stock in a flameproof casserole over a high heat and bring to the boil. Turn the heat down to a simmer, add the dumplings, cover the pot and place it in the oven for 12 or so minutes until the dumplings double in size.

When you are ready to serve, return the shins to the flameproof casserole with the reduced cooking liquid. Bring to the boil, then reduce the heat to medium, cover the pot and simmer for 3–5 minutes until the beef is hot.

Divide the beef shins between 6 plates and spoon over a thin covering of the reduced cooking liquid. Add a marrow bone, carrot and dumpling to each portion and serve immediately.

" This is the best ever beef stew. I know that is quite a claim, but I stand by it!"

Treacle-cured beef and roast potatoes with Yorkshire puddings

Curing the beef in treacle gives a real deep depth of flavour and adds a special touch to an already fantastic cut of meat. My technique for roasting the beef at a very low temperature is the oven equivalent of sous-vide cooking. You really do need an instant-read thermometer for this, and when the internal temperature reaches 55–58°C you will have the most perfect medium-rare beef. Guaranteed!

If you have two ovens, use one to roast the potatoes and Yorkshire puddings at a high temperature and the other to roast the beef at a low temperature. That way you can work out the timings and everything is perfectly cooked and ready to serve at the same time. Sunday lunch has never been easier.

Serves 4–6

200g black treacle
100ml water
1 middle-cut fillet of beef, about 800g
vegetable oil
8 Maris Piper potatoes, peeled and cut into chunks
500g spinach leaves, washed and spun dry
50g butter
salt and pepper, to taste
500ml Red Wine Sauce (see page 239), to serve

For the Yorkshire puddings
450g plain flour
750ml milk
8 eggs

A day ahead, mix the treacle and water together in a large bowl, stirring to dissolve the treacle. Add the beef, cover the bowl with clingfilm and put in the fridge to marinate for 24 hours.

The next day, make the Yorkshire pudding batter at least 4 hours before you plan to cook. Put the flour into a mixing bowl and make a well in the centre. Whisk the milk and eggs together, then slowly whisk them into the flour to form a batter. Do not overmix – some lumps are OK. Leave the batter to stand at room temperature for 4 hours.

To prepare the roast potatoes, preheat the oven to 220°C/Gas Mark 7. While the oven is reaching the correct temperature, bring a pan of salted water to the boil. Add the potatoes, return the water to the boil and blanch them for 8–10 minutes until they are cooked through and tender. Drain them through a colander in the sink and leave to steam-dry for a couple of minutes. Be very careful not to break them up too much.

Heat a thin layer of vegetable oil in a roasting tray on the hob. Add the potatoes and stir them around so they are thinly coated with oil on every surface. Place the tray in the oven and roast the potatoes for 45 minutes, or until crispy and golden brown.

Meanwhile, to finish the Yorkshire puddings, put a small amount of vegetable oil in the base of 8 Yorkshire pudding moulds and put the moulds in the oven while it is heating. When the oven reaches the correct temperature and the oil is very hot, pour in the batter. Return the moulds to the oven and bake the Yorkshire puddings for about 25 minutes, until well risen, puffy and golden brown. You can cook the Yorkshire puddings while the potatoes are roasting.

(continued on page 165)

(continued from page 163)

Remove the potatoes and Yorkshire puddings from the oven and immediately turn the oven temperature down to 60°C/Gas Mark very low (or set to the nearest lowest temperature). Do not cover the roast potatoes with foil or they will lose their crispness.

Remove the beef from the marinade and pat dry. Heat 2–3 tablespoons of the vegetable oil in a large frying pan over a high heat. Add the fillet and fry, turning regularly, until browned all over. Place the fillet in a roasting tray.

When the oven has reached the correct temperature, place the roasting tray in the oven and roast the fillet for 1 hour, or until an instant-read thermometer inserted into the middle of the fillet reads 55°–58°C.

As soon as you take the beef out of the oven, turn the oven temperature up to 180°C/Gas Mark 4. Cover the beef with foil and leave to one side. As soon as the oven reaches the correct temperature, return the potatoes and Yorkshire puddings and reheat them for 5 minutes.

Meanwhile, pour the marinade into a saucepan over a high heat and bring to the boil. Turn the heat down and leave the marinade to simmer, uncovered, until it reduces by half.

Melt the butter in a saucepan over a medium-high heat. Add the spinach with just the water clinging to the leaves and stir until it wilts. Season.

When ready to serve, brush the fillet with the reduced cooking juices, then slice the beef. Spoon a little of the red wine sauce on each plate, then top with the spinach and a slice of beef. Serve immediately with the Yorkshire puddings and roast potatoes.

Tom's Tip
You can also use the treacle cure mix for beef, venison or chicken, and then grill them on a barbecue.

" **Curing the beef in treacle gives a real deep depth of flavour and adds a special touch to an already fantastic cut of meat.** "

Barbecued short rib of beef, British style

This recipe takes a couple of days to prepare to be ready for a special weekend barbecue, but it is one of the best things ever! It's perfect outdoor man food – and proper messy to eat! Try it with a serving of my Warm Tomato, Onion and Bread Salad with Beef Dripping Dressing on page 50.

Serves 6–8

1 x 3.5kg short rib of beef on the bones

For the dry cure
4 tablespoons sea salt flakes
1 tablespoon celery salt
1 tablespoon crushed coriander seeds
1 tablespoon dried herbes de Provence
1 tablespoon garlic powder
1 tablespoon ground ginger
1 tablespoon smoked paprika
1 tablespoon cracked black pepper
2 teaspoons chilli powder

For the barbecue glaze
250g pickled onions, drained and roughly chopped
200g pitted dates, roughly chopped
600ml stout
3 tablespoons prepared English mustard
2 tablespoons Worcestershire sauce
300ml apple juice
3 tablespoons runny honey
3 tablespoons black treacle
3 tablespoons golden syrup
1 tablespoon Tabasco Sauce
1 tablespoon tomato purée
3 tablespoons soft dark brown sugar

Two days before you plan to barbecue, mix all of the dry cure ingredients together, then rub them into the rib of beef so it is completely covered. Place the beef into a large plastic container and cover with the remaining cure mix. Put the lid on the container and place it in the fridge overnight or for 24 hours.

Meanwhile, up to 2 days in advance, make the barbecue glaze. Put the onions and dates in a large heatproof bowl. Bring the stout to the boil in a small saucepan, then pour it into the bowl. Cover the bowl with clingfilm and leave the ingredients to cool at room temperature.

Whisk the remaining barbecue glaze ingredients together in a separate bowl. When the dates have softened and cooled, tip the dates, onions and stout into a blender and blend until the mixture is smooth. Stir this purée into the other glaze ingredients. Set aside until needed.

Once the dry cure has been on the ribs for at least 24 hours, preheat the oven to 130°C/Gas Mark $1/2$. Wash the cure off in cold running water. Place the ribs in a large flameproof casserole, pour over the barbecue glaze and cover the pot. Place the pot in the oven and braise the ribs for 5–6 hours until the beef is very tender. Check occasionally to make sure the glaze doesn't evaporate. If it is reducing down too much, add a little water.

When the beef is tender, remove the pot from the oven and leave the beef to cool in the mixture at room temperature. When everything is completely cool, place the pot into the fridge to chill overnight.

The next day, light your barbecue and leave the coals to become glowing. The copious amount of fat will have set, so remove it and discard. In good advance of wanting to eat, place the covered pot on the barbecue rack and leave it to warm the ribs through. This will take 2–3 hours.

When the ribs are warm, uncover the pot to slowly reduce the glaze with the beef in the pan, basting the ribs every 10 minutes. When the glaze is reduced and coats the beef, remove beef from the pan. It is now ready serve.

Rare bavette of beef and charred onions with mushroom ketchup

This is another classic from my pub's lunch menu. Bavette steak has so much flavour, but can easily be tough if overcooked, so pay attention. The mushroom ketchup provides a savoury acidity to the dish and is a very old English accompaniment. I love to serve this with triple-cooked chips.

Serves 2

rapeseed oil
2 onions, peeled and cut in half through the equator
300ml chicken stock
6 sprigs of thyme
100g butter, cubed
2 bavette steaks, 250g each
juice of $1\frac{1}{2}$ lemons
2 tablespoons wholegrain mustard
2 tablespoons chopped chives
150ml Red Wine Sauce (see page 239), hot
2 large sprigs of watercress, to garnish
salt and pepper, to taste

For the mushroom ketchup
6 Portobello mushrooms, wiped and trimmed
1 shallot, finely chopped
70g demerara sugar
4 tablespoons white wine vinegar
200ml double cream
2 salted anchovy fillets

First, make the mushroom ketchup. Put the mushrooms into a food processor and pulse until they are finely chopped. Transfer the mushrooms to a saucepan over a medium heat and cook, without stirring, until the water comes out from them and they are reduced down. It is important not to stir them immediately. This intensifies the mushroom flavour. When they have reabsorbed the liquid they gave off, add the shallot, sugar and white wine vinegar and bring to the boil, stirring to dissolve the sugar.

Reduce the heat and leave the mix to simmer, uncovered, until all the liquid evaporates. Add the double cream and boil until it has reduced by half. Place in a blender, add the anchovies and blend until smooth. Pass through a fine sieve, cover and chill until needed.

Heat 2 tablespoons rapeseed oil in a frying pan over a medium heat. Add the onions, cut-side down, and sear for 10–15 minutes until blackened and charred. Once coloured, flip the onions over and pour the chicken stock into the pan. Add the thyme and 50g of the butter and bring to the boil. Reduce the heat to low and simmer, uncovered, until the stock has evaporated and the onions are soft. Set aside and keep hot.

Heat 4 tablespoons rapeseed oil in a frying pan over a medium-high heat. Season the bavette steaks heavily and place them into the pan. Add the remaining butter and fry the steaks for about 4 minutes until the butter is foaming and turning nutty brown and the steaks are colouring all around. When the steaks are at this rare stage, squeeze in the lemon juice and baste the steaks with the pan juices. Remove the steaks from the pan, cover with the wholegrain mustard and leave to rest for 8–10 minutes. This is very important, as these steaks can be quite tough if over-cooked or not rested for long enough.

Meanwhile, reheat the mushroom ketchup, if necessary. After the steaks have rested, slice them against the grain and sprinkle with the chopped chives. Pour over the red wine sauce, add the onion halves, garnish with the watercress and serve.

Proper Pub Food

Jacob's ladder and braised carrots with bone-marrow bread pudding

This savoury bread pudding is very rich, so you don't need very much. It serves as a replacement for dumplings and soaks up loads of the rich gravy. Buttered cabbage is the ideal accompaniment for this dish.

Jacob's ladder is an alternative name for short rib of beef, and it's an ideal cut for braising, with a high fat content and stunning flavour. Cooking it on the bone, as in this recipe, also prevents too much shrinkage.

Serves 6

2 bay leaves
1 teaspoon coriander seeds
1 teaspoon whole white peppercorns
6 Jacob's ladder beef cuts, about 250g each
500ml red wine
4 tablespoons rapeseed oil
4 celery sticks, halved
1 large carrot, peeled and halved
1 head of garlic, unpeeled and cut in half through the equator
1 onion, quartered
1.5 litres beef stock
400ml water
250g butter, cubed
150g sugar
1 tablespoon salt
4 star anise
6 carrots, peeled and rubbed with a green scourer until smooth
salt and pepper, to taste

For the bone-marrow bread pudding

2 tablespoons salt
100g bone marrow
100g butter, softened, plus extra for greasing the dish
$1/2$ loaf of white bread, sliced and crusts removed
$1/2$ nutmeg
4 eggs
600ml milk
3 tablespoons chopped parsley

The day before you plan to cook, tie the bay leaves, coriander seeds and white peppercorns together in a piece of muslin. Place the beef, red wine and the muslin bag into a non-metallic container. Cover and place in the fridge for at least 24 hours.

Also the day before you plan to cook, to prepare the marrow for the bread pudding, dissolve the salt in a large non-metallic bowl of water. Remove the marrow from the bone and place it in the bowl. Cover the bowl with clingfilm and place it in the fridge for 24 hours for any impurities to be removed.

The next day, remove the beef from the marinade, pat dry with kitchen paper and leave to one side. Transfer the red wine marinade to a saucepan and bring to the boil, skimming the surface as necessary. Reserve the spice bag.

While the marinade is coming to the boil, preheat the oven to 130°C/Gas Mark $1/2$.

Heat 4 tablespoons rapeseed oil a large frying pan over a medium-high heat. Add the beef and sear on both sides until it turns a lovely dark colour to give some great flavour. Transfer the seared beef to a large flameproof casserole. Add the celery, carrot, garlic, onion and spice bag to the pot on top of the beef. Pour over the beef stock and the skimmed marinade and bring to the boil. Cover the pot and place it in the oven for 3–$31/2$ hours until the beef is tender. Remove the pot from the oven and leave the beef in the pot, covered, for about 1 hour until it is cool enough to handle.

When you take the beef out of the oven, turn the temperature up to 150°C/Gas Mark 2.

Meanwhile, mix the water, butter, sugar, salt and star anise together in a saucepan and bring to the boil, stirring to melt the butter and dissolve the sugar and salt. Add the carrots, turn the heat down to low

(continued on page 170)

(continued from page 169)

and simmer, uncovered, for 45–50 minutes until they are soft and the butter has glazed them.

While the carrots are cooking, make the bone marrow bread pudding. Remove the marrow from the salted water and transfer it to a food processor with the butter. Blend together to make bone-marrow butter. Use this to butter the slices of bread, then season the bread slices with salt and pepper and grate over the nutmeg. Leave the bread to one side.

Whisk the eggs and milk together. Grease a 20 x 10cm ovenproof dish with a little butter and arrange half the bread slices in the dish. Sprinkle with parsley and pour over half the egg mix. Do the same again, then leave to one side for 10–15 minutes while the bread pudding absorbs some of the custard. Place the dish in the oven and bake the bread pudding for 25–30 minutes until it is set and golden brown on top.

Remove the Jacob's ladders from the cooking liquid and leave to one side, covered with kitchen foil to keep the meat warm. Bring the cooking liquid to the boil and boil until it reduces to a sauce consistency. Season.

To serve, divide the pieces of beef between 6 bowls and add a whole carrot to each. Pour over some beef sauce and serve with the bread pudding.

Tom's Tip
If you don't use all the bone-marrow butter it freezes well to use another time.

" Jacob's ladder is an ideal cut for braising, with a high fat content and stunning flavour."

Curried lamb and pearl barley with cucumber raita

This is a real mix of the best of British cooking. Curry is a great underlying taste that goes well with pearl barley and slowly braised lamb necks. I suppose this is my version of a dahl, just using barley instead of lentils. There is a proper mix of spice, acid and savoury in this dish, and cooking the lamb on the bone helps to add more flavour and keep the lamb moist.

Serves 4

75g pearl barley
rapeseed oil
4 lamb necks on the bone, 250–300g each
2cm piece of fresh ginger, peeled and chopped
3 garlic cloves, crushed
1 onion, finely chopped
3 tablespoons Curry Powder (see page 241)
2 teaspoons cracked black pepper
1.75 litres Brown Chicken Stock (see page 240)
 or lamb stock
1 dried red chilli
3 fresh curry leaves
175g swede, peeled and diced
175g turnip, peeled and diced
salt, to taste

For the cucumber raita
$1/4$ cucumber, deseeded and diced
1 teaspoon sea salt flakes
2 teaspoons caster sugar
2 teaspoons white wine vinegar
1 teaspoon ground turmeric
200g plain yogurt
3 tablespoons chopped mint

Soak the pearl parley in cold water to cover for 4–6 hours. Drain the barley and transfer it to a saucepan with more cold water to cover and bring to the boil. Drain again, then leave to cool completely and leave in the fridge until needed.

Heat about 2 tablespoons rapeseed oil in a large flameproof casserole over a high heat. Add the lamb neck pieces and sear them for about 5 minutes until they are dark and caramelised all over. Remove the lamb necks from the pot and use kitchen paper to wipe the pot out.

Heat 3 tablespoons rapeseed oil in the pot over a medium heat. Add the ginger, garlic and onion and fry, stirring, for 3–5 minutes until soften. Add the curry powder and cracked black pepper and fry for a further 1–2 minutes, stirring. Watch carefully that the curry powder doesn't burn.

Add the stock and bring to the boil. Return the lamb necks to the pot and turn the heat down to low. Add the dried chilli and the curry leaves and simmer, covered, for 1 hour. Alternatively, place the covered casserole in a preheated 130°C/Gas Mark $1/2$ oven for 1 hour.

After one hour, add the swede and turnip. Re-cover the pot and return it to the heat or oven for a further 30 minutes. Stir in the blanched pearl barley and simmer, uncovered, for a further 35–40 minutes until the lamb is flaking from the bone and the barley is tender. Remove the pot from the heat and leave to stand, uncovered, for 30 minutes. Season.

Meanwhile, make the cucumber raita. Mix the cucumber with the sea salt flakes and leave for 20 minutes. Wash the salt off the cucumber and pat it dry on a tea towel. Combine the sugar, white wine vinegar and turmeric together in a non-metallic bowl. Stir in the yogurt, mint and cucumber and mix together. Cover and chill until needed.

Reheat the curried lamb and pearl barley and serve with the cucumber raita on the side.

Rolled breast of lamb with cracked wheat, merguez sausages and chilli oil

Lamb breast is one of the most underused, but tastiest cuts of meat around. You do have to work with it to get the most out of it, but it is so worth doing. There is a high fat-to-meat ratio, just like with a pork belly, that helps keep flavour and moisture during slow cooking. There is a lot of North African influence in this dish and it is really suited to a warm summer day.

Serves 6

2 boned breasts of lamb, about 800g each
4 teaspoons ground allspice
rapeseed oil
4 star anise
1 bulb of garlic, unpeeled and cut in half through the equator
1 white onion, quartered
1 litre Brown Chicken Stock (see page 240)
salt and pepper, to taste
crisp cool salad, to serve

For the cracked wheat and merguez sausages
400ml chicken stock
2 fresh kaffir lime leaves
1 lemongrass stalk, outer layer removed and the stalk crushed
thinly pared peel of 1 lemon
1 tablespoon coriander seeds, toasted
2 tablespoons olive oil

2 tablespoons rapeseed oil
1 large red onion, chopped
1 red pepper, deseeded and finely chopped
1 garlic clove, crushed
60g cracked wheat
6 merguez sausages
2 tablespoons chopped flat-leaf parsley leaves
1 tablespoon chopped coriander leaves
1 tablespoon chopped mint leaves
30g raisins
$1/4$ cucumber, deseeded and diced
freshly squeezed juice of 1 lemon

For the chilli oil
6 fresh red chillies, chopped – with seeds and all
3 garlic cloves
250ml olive oil

At least 24 hours before you plan to serve, cut each lamb breast in half horizontally so you have 4 equal pieces. Score the lamb on the inside and rub 1 teaspoon allspice into each piece. Roll up each piece very tightly, like a Swiss roll, and tie with string so they don't unroll.

Heat 4 tablespoons rapeseed oil in a flameproof casserole over a medium-high heat. Add the lamb and sear until browned all over. Add the star anise, garlic and onion and stir around. Pour in the brown chicken stock and bring to the boil, skimming the surface, as necessary. Cover the pot, reduce the heat to low and leave to simmer for 3 hours, or until the lamb is tender. Turn off the heat and leave the lamb to cool in the pot, covered, for 1 hour.

After one hour, remove the lamb and untie. Wrap the lamb pieces, still rolled, tightly in clingfilm, trying as best as you can to keep the shape. Leave to cool completely, then place in the fridge for 24 hours to firm up.

Strain the cooking liquid through a fine sieve and leave to cool completely. Place it in the fridge for 24 hours, so the fat firms up and can be lifted off.

Meanwhile, begin the cracked wheat dish. Place the chicken stock, kaffir lime leaves, lemongrass, lemon peel and coriander seeds in a saucepan over a high heat and bring to the boil. Remove the pan from the heat and leave to one side, covered, to infuse for at least 30 minutes.

Heat the oil in another pan over a low heat. Add the red onion, red pepper and garlic and fry, stirring, for at least 5 minutes until the onion and pepper are softened. Add the cracked wheat and remove the pan from the heat. Strain the infused hot stock through a fine sieve on to the wheat. Cover the pan and leave for 30 minutes, or until the wheat absorbs all the stock.

Meanwhile, make the chilli oil. Purée the red chillies and garlic cloves together in a small food processor. With the motor still running, slowly add the olive oil to make a thin paste. Season, cover and chill until needed.

To finish the cracked wheat dish, heat 2 tablespoons rapeseed oil in a frying pan over a medium-high heat. Add the merguez sausages and fry, stirring for 8–10 minutes until they are cooked through. Remove them from the pan and chop them up, then stir them into the cracked wheat. Add the chopped herbs, raisins and cucumber and season with the lemon juice and salt and pepper. This can be served hot or cold.

Remove the fat from the lamb cooking liquid. Place the liquid in a saucepan over a high heat and bring to the boil. Continue boiling until it reduces down to a sauce consistency. Season.

Meanwhile, unwrap the lamb breasts. Add them to the fat remaining in the pan and fry until browned and crispy on all sides.

To serve, spread a little of the sauce on to 6 plates. Slice the 4 pieces of lamb breast and divide the slices between 6 plates. Serve with the cracked wheat dish and chilli oil and the extra sauce on the side. A crisp cool salad is the ideal accompaniment.

Proper Pub Food

Rump of salt marsh lamb and broccoli stalks with anchovy dressing

You don't have to use salt marsh lamb for this recipe, but it is great if you can get it! Lamb and anchovies are a classic pairing because they work so well together – the lamb fat provides flavour and the rich, salty, savoury kick from the fish is one of the best things ever!

Serves 2

125g butter
1 onion, thinly sliced
4 sprigs of rosemary, tied together
150ml double cream
splash of truffle oil
2 rumps of salt marsh lamb
2 tablespoons rapeseed oil
200ml water
1 large broccoli stalk, quartered and trimmed
salt and pepper, to taste
100ml Lamb Sauce Base (see page 239), boiled
   down to sauce consistency and kept hot, to serve

For the anchovy dressing
150ml rapeseed oil
2 tablespoons dried herbes de Provence
1 tablespoon fennel seeds, toasted
finely grated zest and freshly squeezed juice of 1
   lemon
8 salted anchovy fillets, finely chopped, plus extra,
   to garnish

Melt 50g of butter in a saucepan over a very low heat. Add the onion, rosemary and a good pinch of salt, cover the pan and leave the onions to sweat for 20–25 minutes until softened, but not coloured. Pour in the double cream and bring to the boil, then continue boiling until the cream is reduced by one-third. Discard the rosemary. Transfer the mixture to a food processor, add the truffle oil and process until you have a smooth onion purée, then leave on one side.

To make the anchovy dressing, mix the rapeseed oil, dried herbs, fennel seeds and lemon zest and juice together in a non-metallic bowl. Stir in the anchovies, then leave to one side until needed.

When ready to cook, preheat the oven to 200°C/Gas Mark 6. Season the lamb rumps with salt and pepper. Heat the rapeseed oil in a large ovenproof frying pan over a medium-high heat. Add the rumps, flat side down, and cook for about 8 minutes until they are caramelised and browned. Spoon over some of the anchovy dressing, place the pan in the oven and roast the rumps for 5–6 minutes, in which time they will become medium-rare to medium. Remove the pan from the oven and spoon a little more dressing over the top of the rumps, then leave them to rest, covered with kitchen foil, for 10 minutes.

Melt the remaining butter with the water in another pan and bring to the boil, stirring to melt the butter. Add the broccoli stalk quarters and a pinch of salt and boil for 5–8 minutes until they are just tender.

To serve, place a pool of onion purée on each of the plates. Slice the lamb and rest it on the purée. Spoon a little of the anchovy dressing over the lamb and drizzle some lamb sauce around the plates. Add the broccoli stalks and garnish with anchovy fillets.

Slow-roasted shoulder of lamb with boulangère potatoes

This recipe is great to stick in the oven on a Sunday morning, then go and walk the dogs and call in at the pub for a couple and when you get home the house smells amazing – and lunch is ready. I think I can safely call it the ultimate family lunch!

Pommes boulangère are named after the French term for a bakery. Once every village or town had a baker with big clay ovens. When the baker had finished baking his bread, he would turn the oven off and the residual heat in the oven would slowly cook this fantastic potato dish.

Serves 4–6, plus some for the dogs

6 large waxy potatoes, peeled and thinly sliced
3 onions, thinly sliced
leaves from 1 bunch of thyme
1 shoulder of lamb, about 2kg
1 head of garlic, separated into cloves and peeled
600ml chicken stock
salt and pepper, to taste

Preheat the oven to 130°C/Gas Mark $^1/_2$.

Mix the potatoes, onions and thyme leaves together in a bowl and season. Roughly layer the potatoes and onions in a roasting tray and put the lamb on top, skin side up. Use a knife to pierce the lamb all over, then put a clove of garlic into each hole. Pour over the chicken stock.

Put the baking tray in the oven and roast the lamb for 4–5 hours, until the lamb is tender and the potatoes are cooked through. Remove the tray, cover it with foil and leave the lamb to rest for 20 minutes before carving.

Duck confit with blowtorched chicory and mash

This is my play on Duck à l'orange, a French classic that suits the pub style of cooking. This dish does involve a bit of prep work, but the flavours are outstanding. The curing and confiting processes were originally intended as a way of preserving the duck legs, but the bonus is they end up tasting really lush!

Serves 4

4 cloves
3 dried bay leaves
4 tablespoons sea salt flakes
1 tablespoon demerara sugar
$1/_2$ teaspoon ground mace
$1/_2$ nutmeg, freshly grated
4 duck legs, about 200g each
500g duck fat, melted
100g runny honey
50g butter
250ml Brown Chicken Stock (see page 240)
salt, to taste
1 orange, to garnish

For the blowtorched chicory
700ml water
100ml white wine vinegar
100g sugar
1 teaspoon coriander seeds
1 teaspoon white peppercorns
1 teaspoon salt
2 heads of white chicory, halved lengthways
50g butter

For the mash
800g waxy potatoes, peeled and diced
100ml milk
100g butter

Grind the cloves, bay leaves, sea salt flakes, demerara sugar, mace and nutmeg together with a pestle and mortar. Scatter a layer of this mix onto a non-metallic tray and place the duck legs on top, skin side down. Sprinkle the remaining salt mix on top of the duck, then cover with clingfilm. Place in the fridge and leave for 24 hours.

After 24 hours, preheat the oven to 130°C/ Gas Mark $1/_2$. Rinse the duck legs thoroughly under running cold water. Pat them dry and place them in a flameproof casserole. Cover the duck legs with the duck fat and heat on the hob until the fat reaches 80°C on an instant-read thermometer. Cover the pot and place it in the oven for $2^1/_2$–3 hours until the duck legs are tender. Remove the pot from the oven and leave the duck to cool in the pot, covered, for 2 hours.

When the duck legs are cool, transfer them to a plate, skin side down. Pass the duck fat through a fine sieve, then transfer it to the fridge and save to use another time. It will remain fresh in a sealed container for several months.

To prepare the chicory, mix 500ml of the water, the white wine vinegar, sugar, coriander seeds, peppercorns and salt together in a saucepan over a high heat and bring to the boil, stirring to dissolve the sugar. Add the chicory to the boiling liquid, then reduce the heat to low and poach the chicory for 15–20 minutes until it is just tender. Remove the chicory from the poaching liquid and leave to cool.

Meanwhile, make the mash. Put the potatoes in a saucepan with enough salted water to cover them over a high heat and bring to the boil. Reduce the heat to low and leave the potatoes to simmer for 20 minutes, or until they are tender. Drain the potatoes through a colander and leave them to steam dry. Put the milk and butter in another pan and bring to the boil, stirring to melt the butter. Use a mouli-legume, potato ricer or a masher to mash the potatoes, then return them to the pan, if necessary. Beat in the hot milk and butter and season. Cover the pan and keep the mash warm.

Preheat the oven to 190°C/Gas Mark 5. Place the duck legs in a roasting tray. Place the tray in the oven and roast the duck legs for about 35 minutes until crispy and browned. When they are ready, remove the thigh bones by twisting them out. Place the duck legs, skin side up, on a heatproof plate and set aside.

Put the tray over a high heat on the hob. Add the honey and butter, stirring until the honey dissolves, then leave to bubble until the mixture turns dark amber colour and is caramelised. Watch closely at this point. Pour half of the caramelised mix over the ducks to glaze them. Add the brown chicken stock to the caramel remaining in the tray and bring to the boil, whisking, to make a sauce. Leave to one side until needed.

To finish the chicory, put the remaining 200ml water, the butter and a pinch of salt in a saucepan over a high heat and bring to the boil, stirring to melt the butter. Turn the heat to low, add the chicory halves and reheat them. When they are warm, transfer them to a roasting tray. Use a blowtorch to give the chicory a charred flavour and dark colour.

Divide the mash between 4 plates, add a chicory half to each and place a boned duck leg on top. Pour over a little gravy, then freshly grate the zest of an orange over the top to release the lovely fresh orange oils. Serve immediately.

" **This is my play on Duck à l'orange, a French classic that suits the pub style of cooking. This dish does involve a bit of prep work, but the flavours are outstanding.** "

Slow-roasted duck with braised lettuce and potato pancakes

Everybody loves slow-roasted, crispy duck from a Chinese takeaway, but this is an English version for a more substantial main course.

Serves 4

1 English free-range duck, about 2.5kg
1 teaspoon Szechuan peppercorns, ground
300ml Brown Chicken Stock (see page 240) or duck stock made with the giblets
100g butter, cubed
10 sprigs of thyme
thinly pared peel of 1 lemon
4 Little Gem lettuces, halved lengthways and rinsed
150g runny honey
75ml soy sauce
salt and pepper, to taste
sea salt flakes, to taste

For the potato pancakes
250g cold, dry mashed potato
75g plain white flour
1 teaspoon baking powder
125ml milk
2 eggs
3 tablespoons rapeseed oil

Preheat the oven to 200°C/Gas Mark 4. Pierce the duck skin all over with a small sharp knife, but be careful not to tear the skin. Season the duck with the Szechuan pepper and salt to taste, then place it on a wire rack in a roasting tray. Place the tray in the oven and roast the duck for 25 minutes.

Remove the roasting tray from the oven and pour off and reserve the fat that has accumulated in the tray. Reduce the oven temperature to 110°C/Gas Mark $1/4$. When it reaches that temperature, return the roasting tray to the oven and continue roasting the duck for a further $1^1/_4$ hours, basting with its own fat every 20 minutes.

Meanwhile, mix the stock, butter, thyme and lemon peel together in a large saucepan over a high heat and bring to the boil, stirring to melt the butter. Place the lettuce halves in the stock and cover the pan. Turn the heat down to low and leave the lettuces to simmer for 8–10 minutes until they start to wilt. Remove them from the heat and keep warm.

Remove the roasting tray from the oven and pour off 90 per cent of the duck fat from the tray. Increase the oven temperature to 180°C/Gas Mark 4. Pour the runny honey over the top of the duck, then return the tray to the oven and continue roasting the duck for a further 15–20 minutes, basting every 5 minutes with the pan juices and watching closely that the honey doesn't burn, until the duck is cooked through and tender. On the last baste, add the soy sauce to glaze the duck. Remove the duck from the tray and leave to rest, uncovered, for 45 minutes.

Whilst the duck is resting, make the potato pancakes. Mix the mashed potato, flour and baking powder together in a bowl. Whisk together the milk and eggs, then stir the liquid ingredients into the potato mix to form a batter. Heat the rapeseed oil in a large non-stick frying pan over a medium heat. Drop spoonfuls of the batter into the pan and fry for 2–3 minutes on each side until golden brown. Transfer them to the turned-off oven to keep hot. You should get 12–16 pancakes.

When ready to serve, sprinkle the duck, potato pancakes and braised lettuce with sea salt flakes. Carve the duck and serve with the braised lettuce and the potato pancakes. Spoon some pan juices over the top and tuck in.

Tom's Tip
Any fat leftover after basting the duck while it roasts can be left to cool completely, then stored in the fridge in a sealed container for almost indefinitely to use in other dishes. You can't beat it for frying potatoes in.

Wild rabbit and bacon with dandelion salad and wet polenta

I lived in Norfolk for a short while before opening The Hand & Flowers and I was introduced to the real outdoor way of life, proper country living. It was a fantastic experience for a bloke who has always lived in cities. One night, a local took me out from the pub in his 4x4 to go 'lamping'. This turned out to mean that I had to point a lamp with a red light over a field to catch the eyes of wild rabbits, providing a target for my local shooter friend. We shot loads of rabbits that night, and this is one of the dishes that I was inspired to make.

Serves 2

1 skinless chicken breast fillet, about 150g, diced
1 teaspoon sea salt flakes
$1/2$ teaspoon cayenne pepper
1 egg
150ml single cream
1 rabbit saddle, with liver and kidneys
1 garlic clove, crushed
1 tablespoon chopped flat-leaf parsley leaves
6 streaky smoked bacon rashers, rindless
rapeseed oil
knob of butter
$1/2$ lemon
salt and pepper, to taste

For the wet polenta
400ml milk
1 bay leaf
$1/2$ teaspoon black peppercorns
150g instant polenta
70g butter, cubed
70g Parmesan cheese, freshly grated
1 tablespoon truffle oil

For the dandelion salad
100g dandelion salad leaves (*pis en lit*), rinsed and spun dry in a salad spinner
4 tablespoon extra virgin olive oil
1 tablespoon chopped chives
juice of $1/2$ lemon

Put the chicken, sea salt flakes and cayenne pepper and a food processor and process until the chicken is broken down. Add the egg and process again until incorporated. When fully mixed, add the single cream and blend until a firm mousse forms. Transfer to a bowl, cover with clingfilm and put in the fridge until needed.

Remove the loins, fillets, kidneys and the liver from the rabbit. Trim all sinew from the loin. Dice the liver and the kidney and mix with 4 tablespoons of the chicken mousse. Add the garlic and parsley and mix again.

Lay the rashers of streaky bacon out next to each other on a large sheet of clingfilm. Place another layer of clingfilm on top and roll out with a rolling pin to stretch the rashers. Remove the top layer of clingfilm. Lay the trimmed rabbit loins on the bacon with a 2cm gap between them. Fill this gap with the remaining chicken mousse. Place the rabbit fillets on top and then use the clingfilm to help you roll the bacon over the top to form a sausage-like shape. Tie both ends to secure. Wrap the whole thing in kitchen foil and leave in the fridge to rest for 1 hour.

After 1 hour, bring a large saucepan of water up to the boil over a high heat. Drop the wrapped rabbit into the pan and put a small plate on top to keep it submerged. Turn off the heat and leave the rabbit in the liquid, uncovered, for $1\frac{1}{2}$ hours, or until it cools completely. When it is room temperature, transfer the rabbit to the fridge until needed.

Before you are ready to serve, make the wet polenta. Put the milk, bay leaf and black peppercorns in a saucepan over a high heat and bring to the boil. Turn off the heat and leave to infuse, uncovered, for 10 minutes.

Put the polenta into another pan and strain the infused milk onto the polenta. Place the pan over a medium heat and whisk constantly for 8–10 minutes until the polenta has absorbed the milk and is cooked through and softened. Stir in the butter, Parmesan cheese and truffle oil. Season, but remember the cheese is salty, so you might not need any. Set aside and keep hot.

Remove the rabbit from the foil and clingfilm and pat dry. Heat 2 tablespoons rapeseed oil in a large non-stick frying pan over a medium heat. Add the rabbit and fry for about 8 minutes until browned all over and warmed through. Add the knob of butter and squeeze in the lemon juice. Remove the rabbit from the pan, leave to one side and keep warm. Do not discard the buttery juices.

Quickly assemble the dandelion salad. Mix the dandelion leaves with the olive oil, some of the chives and season.

To serve, divide the polenta between 4 plates. Slice the rabbit and arrange it on the polenta. Drizzle the salad with a little of the buttery juices from the pan and arrange it and the remaining chives around the plate. Serve immediately.

" I lived in Norfolk for a short while... and I was introduced to the real outdoor way of life, proper country living. This is one of the dishes I was inspired to make."

Pot-roasted pheasant, game chips and bread sauce

Here's a proper British dish with all the classic game garnishes. Pheasant is a bit like game for beginners – it's not too strong and is cooked like chicken. This recipe is easy to do – just stick the bird in a pot and put it into the oven. You must be careful not to overcook the pheasant, however, as it has a very low fat content and can dry out.

Serves 2

4 streaky smoked bacon rashers
1 large oven-ready pheasant
4 tablespoons rapeseed oil
4 carrots, peeled and halved
150g pancetta, finely chopped
6 garlic cloves, peeled, but whole
thinly pared peel of 1 orange
$\frac{1}{2}$ bunch of thyme
350ml Brown Chicken Stock (see page 240)
4 potatoes for frying, such as Maris Piper, peeled
vegetable oil, for deep frying
salt, to taste
200g vacuum-packed chestnuts

For the bread sauce
70ml milk
30g butter
30ml double cream
6 white peppercorns
1 clove
1 star anise
$\frac{1}{4}$ teaspoon coriander seeds
20g dry breadcrumbs

To make the bread sauce, put the milk, butter and double cream in a saucepan over a high heat and bring to the boil. Add the peppercorns, clove, star anise and coriander seeds, then remove the pan from the heat. Cover the pan and leave the liquid to infuse for 45 minutes.

Strain the infused liquid through a fine sieve into another pan. Return the liquid to the boil and whisk in the breadcrumbs, whisking until the sauce thickens.

Leave to one side and keep warm.

Meanwhile, preheat the oven to 200°C/Gas Mark 6. Stretch the bacon over the top of the pheasant breasts, then leave to one side.

Heat the rapeseed oil in a flameproof casserole over a medium heat. Add the carrots and fry, turning them occasionally, until they turn a deep caramel colour – the darker the better. Add the pancetta and garlic and fry, stirring, for a further 5 minutes. Add the orange peel and thyme, then place the pheasant on top, pour over the chicken stock and bring to the boil. Cover the pot, then place it in the oven and pot-roast the pheasant for 40–50 minutes until it is tender.

Remove the pheasant from the pot, cover with foil and leave to rest for 20 minutes. Strain the cooking liquid into a saucepan and reserve the carrots, garlic and thyme. Bring the cooking liquid to the boil, skimming the surface as necessary, then reduce the heat to medium and leave the sauce to simmer, uncovered, until it reduces to a sauce consistency. Add the chestnuts right towards the end and stir through. Cover the carrots and garlic with foil to keep warm.

Meanwhile, bring a large pan of salted water to the boil. Use the gaufrette blade on a mandoline to cut the potatoes into thin game chips. Add the game chips to the boiling water and almost immediately take them straight out and drain on a tea towel. Pat them completely dry.

Heat enough oil for deep-frying in a deep-fat fryer or heavy-based saucepan until it reaches 180°C. Add the game chips and fry, stirring constantly, for 3–4 minutes until they become crisp and golden brown. Remove the game chips from the fat and drain on kitchen paper. Season. Fry the game chips in batches, if necessary, reheating the oil between batches. You can keep them warm in the turned-off oven, but don't cover then with foil or they will lose their crispness.

Just before you are ready to serve, preheat the grill to high. Remove the bacon from the pheasant and crisp it up under the hot grill. Use a blowtorch to make the pheasant skin crispy and coloured. Remove the pheasant breasts from the bone and serve with the carrots and garlic, bread sauce, the reduced sauce, the bacon and the game chips.

Venison steaks with red cabbage and potato pancakes

I love a T-Bone steak and I love venison.... I think you can work out the inspiration for this recipe. Red cabbage is a classic accompaniment to venison, but far too often it is stewed and loses its freshness. Instead, I like to serve it with a crunch. There is plenty of acidity and sweetness all over this plate in this recipe, so the balance of flavours is very important. Taste everything as you go along.

Serves 4

50g butter
4 tablespoons rapeseed oil
4 venison T-Bone steaks, about 250g each
$1/2$ lemon
salt, to taste
150g crème fraîche, to serve
1 teaspoon crushed Szechuan peppercorns
juice of 1 lime, to serve
1 recipe quantity Potato Pancakes (see page 181), kept hot, to serve

For the red cabbage
$1/2$ red cabbage, shredded
150g demerara sugar
40g sea salt flakes
20 juniper berries, crushed
50g butter

For the clove sauce
200ml red wine
100ml red wine vinegar
100g redcurrant jelly
4 cloves
500ml beef stock

Thirty minutes before you plan to cook, mix the red cabbage, demerara sugar, sea salt flakes and juniper berries together in a non-metallic bowl and leave for the cabbage to soften.

Meanwhile, make the potato pancakes following the instructions on page 181. Keep them hot in a low oven until ready to serve.

To make the clove sauce, bring the red wine, red wine vinegar, redcurrant jelly and cloves to the boil in a saucepan over a high heat, stirring to dissolve the jelly. Continue boiling until the liquid reduces to a glaze. Add the beef stock, return to the boil and reduce again by half to make the sauce. Pass the sauce through a fine sieve into a bowl to remove the cloves, then leave to one side and keep warm.

Rinse the cabbage thoroughly in running cold water. Melt the butter in a pan over a medium heat. Add the cabbage to it to heat up, but do not overcook. We still want the cabbage to have a crunch to it. Leave to one side and keep hot.

Melt the remaining 50g butter with the rapeseed oil in a large frying pan over a high heat until the butter just starts to turn a hazelnut brown. Season the steaks with a pinch of salt, and add them to the pan and fry for 3–4 minutes on each side until they are a lovely dark colour. Squeeze in the lemon juice and baste them with the pan juices. Do not overcook them, as venison has a very low fat content, so the more well done it is, the drier it will be. Remove the steaks from the pan and leave them to rest, covered with foil, for 10 minutes.

Whilst the steaks are resting, mix together the crème fraîche, Szechuan pepper and lime juice.

To serve, put a couple of pancakes on each plate, add some red cabbage and a venison steak, then pour over the clove sauce. Serve with the spiced crème fraîche on the side.

Venison, peppered sprouts, squash purée and chocolate sauce

This is a full-on winter dish. Venison is one of my favourite meats, full of flavour and so good when served medium-rare. The use of dark chocolate and red wine gives a bitter, rich finish to the plate of food and a real taste of class.

Serves 4

100g butter, cubed
rapeseed oil
4 venison loin steaks, 180–200g each
juice from $\frac{1}{2}$ lemon
2 frankfurters, sliced
2 tablespoons pumpkin seeds
200g Brussels sprouts, quartered
$\frac{1}{2}$ teaspoon cracked black pepper
$\frac{1}{2}$ teaspoon crushed Szechuan peppercorns
$\frac{1}{2}$ nutmeg
200ml Red Wine Sauce (see page 239)
1 tablespoon grated 70% dark chocolate
salt and pepper, to taste

For the squash purée
1 butternut squash
100g butter, cubed
2 shallots, finely chopped
150ml chicken stock
100ml double cream
truffle oil, to taste

First, make the squash purée. Peel the butternut squash, then cut it in half lengthways. Dice the top half and keep the trimmings. Scoop the seeds out from the bottom half and cut into equal chunks of about 2cm. ·

Melt 50g of the butter in a large frying pan over a low heat. Add the shallots and fry, stirring occasionally, until they are softened, but not coloured. Add the 2cm chunks of squash and the trimmings from the top half and continue to slowly cook for 5 minutes. Pour in the chicken stock and

bring to the boil, then continue to boil for about 10 minutes until the squash is tender. Place the contents of the pan in a blender, add the remaining 50g butter, the double cream and truffle oil and blend until smooth. Season and pass the sauce through a fine sieve into a pan. Leave to one side until needed.

To cook the venison, melt 50g butter with 4 tablespoons rapeseed oil in a large frying pan over a high heat until the butter just starts to turn a hazelnut brown. Season the steaks with a pinch of salt, add them to the pan and fry for 3–4 minutes on each side until they are a lovely dark colour. Squeeze in the lemon juice and baste them with the pan juices.
Do not overcook them or they will become dry. Remove the steaks from the pan and leave them to rest, covered with foil, for 10 minutes.

In another frying pan, heat 2 tablespoons rapeseed oil in the pan. Add the frankfurters and fry, stirring occasionally, for about 5 minutes until they are crispy around the edges. Remove them from the pan and drain on kitchen paper. Add the diced squash to the pan and fry, stirring, for about 4 minutes, or until just tender. Return the frankfurters to the pan, add the pumpkin seeds and season.

In another pan, melt the remaining 50g butter over a medium heat. Add the Brussels sprouts and fry, stirring, for 3–5 minutes until they are just tender. Season with the black pepper and Szechuan pepper, grate over the nutmeg and add salt to taste.

Meanwhile, bring the red wine sauce to the boil in a separate pan over a high heat. Whisk in the dark chocolate, then immediately remove the pan from the heat.

Divide the squash purée between 4 plates and place the diced squash on top. Slice the venison and place that on top and pour over a little sauce. Serve the sprouts on the side.

Tom's fried chicken in a basket

This is a really nostalgic dish that reminds me of when I was a naughty boy who had just passed my driving test. We used to go out to a great country pub called The Mill, at Withington, about 10 miles outside Gloucester city centre and in the middle of the countryside. It has the local reputation of being the first pub to serve 'chicken in a basket'. This was a proper posh dish when I was growing up, a great dish in a fantastic setting. This version is inspired by my memories, but with more of a spicy, smoky kick.

Serves 4

9 chicken pieces, such as thighs, drumsticks and
   breasts, all on the bone
500ml buttermilk
100g plain white flour
50g cornflour
2 tablespoons smoked paprika
2 tablespoons sweet paprika
4 teaspoons salt
2 teaspoons dried basil
2 teaspoons dried oregano
2 teaspoons dried marjoram
2 teaspoons dried sage
2 teaspoons chilli powder
2 teaspoons garlic powder
2 teaspoons onion salt
2 teaspoons ground white pepper
vegetable oil
coleslaw, to serve

For the brine
1 litre water
500g sea salt
150g demerara sugar
1 tablespoon black peppercorns
2 cloves
1 bay leaf
1 sprig of thyme

A day ahead, mix all the ingredients for the brine together in a saucepan over a high heat and bring to the boil, stirring to dissolve the sea salt and sugar. Pour into a large non-metallic bowl and leave to cool completely. When the brine has cooled, add the chicken pieces. Cover the bowl with clingfilm and leave it in the fridge for 8 hours.

After 8 hours, remove the chicken from the brine and pat dry. Place the chicken into a large plastic container, pour over the buttermilk and use your hands to make sure each piece is well coated. Cover the container and place it in the fridge for 12 hours.

Just before you are ready to cook, mix the flour, cornflour and all the herbs and spices together in a small roasting tray.

Remove the chicken from the buttermilk and scrape off as much of the buttermilk as possible. One by one, roll each chicken piece in the herb and spice mix, shaking off the excess. Leave to one side and preheat an oven to low.

Heat about 1cm vegetable oil in a frying pan over a medium-low heat. Add only 2 or 3 pieces of chicken at a time and fry for 6–7 minutes on each side until the juices run clear when you pierce the pieces and they are lightly coloured. As each batch is cooked, remove it from the pan, drain well on kitchen paper and keep warm in the oven until all the chicken is fried. Add more oil to the pan as needed.

After all the chicken has been fried, put it in the oven on a high heat for 15 minutes, until the coating is crispy and browned. Serve immediately in a basket with coleslaw on the side.

Hay-baked chicken and roasted celeriac

This dish is so clean and simple. It tastes and smells like a gorgeously sweet hay field, which gives it an authentic, real flavour. There is something very comforting about wrapping up a whole chicken in muslin, swaddling it with hay and baking it in quality cider – giving it all the love it needs to become the best chicken ever.

Don't worry that it looks pale when you uncover it after cooking – a blowtorch will quickly colour and crisp up the skin, and add a delicious charred flavour on top of all that juicy meat.

If you happen to know a friendly farmer, get the hay first-hand as it will be a lot nicer than a pet-shop pack! This is one of my favourite weekend treats – it's perfect for Sunday lunch. I urge every last one of you to give it a go and I promise you'll be eating it again and again!

Serves 4

1 chicken, about 3kg
6 fresh bay leaves
2 bulbs of garlic
600ml cider or scrumpy
1 celeriac
3 tablespoons rapeseed oil
150g butter
1 bunch of thyme
1 lemon, halved
2 tablespoons malt extract
600ml chicken stock
salt and pepper, to taste
1 small bag of hay

Preheat the oven to 200°C/Gas Mark 6.

Place the chicken on top of a piece of muslin, large enough to wrap around it, and season with salt and pepper. Put the bay leaves on top of the chicken. Break apart the cloves of garlic from one bulb, but don't peel them. Give them a bash with the back of a knife and sprinkle them over the chicken. Wrap the chicken tightly in the muslin, then put it in a large flameproof casserole.

Pack hay all around the chicken and pour over half the cider. Cover the casserole and place it in the oven for 1 hour, checking occasionally that the liquid hasn't evaporated. If it needs topping up, use the remaining cider, and then some hot water, if necessary. Pierce the muslin with a knife and stab the chicken in the thigh joint to check if the juices run clear. If not, return the pot to the oven for a further 5 minutes. Leave the chicken to rest in the pot, covered, for 45 minutes.

Meanwhile, peel the celeriac and rub it down with a green scouring pad to make it very smooth and rounded. Heat the rapeseed oil an ovenproof frying pan over a medium heat. Add the celeriac to the pan and fry for 10–15 minutes until it is coloured all over. Once the celeriac is nicely browned, add the butter to the pan with the thyme and the remaining garlic bulb, cut in half through the equator. Baste the celeriac in the butter, then place the pan in the oven for 25–30 minutes until the celeriac is tender all the way through. Baste with butter 3 or 4 times during the cooking time.

When the celeriac is tender, remove the pan from the oven and give a good squeeze of lemon juice over the celeriac and season with salt and pepper. Do not discard the garlic and thyme.

(continued on page 192)

(continued from page 190)

Remove the chicken from the pot and place it on a chopping board. Pass any liquid from the pot through a fine sieve into a saucepan. Add the malt extract and bring to the boil. Add the chicken stock and continue boiling until the liquid reduces to a sauce consistency. Adjust the seasoning, if necessary.

Unwrap the chicken from the muslin and remove the garlic and bay leaves. Use a blowtorch to brown the skin. Serve the chicken whole on a platter with the whole celeriac and with a jug of the gravy. Add the thyme and garlic from cooking the celeriac as a garnish, if you like. Let the diners carve the chicken and cut the celeriac themselves.

"This is one of my favourite weekend treats – it's perfect for Sunday lunch. I urge every last one of you to give it a go and I promise you'll be eating it again and again!"

Turkey roll with Christmas crumble topping and sage and onion stuffing

Christmas is such a great family time and no matter how big or small your gathering is, this is the perfect way to serve turkey. When I was a kid, we used to have a well-known turkey roll on Christmas day and this is my updated, super-tasty version of that supermarket classic. I concede there is quite a lot of work to do here, but so much of it can be done days in advance, so there isn't much Christmas-day pressure.

If you buy yourself an instant-read thermometer, I promise you will have a lovely, moist and succulent turkey breast. It could be the best £10.00 you'll ever spend. Why not ask for one for your Christmas stocking?

Serves 6–8

1 boneless, skinless turkey, 2–2.2kg, butterflied – any butcher will do this for you, and make sure to ask for the bones
20 streaky smoked bacon rashers
150ml Homemade Brown Sauce (see page 22)
Rye Bread Sauce (see page 242), to serve
roasted carrots and parsnips, to serve

For the gravy
2kg turkey bones, chopped – you can get these from your butcher
2 turkey wings, chopped
3½ litres Brown Chicken Stock (see page 240)
150g button mushrooms, wiped, trimmed and sliced
4 banana shallots, sliced
2 celery sticks, chopped
10 sprigs of thyme
50g butter, melted
50g plain white flour
salt and pepper, to taste

For the Christmas crumble topping
100g sourdough bread, torn into pieces and toasted
100g shelled pistachio nuts, peeled
100g Pork Scratchings (see page 102)
50g dried cranberries
2 tablespoons thyme leaves
1 orange

For the sage and onion stuffing
250g butter, cubed
400g onion, finely chopped
800g sausage meat
160g fresh fine breadcrumbs
100g vacuum-packed cooked chestnuts, finely chopped
100g dried cranberries
5 tablespoons chopped sage leaves
1 tablespoon juniper berries, finely chopped
1 tablespoon cracked black pepper
2 teaspoons salt

Up to 2 days in advance, begin the gravy. Preheat the oven to 180°C/Gas Mark 4. Place the turkey bones and turkey wings in the tray and roast them for 30–40 minutes until they are dark brown, but not burnt.

Transfer the bones and turkey wings to a large saucepan over a high heat. Add the brown chicken stock, mushrooms, shallots and celery and bring to the boil, using a large metal spoon to skim the surface, as necessary. Turn the heat down to very low and leave the stock to simmer, uncovered, for 4 hours, or until it is reduced by one-third.

Turn the heat off, add the thyme leaves and leave to infuse, uncovered, for 10 minutes. Pass the stock through a fine sieve into a bowl, then leave to cool completely. Cover and place in the fridge for 12 hours so the fat can set on the top and be removed easily.

(continued on page 195)

(continued from page 193)

When you're ready to finish the gravy, remove and discard the fat. Pour the stock into a saucepan and bring to the boil. Mix the melted butter and flour together to make a paste. Add this mix into the boiling liquid, little by little, whisking constantly and vigorously until the gravy thickens. Season, then pass the gravy though a sieve lined with muslin. It's now ready to serve. Leave on one side until needed.

To make the sage and onion stuffing, melt the butter in a frying pan over a medium heat. Add the onions and fry, stirring, for 3–5 minutes until softened. Tip the onions and butter into a large bowl and leave to cool. When the onions are cool, add the remaining stuffing ingredients and mix together. Leave on one side until needed.

To make the crumble topping, mix the toasted sourdough pieces, pistachio nuts, pork scratchings, dried cranberries and thyme leaves together. Break everything up with your fingers until they are all the same size. Leave to one side until needed.

To prepare the turkey, begin by unrolling it and opening it like a book, smooth side down. Cover the surface with clingfilm and bash it out a little with a rolling pin to make it into a rough square, 1–1$^1/_2$cm thick. Spread a $^1/_2$cm layer of the stuffing mix on to the turkey breast and then tightly roll it up, like rolling a Swiss roll. Wrap it in clingfilm as tightly as you can, then use kitchen string to tie the ends and to secure the roll in a couple of places to help keep its shape. Place the turkey roll into the fridge until needed. You will have more stuffing mix than you will use for the turkey, but do not throw it away. It will be roasted separately. Cover and keep it in the fridge until needed.

When you're finally ready to cook the turkey, preheat the oven to 120°C/Gas mark $^1/_2$. Bring a kettle of water to the boil and pour 400ml boiling water into a roasting tray. Put a wire rack in the tray and place the still-wrapped turkey roll on the rack. Place the tray in the oven and roast the turkey for 1$^1/_2$ hours, or until an instant-read thermometer stuck into the centre of the turkey reads 70°C. Once the correct internal temperature has been reached, remove the turkey from the oven and leave it to rest, still wrapped in clingfilm, for 45 minutes. Do not turn the oven off.

Meanwhile, line a flameproof bowl with the bacon rashers, with plenty of overhang. Add the remaining stuffing, pressing it down, and wrap the bacon ends over the top. Place the bowl in the oven about 15 minutes before the turkey should finish cooking and bake the stuffing for 45 minutes, or until it reaches 70°C on an instant-read thermometer. Remove the bowl from the oven and leave to one side until just before the turkey finishes resting.

Meanwhile, preheat the grill to medium. When you're getting ready to serve, place the bowl with the stuffing under the grill and grill for 8–10 minutes until the top of the stuffing is crispy.

After the turkey has rested for 30 minutes, unwrap it and brush a thick layer of the brown sauce over the top. Use your hands to press the Christmas crumble mix all over and instantly grate over the orange zest to release the oil.

To serve, slice the turkey and serve immediately with the gravy and stuffing. The perfect accompaniments? Rye bread sauce and roasted carrots and parsnips. Enjoy the rest of your Christmas day.

Tom's Tips

If you want to get really ahead, leave the gravy to cool completely after it is thickened, then store in a covered container in the fridge for up to 2 days or freeze for up to 3 months. The sage and onion stuffing can be made up to 2 days in advance and kept in the fridge, and you can stuff and roll the turkey breast a day in advance.

PROPER
PUDDINGS

Apple and toffee crumble tart

This is the ultimate crumble. It has taste, texture, acidity and sweetness. You get toffee apple and apple crumble all together, what more could you want?!

Serves 8

4 Bramley apples
4 Cox's apples
100g butter, cubed
100g caster sugar
finely grated zest of 1 orange
1 cinnamon stick
clotted cream, Vanilla Custard (see page 235), or crème fraîche, to serve

For the toffee
vegetable oil for greasing the baking parchment
450g soft dark brown sugar
125ml water
130g golden syrup
100g black treacle
1 teaspoon cream of tartar

For the pastry
225g butter, softened
125g caster sugar
1 egg yolk, beaten
400g plain white four, plus extra for rolling out the pastry

For the crumble topping
200g plain white flour
100g caster sugar
80g butter, softened
35g ground almonds
10g flaked almonds

First, make the toffee. Line a baking tray with baking parchment, grease it with vegetable oil and leave it to one side. Place the dark brown sugar and water in a saucepan over a high heat and bring to the boil, stirring to dissolve the sugar. Make sure the sugar has completely dissolved before the water boils. Remove the pan from the heat. Add the golden syrup, black treacle and cream of tartar to the pan, return it to the heat and boil until the mix reaches 140°C on an instant-read thermometer. This will take a while, but be patient and don't leave it. It can burn very easily! Once the mix reaches the correct temperature, pour it straight into the lined tray and leave to cool at room temperature.

To make the pastry, place the butter and the sugar into a large mixing bowl and beat together until light and creamy. Add the egg yolk and sift over the flour, then just mix until the pastry comes together. Do not overwork. Wrap the pastry in clingfilm and leave to rest in the fridge for at least 1 hour.

When you are ready to bake the pastry case, preheat the oven to 170°C/Gas Mark 3 and place a 25cm tart ring on a baking sheet lined with baking parchment.

After the pastry has rested, roll it out on a lightly floured surface to about 1/2cm thick. Line the tart ring with the pastry. Press in a piece of clingfilm, then fill with baking beans or rice. Place the baking sheet in the oven and bake the pastry case for 15 minutes, or until it is crisp and golden brown. Very gently, remove the pastry case from the oven and leave to cool on a wire rack.

To make the filling, peel and dice the Bramley and Cox's apples and leave them to one side separately. Melt the butter in a saucepan with the sugar and orange zest, stirring to dissolve the sugar. Add half of the Bramley apples and the cinnamon stick and stir over a medium-high heat until the apples break down into a purée. Add the rest of the diced apples and gently stir for only 1–2 minutes to just soften them, then remove the pan from the heat. Pour the mix into a colander over a bowl to strain off any excess liquid and leave to cool. Remove the cinnamon stick.

Meanwhile, reheat the oven to 180°C/Gas Mark 4. To make the crumble topping, mix the flour, sugar, butter and ground almonds together until the mix resembles large breadcrumbs. Mix in the flaked almonds.

Place this mix in a baking tray and bake for about 20 minutes, until golden brown and crumbly. Make sure you stir it every 5 minutes so it colours evenly. Remove the tray from the oven and leave the crumble topping to cool. Do not turn off the oven.

To assemble the tart, spoon the apple filling into the pastry. Break the toffee into nice-size chunks and place a few over the top of the apple. Completely cover with the toasted crumble and then dot a few more pieces of toffee on top. Place the tart in the oven and bake for 10–12 minutes until the filling is bubbling hot and the toffee has melted. Remove the crumble from the oven and leave to stand for a few minutes. Serve with clotted cream, vanilla custard or crème fraîche... or all of them!

Proper Puddings

Date and toffee puddings with caramelised bananas

I'm sure you'll enjoy these super-sweet and dark puddings. They are very easy to make and best when served warm. This is a pub favourite and always a bestseller when it's on the menu. It's a bit naughty, but satisfying! You can serve these hot, straight from the oven, or leave them to cool slightly, as we do in the restaurant.
Make my ultimate Toffee Sauce to go with the puddings – it's a treacly, caramelly, toasty treat.

Serves 6

250ml water
150ml dark rum
1 vanilla pod, split in half lengthways and the seeds scraped out
250g pitted dates, chopped
150g plain white flour, plus extra for dusting the pan
2 teaspoons bicarbonate of soda
125g butter, softened, plus extra for greasing the pan
125g soft dark brown sugar
3 eggs
2 bananas
demerara sugar for dusting
Toffee Sauce (see page 243), to serve

Bring the water, rum and vanilla pod and seeds to the boil in a saucepan over a high heat. Add the dates, cover the pan, remove it from the heat and leave the dates to soak for 1 hour.

After the dates have soaked, preheat the oven to 180°C/Gas Mark 4 and grease and flour six 10cm ceramic ovenproof dishes. Sift the flour and bicarbonate of soda together and leave to one side.

Beat the butter and soft dark brown sugar together until light and fluffy. Beat in the eggs, one at a time. Beat in the sifted flour, then fold in the date and rum mix.

Pour the batter into the dishes and smooth the surfaces. Place the dishes in the oven and bake the puddings for 12–15 minutes until a skewer stuck in the centre of each comes out clean. Transfer the dishes to a wire rack and leave the puddings to cool for 10 minutes.

Meanwhile, to make the decorative toppings, thinly slice the bananas. Fan the slices into six 10cm circles on a metal baking sheet, then dust each with demerara sugar. Use a blowtorch to caramelise the sugar.

Remove the puddings from the dishes, then use a fish slice to gently transfer the glazed banana circles to the top of the puddings. Serve with the toffee sauce.

If you decide not to serve the puddings while they are still warm, they can be left to cool completely, then wrapped in kitchen foil and stored in an airtight container for 2–3 days.

Bread and butter pudding

No recipe collection should be without a bread and butter pudding. It is such a simple and rich pudding, but so rooted in Great Britain. Served straight from the oven, this is one of the best puddings ever!

Serves 4–6

butter, softened, for greasing the dish and spreading
½ loaf of white bread, about 500g
1 nutmeg
600ml double cream
1 vanilla pod, split in half lengthways and the seeds scraped out
75g caster sugar
8 large egg yolks
150g raisins
demerara sugar for glazing
your favourite ice cream (my favourite is Buffalo Vanilla Ice Cream on page 217), to serve (optional)

Grease an ovenproof serving dish with butter. Remove the crusts from the bread, then slice and butter each slice. Spread the slices out on your work surface and grate the whole nutmeg over them, then leave them to one side until needed.

Put the cream and vanilla seeds and pods into a saucepan over a high heat and bring just to the boil. Whisk the sugar and egg yolks together in a heatproof bowl. Pour the boiling cream onto the egg mix, whisking, then leave to one side to cool a little. Pass the custard through a fine sieve.

Pour a layer of the custard into the greased dish. Sprinkle with some of the raisins and then add a layer of bread. Repeat this process until all the ingredients have been used. Leave on one side to rest for 25 minutes.

Meanwhile, preheat the oven to 130°C/ Gas Mark ½. Place the pudding in the oven and bake for 25–30 minutes until the custard is just set. Remove the dish from the oven and leave the pudding to stand for 10 minutes. Sprinkle a thick layer of demerara sugar over the top and use a blowtorch to caramelise. Serve with ice cream, if you fancy.

"**No recipe collection should be without a bread and butter pudding... this is one of the best puddings ever!**"

Cherry Bakewell tart

Try my Bakewell tart with a difference.
The recipe is such a classic, but I use puff pastry
which gives it a lighter and more indulgent
touch. Fennel herb tastes of aniseed and is a
great match for the cherries.

Serves 8

500g fresh cherries, stoned
100ml cherry brandy, plus a little extra for finishing
500g all-butter puff pastry, defrosted if frozen
icing sugar, for dusting
2 tablespoons fennel herb, to decorate
clotted cream, to serve

For the frangipane
100g butter, softened
100g icing sugar, plus extra for dusting
2 eggs
100g ground almonds
2 tablespoons dark rum

Preheat the oven to 200°C/Gas Mark 6 and line a
baking sheet with baking parchment.

While the oven is heating, make the frangipane. Place
the butter and icing sugar in a bowl and beat together
until light and creamy. Beat in the eggs, then add the
ground almonds and the rum. Leave to one side.

Place the cherries in a baking tray and pour over
the cherry brandy. Place the tray in the oven and
bake the cherries for 10–12 minutes until they start to
dehydrate and the brandy has evaporated. The cherry
flavour intensifies by doing this.

Roll the puff pastry out on a lightly floured surface
until it is about $\frac{1}{2}$cm thick. Use a 30cm plate as a
template and cut out a circle of pastry. Spread the
frangipane 1cm thick over the pastry, leaving about
2cm around the edge. Roll the edge in to form a rim.
Press the dehydrated cherries into the frangipane and
heavily dust with icing sugar. Place the baking sheet
in the oven and bake the tart for 20–30 minutes until
crispy and golden brown.

Remove the baking sheet from the oven and put
a piece of baking parchment on top of the tart.
Place another baking tray on top and flip the tart over.
Take the first tray away and put the tart back into the
oven for a further 10 minutes, upside down, to crisp
up the bottom. Remove the tart from the oven and
leave to cool for 15-20 minutes on a wire rack.

Place a chopping board on top of the tart and flip
it back over, the right way up. Sprinkle the top with a
little more cherry brandy, dust with icing sugar and
use a blowtorch to give a glaze. Scatter the fennel
herb on top and serve with clotted cream.

Gloucester lardy cake with orange caramel

Fresh-from-the-oven lardy cake is a massive childhood memory. Gloucester used to have two or three proper bakeries, and I can remember shopping in town on Saturday mornings with my mum and brother and finishing off with a warm lardy cake... lush!!!

Serves 8–10

375g strong white flour, plus extra for rolling out
20g fresh yeast, crumbled
1 tablespoon sugar
1 teaspoon salt
215ml water, blood heat
200g lard, diced
200g demerara sugar
150g sultanas
150g currants
finely grated zest of 1 orange
$\frac{1}{2}$ nutmeg

For the orange caramel
250g caster sugar
100ml freshly squeezed orange juice

Mix the flour, yeast, sugar and salt together in the bowl of a freestanding food mixer with a bread hook fitted and make a well in the centre. Pour in the water, start the mixer and knead for 5 minutes, or until the dough is smooth and elastic. Cover the bowl with clingfilm and leave the dough to rise at room temperature until it doubles in volume, which will take $1\frac{1}{2}$–2 hours.

To make the orange caramel, put the caster sugar in a saucepan over a high heat to make a dry caramel. By this I mean do not add any water, just melt the sugar in the pan. Once it boils, don't stir. When it is a nice amber colour, pour in the orange juice and remove the pan from the heat. Whisk briskly until all the sugar pieces have dissolved. Leave the caramel to one side to cool.

Meanwhile, grease a 24cm springform cake tin.

Knock the dough back and tip it out on to a lightly floured surface. Roll it out into a 30 x 20cm rectangle. Sprinkle over 75g of the lard, 75g of the demerara sugar, 75g of the sultanas, 75g of the currants and half the orange zest, then grate over half the piece of nutmeg. Fold the dough in half, on to itself, then re-roll out to the same size. It's OK if a little of the stuffing falls out.

Add the same quantity of flavourings, so you have 50g sugar and 50g lard left. Fold the dough in half, on to itself, then use your hands to roll the dough into a ball shape. Place the dough into the prepared tin and press down on it so it fills the tin. Sprinkle the remaining sugar and lard over the top and leave the cake to one side, uncovered, for about 45 minutes until slightly risen.

Meanwhile, preheat the oven to 200°C/Gas Mark 6. Place the tin in the oven and bake the cake for 30–35 minutes until it is risen and golden brown. Transfer the tin to a wire rack and leave the cake to cool for at least 20 minutes before eating.

When ready to serve, remove the lardy cake from the tin. Slice the lardy cake, place on plates and spoon the orange caramel over.

Proper Pub Food

Chocolate and ale cake with muscovado and malt cream

Dark beer and dark chocolate go so well together. They have a very similar bitter taste and when that is combined with a little sugar it makes an excellent cake. At the pub we serve this with a shot glass of dark quadruple ale. The muscovado and malt cream is my nod to the malt taste in the beer.

Serves 8

50g dark cocoa powder
200ml dark ale
175g plain white flour
1 teaspoon bicarbonate of soda
$\frac{1}{4}$ teaspoon baking powder
275g dark soft brown sugar
110g butter, softened, plus extra for greasing the pan
2 large eggs

For the muscovado and malt cream
50g dark muscovado sugar
50g malt extract
pinch of salt
250ml double cream

For the chocolate and ale icing
220g dark chocolate, at least 70% cocoa, broken
220g icing sugar
100g butter, softened
4 tablespoons dark ale

First, make the muscovado and malt cream. Mix the muscovado sugar, malt extract and salt together in a bowl. Whisk in the double cream until it holds a soft peak, then cover and chill until needed.

Preheat the oven to 180°C/Gas Mark 4 and grease a 25cm metal terrine. Put the cocoa powder in a bowl, stir in the dark ale and leave to one side until needed.

Sift the flour, bicarbonate of soda and baking powder together and also leave to one side. Beat the soft dark brown sugar and butter together until soft and creamed. Beat in the eggs, one at a time. Beat in the cocoa mix, then add the flour mix, little by little, and beat it in, making sure each addition is incorporated before adding the next.

Spoon the batter into the prepared tin and smooth the surface. Place the tin in the oven and bake the cake for 30–35 minutes until a skewer inserted in the centre comes out clean and the cake comes away from the sides. Remove the cake from the oven and leave it to cool on a wire rack. When it is cool, remove it from the tin.

While the cake is cooling, make the chocolate and ale icing. Place a heatproof bowl over a pan of simmering water, without letting the bottom of the bowl touch the water. Add the chocolate and stir until it melts. Beat the icing sugar and butter together in another bowl until a soft paste forms. Gradually beat in the dark ale, then fold in the melted chocolate. Spread the icing over the cake and leave to set.

Slice the cake and serve with the muscovado and malt cream.

Barbecued maple cake

Here you go – this recipe is a fun risk to be undertaken when you're feeling brave and bold. We bake this cake in a kettle barbecue, which gives it a fantastic smoky taste. Granted, it is a little unconventional to bake in a barbecue, as the heat is difficult to regulate, but the result gives a completely new dimension to the cake. Once you master this technique you will be baking all sorts of dishes on a barbecue.

Don't worry if you haven't got a barbecue, however, as the cake also bakes beautifully in an oven and you get the smoky taste from the smoked butter, which you can source on the internet.

Serves 6–8

300g caster sugar
200g butter, softened, plus extra for greasing the tin
30g smoked butter
4 eggs
2 extra egg yolks
120g maple syrup, plus extra to serve
400g self-raising white flour

Light a barbecue and leave the coals to become glowing. Alternatively, preheat the oven to 180°C/ Gas Mark 4. Grease a 25cm springform cake tin, line the base with baking parchment and then flour.

Beat the sugar and both butters together until light and creamy. Beat in the eggs, one by one, then beat in the egg yolks and maple syrup. Sift over the flour and beat it in.

Pour the batter into the cake tin and smooth the surface. Place on the barbecue rack, close the lid and wait to see what happens. Just keep checking the cake until a skewer inserted in the centre comes out clean and the cake comes away from the edge of the tin.

Or, if you don't want to live life quite that much on the edge, place the tin in the oven and bake the cake for 35 minutes, or until a skewer inserted in the centre comes out clean and the cake comes away from the edge of the tin.

However you bake the cake, though, leave the cake to cool in the tin for 10 minutes on a wire rack. Turn it out and peel off the paper, then leave it to cool completely. Serve cut into slices with a little maple syrup spooned over.

Tom's Tip
It's important the coals are glowing grey and not red hot when you put the tin on them, or the cake will burn on the bottom. To be on the safe side, rest the tin on a couple hot bricks until you get the hang of baking over coals.

Sesame sponge cake with green tea sorbet and poached plums

This super-moist cake is made with oil instead of butter and brioche crumbs instead of flour. The result is just amazing! The whole dish has a slight Asian tilt and the green tea sorbet is very refreshing and clean. The sorbet is equally enjoyable with a cup of tea or served on its own for dessert.

Serves 6–8

200g caster sugar
90g fresh brioche crumbs
50g ground almonds
50g sesame seeds, toasted
1 teaspoon baking powder
4 eggs
200g tahini paste
100ml rapeseed oil
100ml sesame oil
maple syrup, to serve

For the green tea sorbet
500ml water
125g glucose syrup
100g caster sugar
1 teaspoon green tea powder
freshly squeezed juice of $\frac{1}{2}$ lemon

For the poached plums
4 cloves
4 star anise
$\frac{1}{2}$ cinnamon stick
1 tablespoon coriander seeds
$\frac{1}{2}$ tablespoon black peppercorns
300ml water
200ml dark rum
300g caster sugar
500g plums, stoned and quartered

To make the green tea sorbet, place the water, glucose syrup and sugar in a saucepan over a high heat and bring to the boil, stirring to dissolve the sugar. Remove the pan from the heat and whisk in the tea powder and lemon juice. Leave the sorbet mix to cool completely.

When the sorbet mix is completely cool, pour the mix into an ice cream machine and follow the manufacturer's instructions. Place in a freezerproof container and freeze until it's time to serve.

Meanwhile, poach the plums. Tie the cloves, star anise, cinnamon stick, coriander seeds and peppercorns in a piece of muslin. Place the water, dark rum and sugar in a saucepan over a high heat and bring to the boil, stirring to dissolve the sugar. Add the muslin with all the spices, lower the heat and simmer for 3 minutes. Place the plums in an heatproof bowl, pour the spiced poaching liquid over, add the spice bag and leave to cool completely. Cover the bowl and place in the fridge until needed.

To make the cake, preheat the oven to 130°C/Gas Mark $\frac{1}{2}$ and line a 900g loaf pan with baking parchment. Mix the caster sugar, brioche crumbs, ground almonds, sesame seeds and baking powder together in a large bowl. Whisk the eggs in a bowl, then whisk in the tahini paste, rapeseed oil and sesame oil. Beat the wet ingredients into the dry ingredients to make a cake batter.

Pour the batter into the loaf tin. Place the tin in the oven and bake the cake for between 45 minutes and 1 hour until a skewer inserted in the centre comes out clean and the cake comes away from the edges of the tin. Leave to cool on a wire rack for 10 minutes, then turn out and peel off the paper. Return the cake to the rack to cool completely. It will keep for up to 2 days wrapped in kitchen foil in an airtight container.

Slice the cake and serve with the green tea sorbet and poached plums, drizzled with maple syrup.

Stewed gooseberries with elderflower dumplings and sweet cheese

A refreshing change from more ordinary gooseberry fool or gooseberry crumble – it is like a sweet stew with dumplings, and it really captures the taste of summer. I think gooseberries are one of the most underrated and underused fruit that we have in Britain. Their season is not that long, so make the most of it!

Serves 4

500g gooseberries
150g caster sugar, plus extra, if needed

For the elderflower dumplings
500ml water
355g caster sugar
10 heads of elderflower, plus a few extra flowers, to decorate
finely grated zest and freshly squeezed juice of 3 lemons
125g fresh breadcrumbs
125g grated suet

For the sweet cheese
150g cream cheese
70g icing sugar
1 teaspoon ground mace

To begin the elderflower dumplings, place the water and 300g of the caster sugar in a saucepan over a high heat and bring to the boil, stirring to dissolve the sugar. Place the elderflower heads in an heatproof bowl, pour over the boiling syrup and add two-thirds of the lemon zest and juice. Cover the bowl with clingfilm and leave to one side to cool completely.

Place the gooseberries and the 150g caster sugar in the washed pan over a medium heat and gently simmer, stirring, until the gooseberries have broken down and you have a lovely purée. You may need to add a little more sugar, depending on how tart the gooseberries are. Remove the pan from the heat, cover and leave to one side.

Meanwhile, finish the elderflower dumplings. Mix the breadcrumbs, suet, the remaining 55g caster sugar and the remaining lemon zest and juice together. You may need to add a little water or the elderflower syrup to make the paste a bit moister. Shape into 12 dumplings.

Uncover the elderflower syrup and remove the flower heads, then return it to the boil. Add the dumplings to the pan, reduce the heat to low and gently poach them, uncovered, for 35–45 minutes until they are puffy.

To make the sweet cheese, beat the cream cheese, icing sugar and ground mace together. Cover and chill until needed.

Meanwhile, preheat the oven to 180°C/Gas Mark 4 and line a baking sheet with baking parchment. Remove the dumplings from the syrup and place them on the baking sheet. Place the baking sheet in the oven and bake the dumplings for about 10 minutes until they start to become crisp and lightly brown.

To serve, reheat the gooseberries until just warm, if necessary. Spoon into a bowl, add a couple dumplings, a spoonful of the sweet cheese and a few elderflowers to decorate. Drizzle a little of the elderflower syrup over the top and serve.

Plum fool with pink peppercorn shortbread biscuits

OK, you do need to buy a cream whipper gun for this recipe, but it will make all the difference to the final texture. They don't cost much and are good fun – they are real toys for boys and girls for the kitchen! You can substitute the plum purée in this recipe with any other fruit you like and move the dish with the seasons.

Serves 8

150g butter, cubed
150g caster sugar
2 cinnamon sticks
1kg plums, halved and stoned
freshly squeezed juice of 1 lemon
300ml double cream
300ml milk
6 egg yolks
pink peppercorns, to decorate

For the shortbread biscuits
175g butter, cubed
85g caster sugar
225g plain white flour, sifted, plus extra for rolling out
2 tablespoons pink peppercorns, crushed
demerara sugar for sprinkling

Melt the butter with 100g of the caster sugar and the cinnamon sticks in a saucepan over a medium heat, stirring to dissolve the sugar. Add the plums and lemon juice and stir over a low heat until the plums break down into a purée. Remove the cinnamon sticks, transfer the mix to a blender and blend until smooth. Pass the plum purée through a fine sieve into a bowl and leave to cool completely, then cover and chill until needed.

Bring the double cream and the milk to the boil in the washed pan over a high heat. Whisk the egg yolks and the remaining 50g caster sugar together in a heatproof bowl until fluffy and pale. Pour the boiling cream and milk on to the egg yolks, whisking.

Pour this mix back into the pan, return to the heat and simmer, whisking, until the custard reaches 82°C on an instant-read thermometer. Pass through a fine sieve onto two freezer blocks to stop the eggs from scrambling. Leave to cool completely, then cover and chill until needed.

Meanwhile, make the shortbread biscuits. Place the butter, sugar and flour into a food processor and pulse until the mixture comes together and forms a dough. Add the peppercorns and pulse once more. Remove the dough from the processor, wrap in clingfilm and leave in the fridge for at least 1 hour or up to 4 hours.

When ready to bake, preheat the oven to 150°C/ Gas Mark 2 and line a baking sheet with parchment paper. Roll the shortbread dough out on a lightly floured surface until about 1cm thick. Use biscuit cutters to cut into the shapes that you require and place on the baking sheet. Place the baking sheet in the oven and bake the biscuits for 8–10 minutes until they are baked through and dried. Remove the baking sheet from the oven and quickly sprinkle the biscuits with demerara sugar. Transfer them to a wire rack and leave to cool completely. Store the biscuits in an airtight container until needed.

About 15 minutes before you're ready to serve, stir the custard mix and 400g of the plum purée together, then pass through a fine sieve. Pour this into a cream whipper gun. Charge with 2 chargers and give it a good shake, then leave to settle for 10–15 minutes.

To serve, spoon a little leftover purée into tall glasses or serving bowls. Squirt on the fool mix and sprinkle with pink peppercorns. Serve with the shortbread biscuits. This fool must be eaten straight away.

Brown sugar-cured Devon strawberries and lavender in choux buns

This recipe makes lovely strawberry choux buns, much like summer fruit éclairs. The process of curing the strawberries in the sugar gives them an almost cooked texture, but with a fresh raw taste. If you don't want to go to the trouble of making the choux buns, serve the strawberries on their own or spooned over a scoop of ice cream – try either the Buffalo Vanilla Ice Cream (see page 217) or Strawberry Ice Cream (see page 218).

Serves 6

350g Devon strawberries, halved and hulled
70g demerara sugar
1 tablespoon culinary lavender
100g icing sugar
clotted cream, to serve

For the choux buns
90g plain white flour
$\frac{1}{2}$ teaspoon caster sugar
pinch of salt
60g butter, cubed
100ml water
3 large eggs, beaten

To make the choux buns, preheat the oven to 200°C/Gas Mark 6 and line a baking sheet with baking parchment. Sift the flour, sugar and salt together and leave to one side. Melt the butter with the water in a saucepan over a high heat and bring to the boil. Remove the pan from the heat, tip in the flour mix all at once and beat with a wooden spoon. Return the pan to a medium heat and continue beating for 2–3 minutes until the dough comes away from the side of the pan and forms a ball in the middle. It should look dry, not greasy.

Transfer the dough to a freestanding food mixer with the dough hook attached and beat on medium speed for 5–6 minutes until it cools down a little. Add the eggs, little by little, and continue beating until the dough is smooth and shiny and has a piping consistency. Put the dough into a piping bag with a plain nozzle and pipe 6 buns on to the parchment-lined baking sheet.

Place the baking sheet in the oven and bake the buns for 20–30 minutes until they are risen and golden brown. When they are baked, turn the oven off and open the door, but don't take the buns out. Leave them in the oven for a further 25–30 minutes to cool down and dry out. Store the choux buns in an airtight container until needed.

Meanwhile, place the strawberries on a baking sheet. Sprinkle with the demerara sugar and lavender and leave to cure for 30–40 minutes. The sugar will draw lots of water from the strawberries. Strain the strawberries in a colander over a bowl to keep the juice.

Just before you are ready to serve, stir about 1 tablespoon of the reserved strawberry juice into the icing sugar to make a thick icing, then spread it on top of choux buns. Cut each bun in half horizontally and top with the strawberries and then a dollop of clotted cream. Put the iced lids on top and serve immediately.

Crunchy pears baked with peanut brittle

Pears are one of the great English fruits. They have such a fantastic full and rounded flavour that can work with, hold and withstand big, contrasting tastes. Mixing the soft, fruity pear flesh with the lovely crunch from the peanut brittle is a perfect culinary contrast – and a real treat.

Serves 4

4 pears
100g butter, softened
75g caster sugar
$\frac{1}{2}$ teaspoon ground allspice
1 lemon
Toffee Sauce (see page 243), to serve
crème fraîche, whipped, to serve
1 tablespoon lemon thyme leaves, to decorate

For the peanut brittle
300g caster sugar
150g toasted peanuts

For the crunchy coating
180g cornflakes
140g butter, melted
50g demerara sugar
50g milk powder
pinch of salt

To make the peanut brittle, line a baking tray with parchment paper and leave to one side. Put caster sugar in a saucepan over a high heat to make a dry caramel. By this I mean do not add any water, just melt the sugar in the pan. Once it boils, don't stir. When it is a nice dark colour, stir in the peanuts and immediately pour the mix on to the baking tray. Leave to cool and become crisp.

To make the crunchy coating, preheat the oven to 140°C/Gas Mark 1 and line another baking tray with baking parchment. Mix the cornflakes, melted butter, demerara sugar, milk powder and salt together in a bowl, then spread the mix out on the baking tray. Place the tray in the oven and bake the crunchy mix for 20–25 minutes, stirring every 5 minutes so it colours evenly, until crunchy and toasted. Set to one side and leave to cool.

Turn the oven up to 190°C/Gas Mark 5. Peel the pears and rub them down with a green scouring pad to make them very smooth and remove any peeler marks. Place the pears upright in an ovenproof dish. Mix the butter, caster sugar and ground allspice together and spread evenly over the pears. Place the dish in the oven and bake the pears for 10–15 minutes until they are just tender. Take the dish out of the oven and immediately grate the lemon zest over the pears to release the citrus oils, then squeeze the juice over them.

Meanwhile, crush equal parts of the peanut brittle and the crunchy coating together to make a 'crumble' and set aside until needed.

Brush the hot pears with toffee sauce and then roll them in the 'crumble'. Serve them warm with extra toffee sauce, the crème fraîche and with the lemon thyme leaves sprinkled over.

Buffalo vanilla ice cream

Buffalo milk is very rich and, although this is a very simple ice cream, it tastes fantastic: a little bit farmyard-like with vanilla and sugar. If you don't freeze the mix, it is quite simply a fantastic-tasting custard. And if you do, you'll discover that this is the best vanilla ice cream ever!

Serves 4–6

400ml buffalo milk
200ml buffalo cream
2 vanilla pods, split in half lengthways and the seeds scraped out
8 egg yolks
100g sugar
2 tablespoons glycerine

Put the milk, cream and vanilla seeds and pods into a saucepan over a high heat and bring just to the boil. Whisk together the sugar and egg yolks in a heatproof bowl until fluffy and pale. Pour the boiling cream on to the egg mix, whisking. Pour the mix back into the pan and simmer, whisking, until the custard reaches 82°C on an instant-read thermometer.

Pass the hot custard through a fine sieve into a bowl. Stir in the glycerine. This acts as an anti-freeze and helps the ice cream to stay smooth and ice-crystal free. Leave to one side to cool completely.

When the custard is cool, pour it into an ice cream machine and follow the manufacturer's instructions. Pour into a freezerproof container and freeze for up to 3 months.

"**If you don't freeze the mix, it is quite simply a fantastic-tasting custard. And if you do, you'll discover that this is the best vanilla ice cream ever!**"

Pressed mango and strawberries with strawberry ice cream

When in season, we have some of the best strawberries in the world here in England. The natural sugars from the fruits will stick together when pressed for long enough. After a day of pressing, you have a fantastic, fresh tasting dessert that looks incredible.

If you can get them, Alphonso mangoes from India are the best to use, but they do only have a short season.

Serves 8

4 ripe mangoes, peeled and sliced $\frac{1}{2}$cm thick
1kg strawberries, hulled and sliced $\frac{1}{2}$cm thick
2 tablespoons finely chopped tarragon leaves
demerara sugar for dusting

For the strawberry ice cream
1kg strawberries, hulled
200g caster sugar
500ml single cream
freshly squeezed lemon juice, to taste

To assemble this dish you will need a 22cm square cake tin, a 20cm square cake tin and a baking tray. Make room in your fridge for the baking tray with the stacked tins with a heavy weight on top. At least 24 hours before you plan to serve, line the 20cm cake tin with clingfilm, with plenty of overhang.

Press a layer of mango into the clingfilm-lined tin, covering all gaps, then top with a layer of strawberries, sprinkling tarragon with each layer. Make sure you don't leave any gaps and keep layering until there is no fruit left and the layers are slightly higher than the top of the tin. You should finish with a layer of mango. Fold the clingfilm over the top to seal the fruit in. Pierce the clingfilm with a sharp knife.

Place the 22cm cake tin on top of the filled tin. Turn both tins over so the tin with the mangos and strawberries is now on top. Place the tins on the baking tray and place a heavy weight, such as a full milk carton or cans of tomatoes, on top and put the baking tray into the fridge for 24 hours. The juice should drain through the pierced clingfilm.

Meanwhile, make the strawberry ice cream. Put the strawberries in a heatproof non-metallic bowl with the caster sugar. Cover the bowl with clingfilm and place on top of a saucepan of boiling water, as if you were melting chocolate. Turn the heat down to low and leave the strawberries to stew for 30–40 minutes, until they are very soft and break down.

Remove the pan from the heat, transfer the strawberries to a blender and purée. Pass the purée through a fine sieve into a bowl and leave to cool.

Mix 500g of the strawberry purée and the single cream together. Pour the mix into an ice cream machine and follow the manufacturer's instructions. Transfer the mixture to a freezerproof container and freeze until needed.

The next day, when you are ready to serve, remove the clingfilm from the pressed fruit and reserve the drained juices. Cut the fruit into serving portions. A bread knife works best, but otherwise use a long, thin knife. Thinly sprinkle the tops with demerara sugar and use a blowtorch to melt the sugar and make a crispy caramelised top. Serve the pressed fruit with a scoop of the strawberry ice cream, and the reserved juice, if you like.

Amaretto baba in honey with rosemary-poached peaches

A classic baba is traditionally soaked in rum, but I like to make it with amaretto, because the almond flavour works well with peaches. There is a lot of work to be done here, but you are rewarded with a memorable dessert.

Makes 8

250g plain white flour, plus extra for flouring the moulds
180g caster sugar
20g fresh yeast, crumbled
4 eggs
1 teaspoon salt
90g butter, melted, plus extra for buttering the moulds
250ml water, blood heat
100ml amaretto
4 tablespoons runny honey, to serve
1 tablespoon thyme leaves, to serve
crème fraîche, to serve

For the rosemary-poached peaches
8 peaches, with the skin scored on each
500ml water
300g caster sugar
4 sprigs of rosemary

To make the dough for the babas, put the flour, 30g of the sugar, yeast, eggs and salt into a freestanding food mixer with the dough hook attached and mix until a rich, elastic dough forms. Pour in the melted butter and mix again. Cover the mixer's bowl with clingfilm and leave to one side at room temperature until the dough doubles in volume. This will take at least 1 hour, depending on the temperature of your room.

Meanwhile, make the rosemary-poached peaches. Bring a large saucepan of water to the boil and place a bowl of iced water next to it. Drop the peaches into the boiling water and count to 10. Using a slotted spoon, remove them from the water and put straight into the iced water to refresh. Peel the skin from the peaches, then cut each in half from top to bottom and remove the stone. Place the peaches on to a tea towel and pat dry. Transfer the peaches to a deep baking tray and leave to one side.

In a separate pan over a high heat, bring the water, caster sugar and the rosemary sprigs to the boil, stirring to dissolve the sugar. Pour this over the peaches, then cover the baking tray with clingfilm and leave the peaches to cool at room temperature. When they are completely cool, transfer them to the fridge if you aren't using them immediately.

Butter eight 10cm savarin moulds and lightly dust with flour, tipping out the excess. Leave the moulds to one side.

Once the baba dough has risen, knock it back and put it into a piping bag fitted with a plain nozzle. Pipe the dough into the moulds, only filling them halfway. Transfer the moulds to a baking sheet and leave to rise again for 30 minutes, or until the dough reaches the top of the moulds.

Meanwhile, preheat the oven to 190°C/Gas Mark 5. Place the baking sheet in the oven and bake the babas for 8–10 minutes until risen and golden brown. Remove the babas from their moulds and leave them to cool on a wire rack.

Place the 250ml water, remaining sugar and amaretto in a saucepan over a high heat and bring to the boil, stirring to dissolve the sugar. Place the babas on a tray with a rim, pour the boiling syrup over them, cover the tray with clingfilm and leave the babas to soak up the syrup like a sponge.

Serve the babas warm with 2 peach halves each, drizzled with runny honey, sprinkled with thyme leaves and a nice dollop of crème fraîche on the side.

Tom's Tip
Any leftover babas freeze very well, or if you have any raw dough leftover, put it in a piping bag and deep-fry thin strips of it to make fantastic churros to serve with chocolate sauce.

Grapefruit meringue pies

Easy and so clean tasting, this is a fantastic alternative to lemon meringue pies.

Makes 8

2 pink grapefruits, segmented

For the pastry
225g butter, softened
125g caster sugar
1 egg yolk, beaten
400g plain white flour, plus extra for rolling out

For the grapefruit curd filling
finely grated zest and freshly squeezed juice of 3 pink grapefruits
160g sugar
100g butter, cubed
180g eggs (approximately 4 eggs' worth), beaten
200g extra egg yolks (approximately 10 eggs' worth), beaten

For the meringue topping
150g egg whites (approximately 5 eggs' worth)
300g caster sugar
25g glucose syrup
65ml water

To make the pastry, beat the butter and sugar together in a large bowl until light and creamy. Beat in the egg yolk, then sift over the flour and mix just until the pastry comes together. Wrap it in clingfilm and leave to rest in the fridge for at least 1 hour.

Preheat the oven to 170°C/Gas Mark 3. After the pastry has rested, roll it out on a lightly floured surface until it is about 1/2cm thick. Cut out 8 circles of dough, each large enough to line a 10cm tart tin with a removable base. Reroll the trimmings as necessary. Line the tins, press a piece of clingfilm in each, then fill with baking beans or rice. Place the pans in the oven and bake the pastry cases for 12 minutes, or until crisp and golden brown.

Remove the pastry cases from the oven, remove the clingfilm and beans or rice and leave them to cool on wire racks still in the tins.

Meanwhile, make the grapefruit curd filling. Put the grapefruit zest and juice in a saucepan over a high heat and boil until the juice reduces to a glaze. Add the sugar and butter and return to the boil, stirring to dissolve the sugar. Pour in the whole eggs and the yolks, whisking constantly and vigorously, until the mix thickens and looks like it will almost split. When it is thick, remove the pan from the heat and leave the curd to cool, whisking occasionally. Once the curd is completely cool, transfer it to a food processor and blend until smooth. Cover the curd and chill in the fridge until needed.

To make the meringue topping, put the egg whites in a bowl of a freestanding mixer and beat until stiff peaks form. Mix the sugar, water and glucose syrup together in a saucepan over a high heat, stirring to dissolve the sugar, and heat until it reaches 118°C on an instant-read thermometer. With the mixer running, pour the syrup on to the egg whites and continue mixing until the meringue is cool.

Divide the grapefruit curd between the tart cases, then arrange the grapefruit segments on top of each. Pipe the meringue on top of each, like a hedgehog. Use a blowtorch to lightly colour the meringues, then serve immediately.

Tom's Tip
If you'd rather make one large tart, roll out the pastry as above and line a 25cm tart ring on a baking sheet lined with baking parchment or a 25cm tart tin with a removable base. Press a piece of clingfilm in, then fill with baking beans or rice and bake as above for 15 minutes, or until crisp and golden brown. Gently transfer the pastry case to a wire rack to cool. Make the grapefruit curd and meringue topping as above.

Rum junket
with coffee macaroons

Creamy junket is an English classic you don't often see anymore, but junkets are so easy to make. I serve this version with macaroons, sandwiched together with a rich coffee ganache, to give a little texture and depth to the dessert. I sometimes serve these with crème fraîche on the side, too. Leftover macaroons will keep in a sealed container in the fridge for a couple of days.

Serves 4 (makes about 40 filled macaroons)

600ml full-fat milk
50g caster sugar
1 teaspoon rennet
2 teaspoons dark rum
1 nutmeg, to decorate

For the coffee macaroons
75g ground almonds
75g icing sugar
1 teaspoon ground instant coffee
80g egg whites (approximately 3 eggs' worth)
125g caster sugar
30ml water

For the coffee ganache
100g milk chocolate, broken
100g double cream
1 teaspoon instant coffee

To make the coffee meringues, line 2 baking sheets with baking parchment and leave to one side. Sift the ground almonds, icing sugar and instant coffee through a fine sieve into a bowl. Pour half of the egg whites on top and just fold together gently, then set aside.

Place the sugar and water in a saucepan over a high heat, stirring to dissolve the sugar, and boil until it reaches to 118°C on an instant-read thermometer. Place the remaining egg whites in the bowl of a freestanding mixer and beat until soft peaks form. With the mixer still running, slowly pour in the hot sugar mix and continue mixing until the meringue is

cool. Fold the cooled meringue into the almond and coffee mix, trying not to knock too much air out. Put the mix into a piping bag with a plain nozzle and pipe blobs the size of 10-pence pieces on to the baking sheet. Leave at room temperature for 30 minutes to let the mix form a skin.

Meanwhile, preheat the oven to 150°C/Gas Mark 2. After the meringues have formed their skin, put the baking sheet in the oven and bake for 10–15 minutes until they have a crisp shell on the outside, but are still sticky in the middle. Remove the meringues from the baking sheet and cool them on a wire rack. At this stage you can freeze them for up to a month.

To make the coffee ganache, place the chocolate in a heatproof bowl that fits over a saucepan of simmering water without the bottom of the bowl touching the water and melt, stirring occasionally. Remove the bowl from the pan and tip out the water. Bring the cream and instant coffee to the boil in the pan, then stir the coffee-flavoured cream into the melted chocolate. Pour the mix into a piping bag and leave to cool to a sticky piping consistency that isn't too runny.

When the meringues are cool, stick them together in pairs, using the coffee ganache. Leave to one side if you are serving soon, or place in the fridge for up to a day.

About 2 hours before you want to serve, make the junket. Place the milk and sugar in a saucepan over a medium heat, stirring to dissolve the sugar, and heat until it reaches 37°C on an instant-read thermometer. Pour in the rennet and rum. Pass the junket through a fine sieve into your serving bowls and leave to set at room temperature, which will take about an hour. Freshly grate nutmeg over the tops and put into the fridge for 45 minutes.

Serve the bowls of junket with the macaroons.

Tom's Tip
You'll find small bottles of rennet in the baking section of supermarkets.

Lemon verbena creams with charred lemon and meringues

Lemon verbena is one of the easiest herbs to grow, it comes back every year and it is ideal for flavouring sweet desserts. It has a fragrant, herby, lemon flavour that is very fresh tasting. It you haven't got any lemon verbena, however, sweet cicely or lemon balm also work in this recipe.

This dish has plenty of texture and crunch and blowtorching the lemon segments lift them to a new level. It is also very cool to blowtorch stuff!

Serves 6; makes 30–40 mini meringues

750ml double cream
4 eggs
40g caster sugar
120g fresh lemon verbena, plus extra sprigs, to decorate
2 lemons
demerara sugar for dusting

For the meringues
75g egg whites (approximately 2 eggs' worth)
70g caster sugar
70g icing sugar

Bring the double cream to the boil in a saucepan over a high heat. Whisk the eggs and the caster sugar together in a heatproof bowl until light and fluffy. Pour over the boiling cream and mix together. Pour the mix back into the pan and whisk over a medium heat until it reaches 87°C on an instant-read thermometer. The mixture needs to reach this temperature in order to set. Pass the custard through a fine sieve into a bowl. Stir in the fresh lemon verbena and grate in the zest of one of the lemons. Do not discard the zested lemon. Leave the mix to one side for 25 minutes to cool.

After the mix has cooled, remove the lemon verbena. Pour the mix into a blender and blend until smooth, then pour into 6 serving dishes or ramekins. Transfer them to the fridge for at least 3 hours to set.

To make the meringues, preheat the oven to 110°C/Gas Mark $\frac{1}{4}$ and line a baking sheet with baking parchment.

Whisk the egg whites in a large bowl until soft peaks form. Gradually add the caster sugar and continue beating until it is incorporated. Add the icing sugar and continue to whisk until the meringue is stiff and glossy. Spoon the meringue into a piping bag fitted with a small plain nozzle and pipe mini meringues on to the baking sheet. Place the baking sheet in the oven and bake for about 40 minutes until crispy on the outside and soft in the middle. Remove the baking sheet from the oven and leave the meringues to cool completely. Do not attempt to take them off the baking sheet until they are cool.

When ready to serve, take the set creams out of the fridge and sprinkle with demerara sugar. Use a blowtorch to melt the sugar and glaze them. Segment the lemons and place the segments on a metal baking tray, then use the blowtorch to char them. This will give a lovely toasted flavour to the lemon.

Place the lemon segments on top of the glazed creams, add some meringues and serve. Any leftover meringues will keep in an airtight container for several weeks.

Proper Pub Food

Lemon posset with fennel biscotti

This has been on The Hand & Flowers lunch menu many times, and is a real favourite of mine. My pastry chef loves it when I do put this on the menu, because the posset is so easy to prepare and sets very quickly. If you fancy just making the biscotti, they go very well with a great cup of coffee.

Serves 6; makes about 20 biscotti

450ml double cream
130g caster sugar
freshly squeezed juice of 2 lemons

For the fennel biscotti
450g plain white flour
2 teaspoons baking powder
340g caster sugar
190g butter, softened
4 eggs
100g blanched almonds, toasted and chopped
1 tablespoon fennel seeds
icing sugar for dusting

Mix the cream and sugar together in a saucepan over a high heat and bring to the boil, stirring to dissolve the sugar. Turn the heat down to a simmer and stir for 1–2 minutes until the bubbles are quite large. Add the lemon juice and whisk thoroughly. Pass this mix through a fine sieve into a bowl and leave to cool for about 5 minutes. Skim off any air bubbles, then pour the posset into your serving glasses. Leave to cool completely, then place the bowls in the fridge for at least 2 hours.

To make the biscotti, preheat the oven to 170°C/Gas Mark 3 and line a baking sheet with baking parchment. Sift the flour and baking powder together and leave to one side until needed. Beat the sugar and butter together in a large bowl until light and creamy. Beat in the eggs, one by one. Stir in the flour mix, then fold in the almonds and the fennel seeds.

Divide the dough in half and shape into 2 logs, each about 20cm long and 10cm wide on the baking sheet. Place the baking sheet in the oven and bake the biscotti for 20–25 minutes until golden brown.

Remove the baking sheet from the oven and leave the baked dough to cool on the baking sheet for 10 minutes. Do not turn off the oven.

After 10 minutes, slice both pieces of baked dough widthways into biscotti, 1–2cm thick. Lay the biscotti on to a wire rack that will fit in the oven. Return them to the oven on the wire rack and bake for a further 5 minutes, or until they are crisp and dry. Remove them from the oven and immediately dust with icing sugar. Leave the biscotti to cool completely, then store them in an airtight container for 3–4 days.

When the lemon posset is set, serve it with biscotti on the side.

Chocolate and coffee mousse

This is a perfect dinner party pudding because the work can be done up to two days ahead and it has a real touch of decadence.

Serves 4

170g dark chocolate, at least 70% cocoa, broken, plus extra for decorating
70ml hot espresso
115g caster sugar
splash of water
5 egg whites
2 egg yolks, beaten
120ml double cream, semi-whipped
toasted coffee beans, crushed, to serve
Salt Caramel (see page 243), to serve

Place a heatproof bowl over a pan of simmering water, without letting the bottom of the bowl touch the water. Add the chocolate and espresso and stir until the chocolate melts. Remove the bowl from the heat and leave to one side.

Place the sugar and the water in a saucepan over a high heat and bring to the boil, stirring to dissolve the sugar, then boil until it reaches 118°C on an instant-read thermometer. Place the egg whites in a freestanding food mixer and beat until soft peaks form. With the mixer still running, slowly pour the hot syrup on to the egg whites and continue whisking until the meringue cools.

Beat the egg yolks into the chocolate mixture, then stir in the double cream and fold in the meringue. Divide between 4 bowls, then cover and chill for at least 2 hours or up to 2 days.

Serve decorated with grated chocolate and toasted coffee beans and with salt caramel for pouring over.

Proper Pub Food

Gin and tonic granita with apple caramel

Gin is one of my favourite drinks. It contains so many different botanicals, ranging from herbs and spices through to fruit and vegetables. The apple gin I love most is made and flavoured with Bramley apples, which makes it so quintessentially English, and that's why I recommend it in this recipe. It's a combination you can't beat.

Serves 8–10

220g caster sugar
120ml water
2 Bramley apples, peeled and grated
500ml tonic water
170ml apple gin
freshly squeezed juice of 1 lemon
500ml apple juice
50g butter, cubed
2 Braeburn apples, to serve

Put the sugar and water in a saucepan over a high heat and bring to the boil, stirring to dissolve the sugar. Remove the pan from the heat, add the Bramley apples, tonic water, gin and lemon juice. Leave to cool completely, then pour the mix into a plastic freezerproof container and place into the freezer. Remove it from the freezer every 30 minutes and whisk. It will take 2–3 hours to freeze.

Meanwhile, bring the apple juice to the boil over a high heat and boil until it reduces to a dark caramel. Remove the pan from the heat and whisk in the butter so it becomes glossy and shiny. Leave to one side to cool until needed.

When ready to serve, peel and finely dice the Braeburn apples. Remove the granita from the freezer and break it up with a fork to create a 'slush-puppy' texture. Spoon into individual bowls, sprinkle the Braeburn apples over the tops and serve with the apple caramel.

Spiced orange cake with plum sauce and Christmas pudding ice cream

This is a great alternative festive dessert for everybody who says they don't like Christmas pudding, but still want to enjoy the flavours of Christmas. You can make each component of the dish well in advance so you're not left with loads to do on Christmas Eve.

Serves 6–8

3 oranges, 450g pulp
butter, softened for greasing the tin
300g ground almonds
300g caster sugar
7 eggs
2 teaspoons baking powder
1 teaspoon ground cinnamon
1 teaspoon ground ginger
icing sugar, to decorate
extra peeled oranges, to decorate

For the plum sauce
150g butter, cubed
100g caster sugar
1 cinnamon stick
1.5kg plums, halved and stoned
freshly squeezed juice of 1 lemon

For the Christmas pudding ice cream
375g double cream
375g milk
110g caster sugar
150g egg yolks (approximately 8 eggs' worth)
2 tablespoons glycerine (optional)
500g steamed Christmas pudding, cooled and
  crumbled

To make the plum sauce, melt the butter in a saucepan over a medium heat. Add the sugar and cinnamon stick and stir until the sugar dissolves. Add the plums and lemon juice, turn the heat to low and continue stirring until the plums break down into a purée, which will take about 20 minutes.

Remove the cinnamon stick, then pour the purée into a blender and blend until smooth. Pass the sauce through a fine sieve into a bowl, then leave on one side until needed.

To make the Christmas pudding ice cream, put the cream and milk into a saucepan over a high heat and bring to the boil. Whisk together the sugar and egg yolks in a heatproof bowl until fluffy and pale. Pour the boiling cream on to the egg mix, whisking. Pour the mix back into the pan and simmer, whisking, until the custard reaches 82°C on an instant-read thermometer. Pass the hot custard through a fine sieve into a bowl. Stir in the glycerine, if you are using, and whisk together. It acts as an anti-freeze and helps the ice cream stay smooth and ice-crystal free. Leave to one side to cool completely.

Place the Christmas pudding in another bowl. When the custard is cool, stir it into the Christmas pudding, then pour into an ice cream machine and follow the manufacturer's instructions. Place in a freezerproof container and freeze for up to 3 months.

To make the cake, place the unpeeled oranges and water to cover in a saucepan over a high heat and bring to the boil. Turn the heat down to low and leave the oranges to simmer for 2 hours, or until very soft and tender. Drain the oranges and leave to one side.

Preheat the oven to 180°C/Gas Mark 4 and grease a 24cm loaf tin with butter and line the base with baking parchment.

When the oranges are cool enough to handle, cut each in half and remove the seeds. Place everything but the seeds – peel, pith, fruit and all – in a food processor and process until finely chopped. Weigh out 450g of the chopped oranges and discard the remainder.

Return the 450g chopped orange to the food processor and add the ground almonds, sugar, eggs, baking powder, ground cinnamon and ground ginger and process again until well mixed. Pour the batter into the tin. Place the tin in the oven and bake the cake for 1 hour, or until the cake is set and it comes away from the side of the tin. It is a moist cake, so you can't test it with a skewer. You'll probably have to cover the top of the cake with kitchen foil, shiny side down, after about 40 minutes to stop it from burning.

Remove the tin from the oven and leave the cake to cool completely in the tin on a wire rack. When the cake's cool you can take it out of the tin and peel off the paper. Wrap the cake in kitchen foil and store in an airtight container for up to 3 days.

When you're ready to serve, take the ice cream out of the freezer about 10 minutes in advance to soften just a bit and reheat the plum sauce gently. Dust the cake with icing sugar and slice, then serve with the plum sauce and Christmas pudding ice cream on the side and sliced peeled oranges for decoration.

Tom's Tip

The plum sauce can be made 3 or 4 days in advance and kept in a covered container in the fridge. Reheat gently when ready to serve, letting it down with a little water, if necessary.

Steamed ginger puddings with vanilla custard

Is there anything more British than a great steamed pudding! If you don't like ginger you can make this just with golden syrup, but however you flavour it, make sure you still serve it with proper custard!

Makes 6

200g butter, softened, plus extra for greasing the pudding basins
100ml syrup from the preserved ginger jar
100ml golden syrup
4 tablespoons ginger wine
freshly squeezed juice of $1/2$ lemon
300g caster sugar
4 eggs
2 extra egg yolks
400g self-raising white flour
2 teaspoons ground ginger
75g preserved ginger, finely chopped

For the vanilla custard
575ml double cream
2 vanilla pods, split in half lengthways and the seeds scraped out
6 egg yolks
40g caster sugar

Grease six 200ml dariole moulds or pudding basins with butter and line the bottom of each with a small piece of baking parchment cut to fit, then grease the paper. Cut out 6 pieces of kitchen foil, each large enough to be pleated in the middle and to fit over the top of each with an overhang. Bring a kettle of water to the boil.

Bring the ginger syrup, golden syrup, ginger wine and lemon juice to the boil, stirring to dissolve the syrups, then remove the pan from the heat.

Beat the sugar and butter together in a large bowl until light and fluffy. Beat in the eggs and extra egg yolks. Sift over the flour and ground ginger and then beat into the mix. Stir in the preserved ginger.

Divide three-quarters of the syrup between the dariole moulds, then add the batter, only filling each three-quarters full. Cover the tops with the circle of foil, pleated along the centre to allow the puddings to rise, then securely tie in place. Place into 2 or 3 flameproof casseroles or deep saucepans on upturned saucers and pour in enough boiling water to come half way up the side of the moulds. Cover the pans and simmer over low heat for $1^1/_2$ hours, or until the puddings are well risen. Remove the puddings from the water and leave them to stand for a few minutes before turning out and peeling off the paper. If they stick, run a round-bladed knife around the inside of the moulds.

Meanwhile, make the custard. Put the cream and vanilla seeds and pods into a saucepan over a high heat and bring just to the boil. Whisk the egg yolks and sugar together in a heatproof bowl until fluffy and pale. Pour the boiling cream on to the eggs, whisking constantly. Pour this mixture back into the pan and simmer until it reaches 82°C on an instant-read thermometer. Pass the hot custard through a fine sieve.

Pour the remaining syrup over the hot puddings and serve with the hot custard.

Tom's Tip
This recipe is for individual puddings, but if you want to make a large one use a 1.5 litre pudding basin and steam for 2–3 hours. Be sure to check the water level occasionally and top up with more boiling water, if necessary.

PROPER
BASICS

Beef sauce base

Makes about 1.2 litres

100ml rapeseed oil
400g beef trimmings
2 litres chicken stock
4 star anise
$\frac{1}{2}$ bunch of thyme
1 head of garlic, unpeeled but cut in half through
   the equator
salt, to taste

Heat the rapeseed oil in a large saucepan over a high heat. Add the beef trimmings and fry them, stirring occasionally, until browned and almost burnt – but definitely not burnt! Add the chicken stock and star anise and bring to the boil. Add the thyme and garlic. Reduce the heat to very low and leave to simmer, uncovered, for 2 hours, or until the stock has reduced by one-third. Season and pass the stock through a sieve lined with muslin. Leave to cool completely, then cover and chill for 12 hours so any fat will set and can be removed.

This beef base it now ready to use in any recipe that calls for beef stock, or it can be reduced down to use as a sauce. It will keep for up to 3 days in the fridge or can be frozen for up to 3 months.

Beef gravy

This is my basic recipe for making perfect gravy. It is easier than it looks or sounds and once you've made it you'll make it again and again. You can use duck, lamb or venison bones as appropriate, so basically any 'red' meat.

Makes about 1.5 litres

1.5kg beef bones, chopped quite small – ask the
   butcher to do this if you don't have a cleaver
1 pig's trotter, split lengthways – ask the butcher to
   do this if you don't have a cleaver
2.5 litres Chicken Sauce Stock Base (see page 240)
$\frac{1}{2}$ bottle (750ml) red wine
2 tablespoons redcurrant jelly
1 bunch of flat-leaf parsley, tied together
1 tablespoon cornflour (optional)
salt, to taste

A day before you are going to use the gravy, preheat the oven to 200°C/Gas Mark 6 and put the bones in a roasting tray. Put the tray in the oven and roast the bones for 30 minutes, or until dark brown, but not burnt.

Transfer the bones to a large saucepan over a high heat. Add the pig's trotter, chicken sauce stock base, red wine and redcurrant jelly and bring to the boil, stirring to dissolve the jelly. Use a large metal spoon to skim the surface, as necessary. Reduce the heat to very low and leave to simmer, uncovered, for 3 hours, or until the liquid has reduced by one-third.

Turn the heat off, add the parsley – stalks and all – and leave to infuse, uncovered, for 10 minutes. Pass the sauce through a fine sieve into a bowl, then leave to cool completely. Cover and place in the fridge for 12 hours so any fat will set and can be removed.

When you're ready to use, remove and discard the fat. Pour the sauce into a saucepan and bring to the boil, then boil until it reduces down to sauce consistency. If you want your gravy a little thicker, blend the cornflour with 1 tablespoon of the sauce, then pour it into the pan and continue simmering, whisking vigorously, until it has thickened. Season, then pass the gravy though a sieve lined with muslin and it's ready to serve.

Tom's Tip
Any leftovers, before or after the gravy is thickened with cornflour, can be left to cool completely, then kept in the fridge for up to 3 days or can be frozen for up to 3 months.

Lamb sauce base

Makes about 1 litre

1kg lamb bones, chopped
2 litres Chicken Sauce Stock Base (see page 240)
$^1/_2$ bunch of rosemary

Preheat the oven to 180°C/Gas Mark 4. Put the lamb bones in a roasting tray and roast for about 40 minutes until dark golden brown. Transfer them to a saucepan over a very low heat with the chicken sauce stock base and leave to simmer for 4–6 hours until the quantity reduces by half. Remove the pan from the heat, add the rosemary and leave to infuse, uncovered, for 30 minutes.

Pass the stock through a fine sieve lined with muslin. Leave to cool completely, then cover and put in the fridge for 12 hours so any fat will set and can be removed.

This lamb base is now ready to use in any recipe that calls for lamb stock, or it can be reduced down to use as a sauce. It will keep for up to 3 days in the fridge or can be frozen for up to 3 months.

Red wine sauce

Makes about 900ml

2 litres Chicken Sauce Stock Base (see page 240)
1 bottle (750ml) red wine
150g redcurrant jelly
100g frozen blackberries
1 onion, chopped
4 celery sticks, chopped
handful of parsley stalks
salt and pepper, to taste

Mix the chicken sauce base, wine, redcurrant jelly and blackberries together in a saucepan over a high heat and bring to the boil, stirring to dissolve the jelly. Add the onion and celery and continue boiling until it reduces down to one-third of its original volume, skimming the surface as necessary.

Remove the pan from the heat, add the parsley stalks and leave to infuse, uncovered, for 10 minutes. Pass the liquid through a sieve lined with muslin and leave to cool completely. Cover and chill for 12 hours so any fat will set and can be removed.

After you remove the fat, place the liquid over a low heat and leave it to simmer, uncovered, until it reduces down to a sauce consistency. Season.

Chicken sauce stock base

Makes about 7.5 litres

1kg chicken wings
2 pig's trotters, cut in half lengthways
1kg chicken carcass, chopped
4 celery sticks, cut in half
1 head of garlic, unpeeled, but cut in half through
   the equator
1 onion, chopped
200g canned tomatoes
10 litres water

Preheat the oven to 180°C/Gas Mark 4. Put the chicken wings in a roasting tray and roast for about 30 minutes until dark golden brown. Make sure they don't burn. Transfer them to a large saucepan. Add the trotters, carcass and the vegetables. Pour in the canned tomatoes and the water and bring to the boil, skimming the surface as necessary. Reduce the heat to very low and leave the stock to simmer, uncovered, for 6–8 hours, until reduced by one quarter. Pass through a fine sieve lined with muslin or a tea towel. Leave to cool completely, then transfer to the fridge for 12 hours so any fat will set and can be removed.

   This chicken base it now ready to use in any recipe that calls for chicken stock, or it can be reduced down to use as a sauce. It will keep for up to 3 days in the fridge or can be frozen for up to 3 months.

Brown chicken stock

Makes about 2 litres

2 kg chicken wings
3 litres Chicken Sauce Stock Base (see above)
salt, to taste

Preheat the oven to 180°C/Gas Mark 4. Put the chicken wings in a roasting tray and roast for about 30 minutes until dark golden brown. Make sure they don't burn. Transfer them to a large saucepan, cover with the chicken sauce base and bring to the boil. Reduce the heat to very low and leave to simmer, uncovered, until reduced by one-third. Season and pass through a sieve lined with muslin. Leave to cool completely, then cover and chill for 12 hours so any fat will set and can be removed.

   This brown chicken stock is now ready to use, or it can be reduced down to use as a sauce. It will keep for up to 3 days in the fridge or can be frozen for up to 3 months.

Curry powder

Makes about 12 tablespoons

2 tablespoons ground chilli
2 tablespoons ground ginger
2 tablespoons garam masala
1 tablespoon star anise
1 tablespoon cardamom seeds
1 tablespoon coriander seeds
1 tablespoon cumin seeds
1 tablespoon black onion seeds
1 tablespoon yellow mustard seeds
1 tablespoon whole black peppercorns
$\frac{1}{2}$ cinnamon stick

Preheat an oven to 180°C/Gas Mark 4. Mix all the spices together in a dry baking tray. Place the tray in the oven and roast the spices for 10 minutes. Remove the tray from the oven and stir, then return it to the oven and roast the spices for a further 4–5 minutes until they look and smell toasted, but not burnt! Immediately tip the spices out of the pan and leave to cool.

Transfer the spices to a spice grinder and grind, then sift through a fine sieve to leave a powder. Store in an air tight container until needed.

Pickle mix

Makes about 1.5 litres

1 litre white wine vinegar
250ml water
500g caster sugar
5 star anise
2 cloves
1 cinnamon stick
2 tablespoons white peppercorns
1 tablespoon coriander seeds
1 tablespoon fennel seeds

Put all the ingredients in a large saucepan over a high heat and bring to the boil, stirring to dissolve the sugar. Reduce the heat to low and leave the mix to simmer, uncovered, for 10–15 minutes.

Remove the pan from the heat and cover the top with clingfilm, then leave to infuse and cool completely.

Pass the mix though a fine sieve, then store in a sealed container in the fridge. It will last for ages.

Soda bread

Makes 2 loaves

750g plain wholemeal flour
750g strong white flour, plus extra for dusting
75g butter, melted
4 teaspoons bicarbonate of soda
1 tablespoon salt
2 teaspoons cracked black pepper
1.25 litres buttermilk

Preheat the oven to 200°C/Gas Mark 6. Put both flours, the butter, bicarbonate of soda, salt and cracked pepper in a large bowl. Stir in the buttermilk and use your hands to mix together until a soft dough forms. Divide the dough in half and pat into 2 loaves on a baking sheet.

Dust each loaf with a little extra flour and bake for 45–50 minutes until they are risen and golden brown. Transfer to a wire rack and leave to cool completely.

Rye bread sauce

Serves 6–8

$1/2$ loaf rye bread, sliced
200ml milk
100ml double cream
50g butter, plus a little extra to finish
2 star anise
2 cloves
1 teaspoon coriander seeds
1 teaspoon ground cinnamon
$1/2$ teaspoon white peppercorns
$1/2$ teaspoon fennel seeds
salt and pepper, to taste

Preheat the oven to 120°C/Gas Mark $1/2$. Lay the bread slices in a single layer on a baking sheet. Place the baking sheet in the oven and toast the bread for about 1 hour until the slices are completely dried out. Remove them from the oven and leave to cool completely.

When the bread slices are cool, crumble them into a blender or food processor and blend until very finely ground, like a powder. Leave to one side until needed.

Place the milk, cream, butter and all of the spices in a saucepan over a high heat and bring to the boil. Remove the pan from the heat, cover with clingfilm and leave to one side until the mixture cools. Pass the spiced milk through a fine sieve, then place in the fridge until needed.

Measure 300ml of the spiced milk and cream mix into a saucepan over a high heat and bring to the boil. Turn the heat down to low, add 30g of the dry rye breadcrumbs and whisk for 6–8 minutes until thickened. Stir in a little butter, if needed. Season and serve. If you've made this in advance, reheat it very slowly over a low heat and add a little extra milk if it needs letting down.

Toffee sauce

Makes about 750ml

175g demerara sugar
170g butter, cubed
1 tablespoon golden syrup
1 tablespoon black treacle
500ml double cream
pinch of salt

Put the sugar, butter, golden syrup and treacle in a saucepan over a high heat and bring to the boil, stirring to dissolve the sugar. Continue boiling until the sauce becomes a golden caramel colour. Pour in the cream to stop the cooking. Add the salt, then pass the sauce through a fine sieve into a bowl and serve warm.

Leave any leftover sauce to cool completely, then keep in a covered container in the fridge for a couple weeks. Reheat gently to serve.

Salt caramel

Makes 300ml

80ml water
1½ teaspoons salt
200g caster sugar

Place the water and salt in a saucepan over a medium heat and stir to dissolve the salt. Just leave to one side to keep warm.

Place the sugar in another saucepan over a high heat and make a dry caramel. By this I mean do not add any water, just melt the sugar in the pan. Once it boils, do not stir. When it is a nice amber colour, carefully stir in the warm salted water. The water has to be warm, otherwise it will 'shock' the sugar too much – if this happens, the sauce will explode and be very dangerous!

Pour the caramel into a bowl and leave to cool to room temperature to serve.

Tom's Tip

This can be made up to a month in advance and kept in a covered container in the fridge. Just remember to bring it back to room temperature before serving. You can reheat it very slightly, if you need to.

Mulled cider

At Christmas you could serve mulled wine, but I'm a proper West Country boy and mulled cider is more up my street. Get yourself a really good country cider – cloudy or clear; it doesn't matter so long as it tastes great.

Makes 8 glasses

10 cardamom pods
4 star anise
3 fresh bay leaves
1 large cinnamon stick, broken in half
1 teaspoon black peppercorns
2 litres good cider
150g soft dark brown sugar
1 vanilla pod, split in half lengthways and the seeds
   scraped out
150ml dark rum
 thinly pared peel of 1 orange

Tie the cardamom pods, star anise, bay leaves, cinnamon stick and peppercorns together in a piece of muslin. Pour the cider into a large saucepan over a high heat. Add the brown sugar, vanilla seeds and pod and the muslin bag and bring to the boil, stirring to dissolve the sugar. Reduce the heat to low and leave the cider to simmer, uncovered, for 20 minutes. Stir in the dark rum and orange peel. Remove the pan from the heat and serve.

INDEX

Hot salt-beef bagels with pickled
vegetables and black pepper cream
cheese 154

R